♥ ♥ ♥

♥♥Life
Tastes Better
Than
Steak♥♥

COOKBOOK

Heart Healthy
Reversal Recipes

**The fat free cookbook that comes straight
from the hearts of those who wrote it: the
patients and families of a successful heart
disease reversal program**

Gerry Krag, MA, RD and
Marie Zimolzak, DTR, editors

♥ ♥ ♥

All recipes in *The "Life Tastes Better Than Steak" Cookbook* have been developed by patients, staff and friends of the Downriver Reversal Team. Some have been modified from traditional recipes. Should any published or copyrighted recipe appear in the book, it is unintentional.

While the information in this book may be beneficial to heart patients, it is not to be interpreted as medical advice or consultation for any specific condition.

No portion of this publication may be reproduced, reprinted or otherwise copied for distribution purposes without the express written permission of the authors and publisher.

ISBN #0-932212-90-5

Library of Congress Catalog #96-084503

First Edition 1996
Reprinted November 1999

Copyright ©1996 by

Avery Color Studios, Inc.
Gwinn, Michigan

and

Downriver Cardiology Consultants
Trenton, Michigan

While we have made every effort to be accurate, the nutrient calculations in this cookbook cannot be guaranteed. Because ingredients and nutritional content of prepared and processed foods are sometimes modified over time, the assessments may vary.

♥ ♥ ♥

Table of Contents

Foreword 1

Welcome 2

What is the Downriver Reversal Team? 3

What is the Reversal Eating Plan? 4

About the Recipes 7

What Keeps People on the Program 11

Reversal Team Grace 18

Recipes

    Appetizers 19

    Salads 35

    Soups 57

    Breads 81

    Main Dishes 105

    Side Dishes 193

    Desserts 225

Index 285

Every recipe in this cookbook is free of saturated fat. The trivial amounts of dietary fat shown in the nutritional analysis is fat that is found naturally in the low fat ingredients. There is no added fat in any recipe other than an occasional small amount of vegetable oil cooking spray.

♥ ♥ ♥

How This Cookbook Was Named

When a relative from Massachusetts had a heart attack, Gerry Krag mailed recipes, an eating plan, menu ideas and a very long letter of support. Later his wife told Gerry that it was the last sentence in that letter that really hit home. That sentence was the title of this book: *"Life Tastes Better Than Steak."*

We have used those same words with newly diagnosed cardiac patients as they began the rehabilitation phase of treatment. When a patient longs for cheese, we say "Life tastes better than cheese." When a patient craves bacon and eggs, we say "Life tastes better than bacon and eggs." Any fatty food will fit in the sentence. It puts things in perspective. For high risk heart patients, life can take on a new meaning, especially for those who have had a brush with death. Staying alive, healthy and independent can become more important than eating fatty foods.

We have seen people give up food that they never thought they could or would. Part of the motivation for this change was feeling better physically. In addition, these patients liked being in control of their heart disease, rather than having the disease control them. Through the years, we have seen people from all walks of life reverse their heart disease. It has been an unparalleled and joyful experience.

This cookbook was developed for people with blockages in their coronary arteries. If you or someone you love has blockages, these recipes will provide nourishing, tasty food that will be a vital component to the reversal process. "Life Tastes Better Than Steak" may be just the words to help motivate someone to change. These recipes can provide the way.

♥ ♥ ♥

Reversal Team Staff

Joseph C. Rogers, D.O. . . . Medical Director
Dave Durbin, B.A.A. . . . . Program Director, Exercise Physiologist, Group Facilitator
Beverly A. Grobbin . . . . . Data Manager, Exercise Program, Group Facilitator
Shaun Pochik, EMT-P . . . Exercise Rehabilitation Technician
Pat Nevin-Normandin, B.S. Yoga Instructor, Group Facilitator
Helene Rottenberg, M.A. . . Yoga Instructor
Babsi Riegler, B.A. . . . . . . Yoga Instructor
Gerry Krag, M.A., R.D. . . . Consulting Nutritionist, Food Service, Group Facilitator
Marie Zimolzak, DTR . . . . Consulting Nutritionist, Group Facilitator
Betty Verdone . . . . Food Co-op
Maureen Paulin, B.S. . . . . Volunteer Dietetic Intern
Al Lorenz . . . . Food Service
Justin Clemens . . . . Food Service

A Special Thanks

Recipes . . . . Downriver Reversal Team patients,
                                friends, and staff
Special Assistance . . . . Frank Zimolzak
                                Mike Krag
                                Judy Phillips
                                Bob Shank
                                Diane Boehmer
                                Estella Johnson
                                Maureen Paulin
Ongoing Support . . . . Joseph C. Rogers, DO
                                Felix J. Rogers, DO,
                                Joseph T. Rogers, DO
                                Sarah Jessup, DO
                                Paul R. Miluk, DO

Welcome

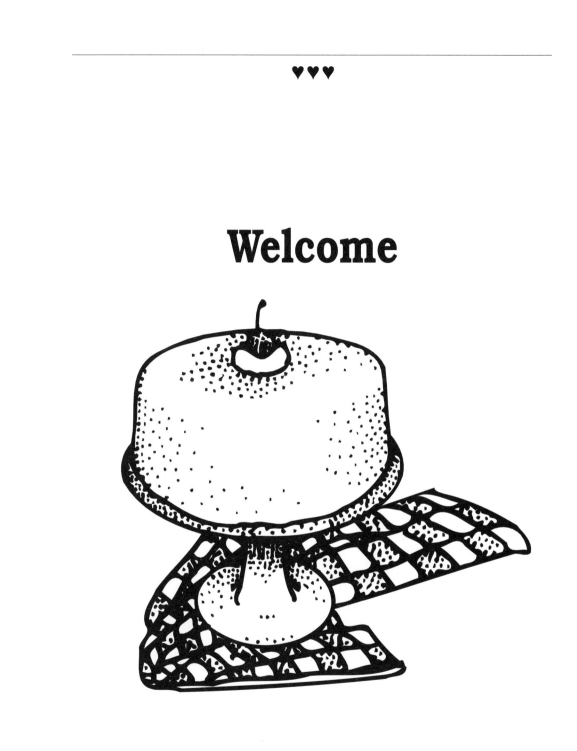

♥ ♥ ♥

Foreword

One of the ironies of modern medicine is that it has required our sophisticated technology to prove what we have always suspected — that healthy lifestyles lead to healthier and longer lives. Surprisingly, an aggressive approach to lifestyle modification can even reverse some of the years of wear and tear.

This cookbook offers part of the cure for heart disease. The reason more patients don't follow this type of diet is that their physicians just assume that no one will adhere to the vegetarian low-fat concept. Doctors forget that the motivation for health is so strong. These recipes are a testimony to the ability of patients to change their dietary habits.

I have been pleased to watch this book develop as a need first expressed by the patients, and then answered by themselves. As you read the recipes, you will begin to sense the "flavor" of this exceptional group of individuals. They are outstanding in their zest for life and sense of community. Their favorite recipes are a way of sharing with each other and with you.

Best wishes for good health and enjoyable dining!

Joseph C. Rogers, D.O., Medical Director
Downriver Reversal Team

♥ ♥ ♥

Welcome

Running a program like the Downriver Reversal Team is a great experience. Some people start the program and they can hardly climb stairs. A few months later they can walk up stairs with no effort. We wish all cardiac patients would consider the Reversal Program. Unfortunately, a lot of patients have excuses and as an exercise physiologist, I think I've heard them all:

It's too hot. It's too cold. It's raining. It's snowing. I've been on my feet all day. I'm too old for exercise. I don't have time.

I can't eat that way. I need meat for protein. I'm too old to change my eating habits. One steak isn't going to kill me. Once in a while, I have to eat something good. I don't like eating that stuff. Vegetarians are weird. Yoga is weird. I'm too old to stretch. I don't believe in yoga. It is too hard. One cigarette isn't going to kill me. How about if I just cut back. I can't quit — I've already tried.

Making excuses is easy. Making changes in your lifestyle is challenging, but rewarding. Don't take the easy way out. If you want to feel better, you've got to make the effort and find reasons for making changes instead of excuses not to! These recipes will make it easier for you to change. Go for It!

Dave Durbin, Director
Downriver Reversal Team

♥ ♥ ♥

What Is The Downriver Reversal Team?

Dean Ornish, M.D. published a scientific report in 1990 documenting that heart disease could be reversed. This was revolutionary, and 82% of his research patients in California showed a reversal in the blockages of the arteries to their hearts. Dr. Ornish used a very low-fat vegetarian diet, exercise, yoga, and stress management. It worked in California, but would it "play" in Trenton, a small suburb just outside Detroit, Michigan?

Dr. Joseph C. Rogers believed it would and in September, 1992, he assembled a group of health professionals to help him. Four brave patients came forward to start the program. Since then, the program has grown and now has over 100 patients following the protocol. Like Dr. Ornish's original patients, these have "boldly gone where no one dared." They have become dedicated vegetarians. They have exercised unfailingly. They have stretched into unusual yoga positions. They have learned to relax deeply. Most importantly, they have learned to share their feelings with others in a support group environment. The sharing and caring concerns that are a part of the support group meetings have assisted in opening up many hearts. The results have been extremely positive. Nearly 90% of those patients who have been in a year or more have improved or stabilized their heart disease. Patients have lower cholesterol, good steady weight loss, improved stamina and endurance, and almost no angina. They feel good!

People often ask about the Reversal Team patients. "Don't they crave meat? Don't they feel deprived?" Once adjusted to the program, these patients usually do not miss meat nor do they feel deprived. They are eating the foods they like and have come to prefer. If you think they are deprived, just try some of the delicious recipes in this book, including potato salad, cabbage rolls, grilled cheese sandwiches, lasagna, desserts of all kinds, and a myriad of other great foods. They are the gift to you from the patients and staff of the Downriver Reversal Team. ***Bon appetit!***

♥ ♥ ♥

What is the Reversal Eating Plan?

The Reversal Eating Plan is a simple vegetarian diet. No meat, poultry, or fish are eaten. It is also a "no added fat" program. No oils, including olive, peanut or canola oil, are used. Foods that have added oils are not eaten. For example, tabouli salad prepared the traditional way is not eaten because it is prepared with a significant amount of olive oil. Tabouli salad prepared without olive oil is acceptable since there is no added fat. Nuts or seeds are not eaten, except a small amount for garnish, occasionally. Dairy foods with fat such as cheese and milk are not used. Egg yolks are not used, but egg whites and fat free egg substitutes may be eaten freely. Vegetable cooking spray is used, but sparingly.

You can eat a variety of foods and be well nourished. Most people find they can eat a fair amount of food and not gain weight. If you are following the eating plan the right way, you should not experience excess hunger. You may need to snack between meals because low-fat foods move through the digestive tract rather quickly.

Besides lowering their fat intake, about 30% of people with heart disease need to modify their food intake for sodium. Some patients need to watch excess sugars and calories to prevent triglycerides from rising. Most will benefit by giving up caffeine, especially those with irregular heart rhythms, insomnia, blood sugar fluctuations, or those who feel uptight and stressed out.

Most people adapt well to the new eating pattern. As the weeks and months pass, the new way of eating becomes preferred — mainly because you feel so much better. This is a very energizing way to eat. It is also an excellent method for weight control. By eating a simple vegetarian diet, your body will be released of the burden of dealing with excess fats and calories. Give your heart and body a break and follow the Reversal Eating Plan today!

In the beginning, it is hard for most of the patients. After all, this way of eating is a big change from the typical American diet. The first six to nine weeks are the toughest, especially for those who continue to eat fat. Patients who really follow the program do better. After the initial adjustment, it gets easier. Cravings decrease and foods start tasting good. Gradually, patients develop a

♥ ♥ ♥

preference for low-fat vegetarianism. They are motivated to continue because they start to feel better. Their bodies no longer have to deal with the digestion and metabolism of large amounts of fat. With less fat going in, there is less fat to cause complications, such as the clotting and arterial spasms associated with high fat meals. The Reversal Team Members also stay motivated because they have the support and help of their fellow patients and the staff. It is much harder to follow this way of eating if you are trying to do it alone without any support.

If you live in the Detroit area, and are interested in finding out about participation in the Downriver Reversal Team, call 313-675-2233 and we will send you a brochure about the program. If you are not from the area, another option is to find a registered dietitian who will help you with the dietary components of the program. A national referral system for dietitians can be reached by calling 1-800-366-1655.

To make sure that the patients in the Downriver Reversal Team are getting the vitamins and minerals they need, we do recommend a daily multiple vitamin with iron and vitamin B12.

♥ ♥ ♥

To learn more about the diet followed by the Downriver Reversal Team, stop by your favorite bookstore and purchase a copy of our recommended 96-page booklet, *The Reversal Eating Plan – Diet for a Clogged Artery*, published by Avery Color Studios (1-800-722-9925). This is the eating guide that has helped these patients change their eating habits. *The Reversal Eating Plan* is written in clear, easy-to-understand language. It leads you step-by-step through the process of change. *The Reversal Eating Plan* includes a fat gram counter and pages for you to keep food records — all in one handy booklet. *The Reversal Eating Plan* teaches you how to eat in a balanced way while cutting your intake of fat and animal based foods. You will learn how to determine if you are getting enough protein and nutrients to stay healthy and how to cut back on dietary fat.

♥ ♥ ♥

A Total Approach

To reverse heart disease, diet is not the only consideration. You must also work on stress management and exercise. If you can't find a total program in your area, look at schools and hospitals for classes in yoga, stress management, and exercise. To be successful, you need to develop and use relaxation skills every day to slow your body's production of cholesterol. In addition, learning how to communicate effectively will improve your relationships with friends, family members, and co-workers. Good communication can relieve stress.

Words Of Caution

Patients in the Downriver Reversal Program follow the following precautions:

1. Do not over exert, especially in competitive sports or in physical tasks that are very strenuous. Patients who push themselves physically have been known to have complications.

2. Do not eat a large amount of fat at one time. (If you are really on the program, you don't need to worry about this.) Once your body adjusts to low-fat eating, a large intake of fat grams will make you sick. You will have difficulty digesting the fat through the intestine. You may experience a bloated feeling that is very uncomfortable, or other complications.

3. Eating large high fat meals may cause arteries to constrict and blood to clot. More heart patients are seen in emergency rooms the day after major holidays and after birthdays, so don't succumb to "party attack." Protect yourself — it is your life. Don't let a "friend" or relative persuade you to eat a higher fat food "just this once."

4. Learn to change your behavior around stressful situations. Stress brings on high blood pressure and increased heart rate. Stress also causes your body to release chemicals that can constrict arteries, clot blood and increase cholesterol production. You need protection from this. When angry or upset, practice deep breathing, yoga and other stress management skills.

♥ ♥ ♥

About The Recipes

The recipes in this book reflect the diverse backgrounds of the patients in the program. There are favorites like lasagna and minestrone, stuffed peppers and potato soup. There are many duplicates that we deliberately included. Each is somewhat different. It is the reader's job to decide which recipe reaches out and beckons. Will it be simple and fast or complex and time consuming? Will it be comforting and familiar or exotic and exciting? We feel there is something for everyone and the preparation times will help you decide.

ABC's of the Reversal Eating Plan

A. Fat gram intake of 12 - 14 grams per day
B. Vegetarian eating — no meat, poultry, fish
C. No added fats — fat or oil is not added to any food
D. Higher fat foods are not used — egg yolks, regular cheese, nuts, whole milk, seeds, avocado, olives
E. No "Fat Free" foods with fat in the ingredient list, ie., whipped topping mix, dairy creamers, etc.

Use These Foods Daily:

A. Fat free dairy foods
B. Fat free egg substitutes and egg whites
C. Fat free meat substitutes such as fat free soy burgers, textured soy protein, and wheat gluten
D. Fat reduced tofu and other fermented soy products
E. Dried beans and peas
F. Breads, cereals, pasta, starches
G. Vegetables and fruits

To Make Foods Taste Good:

Use these ingredients for Sauces, Gravies, and Seasoning:
A. Fat free vegetable broth
B. Fat free meat based broth
C. Herbs and seasonings
D. Fat free butter flavored sprinkles and liquids
Also used but in very small quantity: vegetable cooking spray

What About Sodium?

About a third of the patients in the Downriver Reversal Team need to watch their sodium intake. The rest have greater flexibility with salt. Some recipes in the book have higher levels of sodium. If you are watching your sodium intake, please pay attention to the sodium content of the recipes. Do not use the recipes that have levels that would be too high for you. Some recipes can be prepared with less sodium by modifying an ingredient. For example, using "no added salt" tomato products can lower the sodium in several recipes.

What About Sugar?

About 15 percent of the Reversal Team is diabetic. These patients have done extremely well and most are taking fewer medications since joining the program. However, they still need to watch their intake of refined sugar and excess calories. Some recipes in this book contain sugar. Many of these can be prepared with sugar substitutes. If a food is to be cooked, use a substitute that is stable with heat such as "Sugar Twin™." If it is not cooked, aspartame ("Nutrasweet™") can be used. Rely on the product label for information about the quantity to substitute. The greatest danger of sugar is the extra calories.

What About Calories?

Many people who follow a low-fat vegetarian diet find that weight loss comes fairly easily and naturally for the first six weeks or so. After that, weight tends to plateau. It is important for heart patients to remember that reducing dietary fat is one of the most powerful actions to take. When weight reaches a plateau, do not give up! Continue to eat in a low-fat way and your body will reap the benefits, even if the scale doesn't seem to reflect all your hard work. A second consideration is that calories do count. If you are eating too much food, even fat free food, you will gain weight. So eat well, but eat reasonably, too. Skipping meals causes people to eat more later, so try to avoid this unfortunate situation. Eat frequently to quell hunger, but don't overeat, particularly at night.

♥ ♥ ♥

A Few Words About Special Ingredients

Dairy: All dairy products used in recipes should be fat free, including cheeses. Overheating or overcooking fat free dairy foods will cause them to become tough. Use low to moderate temperatures. When selecting dairy products, check the ingredient list for fat. If there is fat in the ingredient list, do not use the product. An example is liquid "fat free" dairy creamer. This product often has hydrogenated soy oil as the second or third ingredient. The size of serving will be one tablespoon and the amount of fat will be less than .5 grams/serving, low enough to qualify for the fat free designation. If you consume 1/2 cup of this, you are getting close to 4 grams of fat.

Eggs: Use egg whites or fat free egg substitutes such as Egg Beaters™. Always use moderate heat, because overcooking fat free egg products will cause them to be tough. Egg yolks contain fat and are not used.

Broth: When a recipe calls for a fat free broth, look for fat free vegetable broth. Some brands are very high in sodium. It is easy to make your own broth by simmering vegetables and herbs in water for several hours and straining the liquid. Fat free meat broths are also available in cans and as bouillon. If you choose to use these, it is recommended that you refrigerate and strain off any fat residual that coagulates after chilling. Home made meat based broths can also be refrigerated to remove the fat. However, you must be very careful, because any fat left in the broth is harmful to the patient with blocked arteries.

Soy Protein: Many recipes call for soy burger or soy nuggets. A variety of soy burger products are in the marketplace. We recommend the fat free versions such as Tree of Life™ brand fat free textured vegetable protein. Check your local health food store for soy burger products. For some recipes, you may wish to crumble pre-formed soy burgers, such as Boca Burgers™, for inclusion in recipes. Those who are watching sodium should check the sodium levels on flavored soy products. While most soy products are low in sodium, some of the flavored soy products may have high levels of salt and monosodium glutamate. Soy products, like textured soy protein and tofu, help lower cholesterol and triglycerides and are an important protein source for vegetarians.

Dried Beans: Use either dried or canned. When using canned or cooked beans, rinse them to remove extra sodium and gas residue. A cup of dried beans is equivalent to two cups of canned or cooked beans, so you should adjust the quantity based on this ratio. Always soak beans overnight or do a rapid soak by bringing them to a boil and cooking for ten minutes. Turn off heat and let them soak, covered, for 1-2 hours. Dried beans lower cholesterol and triglycerides. They also help to stabilize blood sugar levels in diabetics and hypoglycemics. Dried beans are an excellent source of protein and they keep the digestive tract healthy.

Vegetable Oil Cooking Spray: Each one second spray often represents .5 to 1.0 fat grams. These are not truly fat free, despite the label. If the ingredient list has fat, then the product will have fat. Legally, a product can be called fat free when it has less than one half of a fat gram per serving. Use sprays very sparingly. If you are going to saute onions or stir fry vegetables, use water, wine or broth.

Fat Free Foods: Always read the ingredient list because many fat free foods contain fat. Even though the nutrition label says "zero fat grams," if there is fat in the ingredient list, there will be fat in the food. Avoid oils, hydrogenated oil, cream, whole milk, butter, beef fat, coconut oil and palm kernel oil.

♥ ♥ ♥

What Keeps People on the Program?

Members of the Downriver Reversal Team come from all parts of the metropolitan Detroit area once a week to attend sessions in stress management, nutrition, exercise and yoga. A vegetarian meal is also part of the program. This is a big commitment and, for many, a long drive. They continue to attend and participate because the program works and they feel better. To demonstrate this, here are some testimonials from the patients:

"I was in bad shape, taking about 9 nitrobids each day for frequent, painful angina. Within four weeks of joining the Reversal Team, my angina was almost gone and I have not had to take any nitrobid since that time. I have lost 60 pounds and feel great. I am physically, mentally, and spiritually better off than I have been in years. Before I started the program, my doctor said I needed bypass surgery. Now, I am no longer a candidate for surgery and he is recommending the program to his patients."

Paul Bodrie, Catholic lay pastoral assistant — heart attacks in 1989 and 1992, angioplasty in 1989

"Since starting the program, my cholesterol has gone down to 132 and I've lost 35 pounds. I feel more energetic and I look forward to everyday activities with added zest that I didn't have before. The further I get into this program, the less desire I have for high fat foods or meat."

Don Mitchell, 67, retired elementary school principal, golf course supervisor, and magician — bypass in 1991

"My family is surprised at the way I am eating, as my niece said I had never eaten a green vegetable in my life. It even surprises me. I have lost 37 pounds and as a result of the program, I have reduced my diabetic medicine. When I entered the program I was taking four micronase and seven units of insulin a day. Now I take 1/2 micronase a day."

Margaret Flanigan, retired accountant — heart attack in 1973

♥ ♥ ♥

"I came into the program with a lot of stress in my life. The diet and the program have controlled the elevation of my cholesterol and hypertension and brought me to a positive attitude and more ambition to exercise."

Ethel E. Kennedy, dental assistant — elevated cholesterol and hypertension

"Starting to be a vegetarian at the beginning was hard. Now the food tastes great. I've been on the program since 1992. I feel better and I look better. My blockage has reversed. I lost 25 pounds."

Joe Borawski, retired mail carrier, bypass surgery in 1988

"Becoming a vegetarian was easy. I was determined not to repeat my medical history. The best benefit of the program is the weight loss and the new energy I feel. The unexpected benefit was my husband joining me as a vegetarian — he has lost over 30 pounds without trying. My daughters were so impressed they started an exercise and veggie program on their own!"

Judith Caplan Phillips, general manager of an ad specialty supplier — bypass in 1992 and diabetes

"I've been a strict vegetarian since 1992. If I had been a strict vegetarian for the past twenty years, I would have alleviated my heart disease and stabilized my diabetes, eliminating all its collateral complications. Being a strict vegetarian, I find I have stabilized my heart disease and diabetes. I believe being a strict vegetarian has improved my chances for a longer and better quality life."

Carmine Verdone, retiree — five heart attacks, bypass in 1983, stent surgery in 1994, diabetes

"Being in this program is a good way to live. Health, strength, and good friends — a good way to live!"

Peggy Ray, housewife — coronary artery disease and diabetes

"I feel this program is adding years to my life. My heart surgery saved my life, but even after the surgery, I didn't feel good. The diet is keeping me alive and I feel good."

Pat McKenna, 61, housewife — bypass in 1991

♥ ♥ ♥

"With a dedicated staff and the help of the support group, you can't go wrong. I've lost 28 pounds and my cholesterol numbers are right where they should be. I plan on being around for a long time! A big part of the program's success is the support group and of course Dr. Rogers. Without him, there would be no program. My latest thallium stress test showed significant improvement."

Pat Beaudrie, 59, retiree — heart attack and bypass surgery in 1989

"I never thought I would ever become a vegetarian. It is real healthy for you. The doctors didn't know what my alternatives would be. I had 95% blockage in one artery and 65% in another. Diet and exercise opened up the arteries without surgery."

Helen Moses, housewife — coronary artery disease

"I thank God I was informed about this program and I pursued it until I joined the Downriver Reversal Team. Both my weight and my cholesterol are down. I'm avoiding surgery and feeling better than I ever have. In 1995, I was shown reasons why I should stop eating sugar. I thought I felt great before, but now I'm at a whole other level of "feeling great." My weight loss had plateaued, but since giving up sugar, I have lost an additional 20 pounds to the total of 50 lost since joining the program. My cholesterol is almost down to 150 and my triglycerides are now 88. I continue to learn better ways to keep me off the operating table as I continue to participate in the program."

Al Spiteri, 52, journeyman, hydraulic repair for
Ford Motor Company — heart attack in 1993

"I didn't want unnecessary surgery and was able to correct my blockage through the program. A heart catheterization showed a complete reversal of my blockage. I have lost 70 pounds and my cholesterol has come down from 270 to 177. This program really works! I am in better shape than my doctor — at least that is what he says!"

Virginia Coffee, 53, elementary school custodian —
coronary artery disease

"Since entering the program, I have not had any angina attacks. I have more energy and have lost 15 pounds. I don't find the diet hard at all except when I travel."

Larry Hardin, die and tool maker, cross country biker
and bypass surgery candidate in 1993

"After my angioplasty, I didn't think I needed to go on such an extreme diet. A few months later, I began having angina again and decided to give it a try since the surgery hadn't worked and I wanted to avoid a bypass. I found that the diet really isn't that hard to follow once you just decide to do it. And I feel a lot better — seldom have angina. I've lost 20 pounds without going hungry, and after one year, my thallium stress test showed a significant improvement. I eat a lot of food, it is just very low fat."

Lou Hayward, computer programmer —
angioplasty in 1993

"The hardest part of deciding to start the program was becoming a vegetarian. Once I got started, with great help from the staff and the support group, it felt natural and I don't miss eating meat at all."

Sally Roulinson, 58, seamstress, artist, housewife —
heart attack in 1990, angioplasty in 1993, bypass in
1995

"Breathing is easier, I feel stronger through my breathing. It was heavy and laborious before and I tired easily. Now I feel stronger. I sleep well. The joy of walking, exercising, and being in tune physically is just great. If my thallium had stayed the same, I would have been happy. Imagine how I felt when it showed great improvement after one year."

Neva Neubecker, housewife — bypass in 1992, diabetes

". . . this threw me for a loop. I really believed that my chest pain was from a hiatal hernia. When I was told it was heart disease, all I did was cry. Then I started the program and soon I knew that I could get better. When I first started the program, I could not go up stairs, could not walk to my corner, could not do the dishes or even hang up clothes without my chest hurting. I had little stamina and felt tired all the time. I listened and learned and exercised and followed the eating plan and now I can walk up 2-1/2 flights of stairs without a problem. I can walk all over without getting tired. My exercise tolerance on the treadmill and stationary bike has improved dramatically. My ten year old goes right along with me and she is proud of what I've done and she plans to stay healthy, too. If you are thinking about following a reversal program, give yourself a break and do it — trust and you will get better every week."

Kathryn Curry Peters, homemaker —
blocked arteries

♥ ♥ ♥

"Having been an emergency medical technician for several years, I have taken many coronary victims to the hospital, never dreaming that I would be one myself. In January of 1995, my blood pressure was off the charts; signs and symptoms of heart trouble were present. I was admitted to the hospital. After several tests were run, it was determined that I had several blocked arteries. I looked at my options and I chose the Downriver Reversal Team program. Between the vegetarian diet, stress management and counseling by the program staff, the changes in my life have been dramatic. My weight is down by 35 pounds, my blood pressure is under control, and my total cholesterol is down from over 300 to 124. Thank God for this life saving program."

Chuck Hodge, journeyman millwright and volunteer
firefighter — blocked arteries

"It is clear to me now that my life-long unhealthy lifestyle and poor eating habits contributed to my heart disease. Since that awareness and since joining the Reversal Program, my health has improved dramatically. Adhering to the vegetarian diet and principles taught by the dedicated staff is already reversing my heart disease."

Ronald Konopka, auto stylist — angioplasty in 1988 and
1990, quadruple bypass in 1994

*"I have experienced improved health in general and a more positive outlook about life. I would never have gone anywhere without the large size bottle of Tums. Now, I never take **any** at all! It is a wonderful support team."*

Kathy Mullen, 52, insurance and investment representative
— elevated cholesterol and irregular heart beat

"When I found out from my doctor that I had blocked arteries along with a history of elevated cholesterol, I decided to do something about it. I had heard about the Reversal Program from two friends who were in it and they were doing well. Since I joined the program, I have lost weight, my cholesterol has dropped over 150 points, and my blood pressure readings are great! Now when I walk, I can do so without gasping for air. I like the vegetarian diet and exercise has gotten to be a habit. But I know I couldn't have come this far without the weekly group support. I credit this program for giving me a better and longer life."

Phyllis Dzwigalski, 68, retired educator — blocked
arteries, elevated cholesterol, hypertension

"The Downriver Reversal Team is a great program and a great help due to the team support offered to us. For the past three years, I have driven over 145 miles round-trip from home to Trenton, Michigan, to attend. I surely wouldn't be doing this if I didn't think it was important. I continue to embrace the principles of the program and will do so for the rest of my life."

Jim Gilleran, president of a lumber and wood products company — blocked arteries

"I believe that if I had not joined this reversal program a year ago, I would have had a heart attack by now. I would recommend it for anyone, even those in good health, as a preventative to heart disease"

Jeanne Eckert, 62, homemaker and gardening expert — blocked arteries

"Since joining the Downriver Reversal Team, I've lost 27 pounds and increased my walking speed. My cholesterol is down to 155 from 215. My legs don't ache anymore and on my last stress test, I went beyond all previous stress test times and speeds. My cardiologist said if all his patients got on this program, he'd be out of business in a year. For all the above reasons, I will remain in the program until they plant me in the ground."

Lou Bergeron — two heart attacks and bypass surgery in 1987

"Eight years ago I was told I had triple vessel disease and needed a bypass. With diet, medication and exercise, I've been able to avoid having the bypass surgery, but I felt I needed more. I found what I needed with this program and I've been able to keep running marathons."

Ray Gomez, 64, retired — blocked arteries

"The Reversal Program has empowered me with knowledge, skills and the belief in myself that I can live a healthy, creative and full life. I give thanks to the wonderful team of professionals and the always kind, insightful and sensitive participants."

Gene Pluhar, 52, high school art teacher — heart attacks in 1992 and 1995

"Of course, the best exercises for the heart are lifting others up and learning not to take life so seriously — learning to laugh at ourselves. I feel extremely priv-

eleged to be part of this group — growing in awareness and being transformed physically, mentally, spiritually. I feel more alive and whole today than I was ten years ago."

Libbett Miford, 39, kidney-pancreas transplant in 1992; heart attack, triple bypass in 1994.

"Before joining this program, I had a heart attack. One artery was 90% blocked and so I had an angioplasty. Then I attended cardiac rehabilitation, but never followed up. One year later, another artery was 90% blocked, plus the first artery was starting to block again. I had a second angioplasty. So I decided to join the reversal program and now my cholesterol is down from 243 to 129. My weight has gone from 210 to 175. Plus the other numbers are where they should be. So you see, the program does work. I would highly recommend it. Also, I would like to say that I feel great. I have more energy than before — best in three years. The staff that runs the program are great — very supportive. Plus the members are the most supportive people that you can find. I am very proud to be a member of this program."

Fred Calderone, 69, retired diesel mechanic — blocked arteries, heart attack in 1993, angioplasties in 1993 and 1994

"Dr. Joseph Rogers deserves the Humanitarian of the Year Award! Because of his compassion and generosity in starting the Downriver Reversal Team program, I feel (and look) 20 years younger, weigh 30 pounds less, my blood pressure has stabilized and I'm playing better tennis than ever. To say my heart is overflowing with gratitude would be putting it mildly. Thanks, Jody!"

Sally C. Mackintosh, 60, retired General Motors employee — coronary artery disease

♥ ♥ ♥

♥ ♥ ♥

Reversal Team Grace

Dear God
Bless this food to our use
And us to Thy service
We praise and thank You
For the many blessings
You have given us
Thank You for healing our hearts
Thank You for making us better communicators
Thank You for calming our spirits
Be in our hearts as we go through
The week ahead
Help us always to be mindful of the needs of others
And to be thankful in all things
Amen

Appetizers

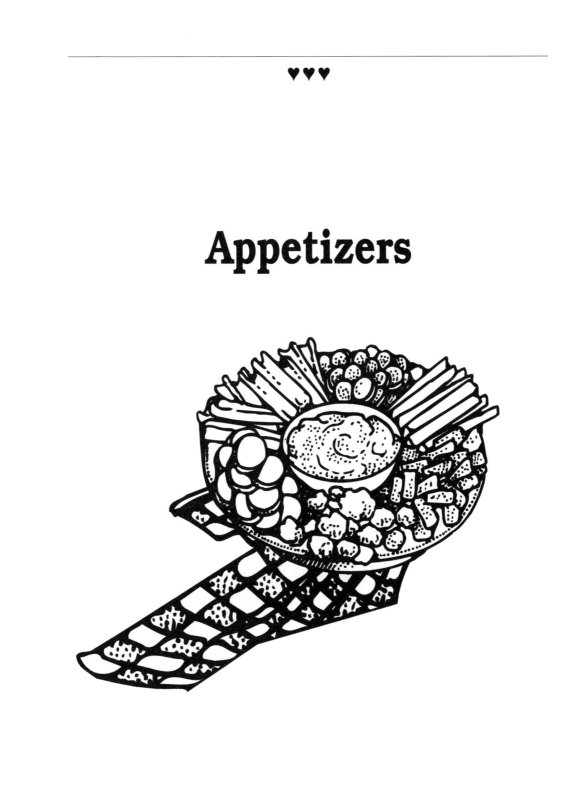

Appetizers

Taco Chips 21

Spinach Dip 22

Mexican Bean Dip 23

Curried Yogurt Dip with Broccoli .24

Pickled Plum Mayonnaise 25

Bob's Special Vegetable Pate 26

Tofu Cucumber Dip 28

Deviled Eggs 29

Triple Deck Mexican Tortillas . . .30

Garbanzo Ghanoush 32

Salsa Grande 33

♥ ♥ ♥

Taco Chips

A great alternative for fried store-bought chips

Serves 12, each serving is eight chips

Preparation: :10   Cook :10   Stand :00   Total :20

Ingredients:

12   fresh or thawed frozen corn tortillas
      liquid Butter Buds™
      garlic powder
      onion powder
      seasoned pepper or cayenne pepper

Cut each tortilla into eight pie shaped pieces. Prepare Butter Buds™ according to label. Lightly spread on each chip. Sprinkle with seasoning (or leave plain for corn chips). Bake on cookie sheet at 400 for about 5 minutes on each side, until crispy. If desired, add more seasonings when you turn the chips.

Option: Use split pita bread cut in wedges instead of tortillas.

Nutrition: (per serving): 71 calories

Saturated fat . . . . 0 g
Total Fat . . . . 1 g   (14% of calories)
Protein . . . . 2 g   (12% of calories)
Carbohydrates . . . . 13 g   (74% of calories)

Cholesterol . . . . 0 mg   Sodium . . . . 54 mg
Fiber . . . . 1 g   Iron . . . . 1 mg
Vitamin A . . . . 29 IU   Vitamin C . . . . 0 mg

Source: Gerry Krag is the consulting nutritionist and group facilitator for the Downriver Reversal Team.

♥ ♥ ♥

Spinach Dip

Enjoy this at your next party

Serves 8 — Each serving is about 1/3 cup

Preparation: :10   Cook :00   Stand 4:00   Total 4:10

Ingredients:

1	10 ounce package frozen chopped spinach, thawed and squeezed dry
1	package dry vegetable soup mix, fat free
1	cup fat free sour cream
3/4 -1	cup fat free mayonnaise
1	4 ounce can water chestnuts, chopped
3	green onions, chopped, optional

Stir all ingredients together. Cover and refrigerate for 4 hours or more (overnight is better). Stir before serving. Serve with fat free bread rounds or fat free crackers.

Nutrition: (per serving): 45 calories

Saturated fat . . . . 0 g
Total Fat . . . . 0 g   (8% of calories)
Protein. . . . . 2 g   (15% of calories)
Carbohydrates . . . . . . 9 g   (76% of calories)

Cholesterol . . . . 0 mg   Sodium . . . . 612 mg
Fiber . . . . 1 g   Iron . . . . 1 mg
Vitamin A . . . . 2752 IU   Vitamin C . . . . 9 mg

Source: Mary Lou Radcliffe Shabinaw is the sister of Bill Radcliffe. Bill has coronary artery disease.

♥ ♥ ♥

Mexican Bean Dip

Great for Company

Serves 16 — Each serving is about 1/3 cup

Preparation: :05   Cook :10   Stand :30   Total :45

Ingredients:

1	14 ounce can fat free refried beans
8	ounces fat free cream cheese
16	ounces fat free picante sauce
12	ounces fat free pizza cheese
1	cup lettuce
1	large tomato

Let the cream cheese soften at room temperature. Mix cream cheese and refried beans together. Spread into a square baking pan (8 x 8 or larger).

Pour the picante sauce over the beans mix and sprinkle the cheese on top. Bake at 350 degrees for ten minutes. Meanwhile, chop the lettuce and tomato. Sprinkle them on top. Serve with fat free corn chips.

Option: This is also good served cold.

Nutrition: (per serving): 88 calories

Saturated fat . . . . 0 g
Total Fat . . . . 1 g (3% of calories)
Protein. . . . . 11 g (50% of calories)
Carbohydrates . . . . . . 10 g (47% of calories)

Cholesterol . . . . 4 mg	Sodium . . . . 711 mg
Fiber . . . . 1 g	Iron. . . . . 1 mg
Vitamin A . . . . 251 IU	Vitamin C . . . . 20 mg

Source: Kathy Williams is a homemaker who had bypass surgery in 1990.

♥ ♥ ♥

Curried Yogurt Dip with Broccoli

A great appetizer or healthy snack

Serves 4 — Each serving of dip is about 1/4 cup

Preparation: :10 Cook :02 Stand :30 Total :42

Ingredients:

1   cup plain fat free yogurt
1   teaspoon curry powder
1   teaspoon paprika
1   teaspoon ground coriander
1/2 teaspoon ground cumin
1   pound broccoli florets

In a small bowl, combine yogurt and spices; refrigerate. Blanch broccoli in boiling water for 2 minutes; drain and pat dry. Cool. Serve with yogurt dip.

Nutrition: (per serving): 47 calories

Saturated fat . . . . 0 g	
Total Fat . . . . 1 g	(12% of calories)
Protein. . . . . 4 g	(31% of calories)
Carbohydrates . . . . 7 g	(58% of calories)
Cholesterol . . . . 0 mg	Sodium . . . . 32 mg
Fiber . . . . 2 g	Iron . . . . 2 mg
Vitamin A. . . . . . . 2107 IU	Vitamin C . . . . . . 107 mg

Source: Carol Rhora is a neurodiagnostic technician who had a heart attack in 1992 and has hypertension. *"If not for this program, I feel that I would have had another heart attack."*

♥ ♥ ♥

Pickled Plum Mayonnaise

Great on veggie burgers and vegetables

Serves 64 – each serving is 1 tablespoon

Preparation: :05   Cook :00   Stand :00   Total :05

Ingredients:

3-3/4   cups fat free mayonnaise
1/4   cup plum sauce, pickled, such as Eden® Pickled Plum Sauce
1   dash black pepper

Place ingredients in bowl and whisk until well blended. This sauce adds zip to potato salad and vegetables.

Nutrition: (per serving): 1 calorie

Saturated fat . . . . 0 g		
Total Fat . . . . 0 g	(1% of calories)	
Protein. . . . . 0 g	(1% of calories)	
Carbohydrates . . . . 0 g	(98% of calories)	
Cholesterol . . . . 0 mg	Sodium . . . . 140 mg	
Fiber . . . . 0 g	Iron . . . . 0 mg	
Vitamin A. . . . . 1 IU	Vitamin C . . . . 0 mg	

Source: Bob Shank is a retired Episcopal priest with multiple risk factors for coronary artery disease. Bob is now the executive director of the Cranbrook Peace Foundation.

"The path to healing a heart is much like the peace process. It takes openess, clear communication and persistence. Neither is easy, but the rewards are well worth the effort."

♥ ♥ ♥

Bob's Special Vegetable Pate

A delectable and colorful appetizer or side dish

Serves 10

Preparation: 1:00 Cook 2:00 Stand 2:00 Total 5:00

Ingredients:

	vegetable oil cooking spray	1	tablespoon lemon juice
3/4	cup apple juice	1	small white onion, chopped
1/2	cup scallions, or leeks, white part only	2	tablespoons dry white wine, or sherry
1	10 ounce package frozen chopped spinach		salt to taste
			ground pepper to taste
2	8 ounce packages fat free egg substitute	3	carrots, large, cooked until soft
3/4	cup evaporated skim milk	2	tablespoons unbleached flour
1/2	cup bread crumbs, dry, whole wheat	1/4	teaspoon ground ginger
1/2	cup fat free cottage cheese	1/4	teaspoon nutmeg
8	ounces fresh mushrooms		chopped parsley

Heat oven to 350°F. Lightly spray a 9 x 5 loaf pan with vegetable oilcooking spray.

Layer 1: Saute the scallions in 1/2 cup of the apple juice until translucent. Add the spinach and saute for three more minutes. Remove from heat. In a medium bowl, combine egg substitute, 1/2 cup of the evaporated milk, 1/4 cup bread crumbs, and the cottage cheese. Add the spinach mixture and mix well until blended. Spoon into the prepared pan and smooth the surface.

♥ ♥ ♥

Layer 2: Trim the mushrooms and wipe them clean. Toss six perfect mushrooms with the lemon juice and set aside. Chop the remaining mushrooms. Spray the bottom of a saucepan with vegetable oil cooking spray. Saute the reserved six mushrooms for five minutes. turning often. Lift out and arrange them in the pan over the spinach. Saute the chopped mushrooms and onion in the same saucepan with 1/4 cup apple juice until translucent. Stir in the wine or sherry. Season to taste with salt and pepper. Remove from heat. Add the egg substitute and 1/4 cup of the bread crumbs. Spoon the mixture over the spinach layer.

Layer 3: Puree the carrots in a food processor or blender until smooth. Spray a saucepan with vegetable oil cooking spray. Mix together the flour, 1/4 cup of evaporated milk, the ginger and nutmeg. Cook, stirring constantly until the mixture comes to a boil. Remove from heat and mix in remaining 1/2 cup egg substitute and the carrot puree. Spoon over the mushroom layer.

Cover the pan with waxed paper and then foil. Set in a large, deep pan. Pour boiling water into the outer pan to a depth of two inches. Bake until pate feels firm to the touch, about two hours. Transfer the pan to a wire rack and let cool for at least one hour. Refrigerate overnight. Let it come to room temperature before serving. Run a thin knife around the pate and turn it out on a plate. Invert the pate onto a parsley-covered plate so the pate is upright and garnish with chopped parsley.

Nutrition: (per serving): 102 calories

Saturated fat . . . . 0 g		
Total Fat . . . . 1 g	(5% of calories)	
Protein. . . . . 9 g	(34% of calories)	
Carbohydrates . . . . . . 17 g	(61% of calories)	
Cholesterol . . . . 2 mg	Sodium . . . . 206 mg	
Fiber . . . . 1 g	Iron . . . . 2 mg	
Vitamin A . . . . 8442 IU	Vitamin C . . . . 20 mg	

Source: Bob Shank is a retired Episcopal priest with multiple risk factors for coronary artery disease. Bob is now the executive director of the Cranbrook Peace Foundation.

♥ ♥ ♥

Tofu Cucumber Dip

A healthy appetizer for all occasions

Serves 8 — Each serving is about 2 tablespoons

Preparation: :10   Cook :00   Stand :00   Total :10

Ingredients:

1	8 ounce package Mori-Nu™ Light tofu
2	tablespoons soy sauce
1	small cucumber, chopped
1	tablespoon dried dill weed
1	pinch paprika, optional
1	pinch cayenne, optional

Combine all ingredients in a blender or food processor until creamy. Serve with vegetables, fat free chips or baked potatoes.

Note: Recipe was calculated using Mori-Nu™ 1% fat tofu.

Nutrition: (per serving): 22 calories

> Saturated fat . . . . 0 g
> Total Fat . . . . 0 g   (20% of calories)
> Protein. . . . . 3 g   (49% of calories)
> Carbohydrates . . . . 2 g   (31% of calories)
>
> Cholesterol. . . . . 0 mg   Sodium . . . . 289 mg
> Fiber . . . . 0 g   Iron . . . . 2 mg
> Vitamin A. . . . . 10 IU   Vitamin C . . . . 1 mg

Source: Babsi Riegler is a yoga instructor for the Downriver Reversal Team. She has a degree in psychology.

♥ ♥ ♥

Deviled Eggs

A low-fat alternative to the real thing

Makes 24

Preparation: :20   Cook :10   Stand :30   Total :60

Ingredients:

1	16 ounce can garbanzo beans, drained and rinsed
1/4	cup plain fat free yogurt
1	tablespoon Dijon mustard
1	tablespoon lemon juice
1	clove finely chopped garlic
	salt and pepper, to taste
12	hard boiled egg whites, halved

Blend, beat, mash or chop beans. Add yogurt, mustard, lemon juice, salt, pepper and garlic. Mix well and fill egg whites. Chill well and enjoy.

Option: Garnish with hot sauce just before eating.

Nutrition: (per serving): 41 calories

Saturated fat . . . . 0 g		
Total Fat . . . . 1 g	(12% of calories)	
Protein. . . . . 3 g	(34% of calories)	
Carbohydrates . . . . 5 g	(54% of calories)	
Cholesterol . . . . 0 mg	Sodium . . . . 105 mg	
Fiber . . . . 0 g	Iron . . . . 1 mg	
Vitamin A. . . . . 5 IU	Vitamin C . . . . 1 mg	

Source: Elsie Sarnecky is a retired food service worker with high blood pressure and multiple risk factors for coronary artery disease.

Triple Deck Mexican Tortillas

A great appetizer

Serves 16

Preparation: :20   Cook :20   Stand :05   Total :45

Ingredients:

1   10 ounce package frozen spinach, thawed and drained
1-1/2   cups fat free cottage cheese
1   16 ounce can fat free refried beans
2   tomatoes, diced
6   10-inch flour tortillas, fat free
2   cups grated fat free cheddar cheese
1/2   green or red bell pepper, chopped
1/2   small onion, chopped
        jalapeno pepper, as desired

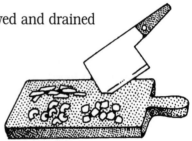

Mix spinach and cottage cheese. In another bowl, mix the beans and half of the chopped tomato. Spray a cookie sheet lightly with vegetable oil cooking spray. Place two tortillas on the sheet and spread each with all the spinach mixture. Put a second tortilla over each and spread all the bean mixture on top of each. Top each with 1/2 cup cheese. Put another tortilla on each and top with green pepper and onion. Bake in a 400°F oven for 15 minutes or until brown on edges. Remove from oven and top with remaining cheese and tomato. Return to oven and bake until cheese melts, about 5 minutes. Let stand five minutes. Cut each into 8 pie shaped wedges and serve. Top with salsa.

♥ ♥ ♥

Nutrition: (per serving): 149 calories

Saturated fat . . . . 0 g		
Total Fat . . . . 0 g	(2% of calories)	
Protein . . . . 13 g	(35% of calories)	
Carbohydrates . . . . . . 23 g	63% of calories)	

Cholesterol . . . . 2 mg	Sodium . . . . 423 mg
Fiber . . . . 1 g	Iron . . . . 1 mg
Vitamin A . . . . 1520 IU	Vitamin C . . . . 12 mg

Source: Richard Mills and Cheryl Taylor. Richard owns a company that installs custom fences. He had a heart attack in 1985 and angioplasty in 1985 and 1986.

"I've been in the program since 1993. The build up in my carotid arteries has decreased dramatically. I have more endurance and I feel great."

♥ ♥ ♥

Garbanzo Ghanoush

A variation of the middle eastern Baba Ghanoush

Serves 8 — Each serving is about 1/4 cup

Preparation: :15   Cook :25   Stand :00   Total :40

Ingredients:

1	cup fat free broth	1/2	teaspoon paprika
1	eggplant	16	ounces canned chickpeas
1/2	onion, chopped	2	tablespoons lemon juice
1/4	teaspoon salt		chopped fresh parsley for garnish
3	cloves garlic, minced		
1/4	teaspoon seasoned pepper		

Peel eggplant and cut in one inch cubes. Saute the eggplant, onion, garlic and seasonings in broth until the eggplant is soft and very tender and the liquid is completely evaporated. Drain and rinse chickpeas. Blend the eggplant with the chickpeas and lemon juice until smooth in a food processor or blender. Use as a dip with fat free chips or with whole grain pita bread. Serve either hot or cold.

Nutrition: (per serving): 82 calories

Saturated fat . . . . 0 g		
Total Fat . . . . 1 g	(8% of calories)	
Protein . . . . 3 g	(17% of calories)	
Carbohydrates . . . . 16 g	(75% of calories)	
Cholesterol . . . . 0 mg	Sodium . . . . 262 mg	
Fiber . . . . 1 g	Iron . . . . 1 mg	
Vitamin A . . . . 111 IU	Vitamin C . . . . 5 mg	

Source: Babsi Riegler is a yoga instructor for the Downriver Reversal Team. She also has a degree in psychology.

♥ ♥ ♥

Salsa Grande

Easy to prepare

Serves 8 — Each serving is about 1/3 cup

Preparation: :15   Cook :00   Stand :30   Total :45

Ingredients:

16	ounces canned stewed tomatoes, low salt
1	clove garlic, minced (or more, if you prefer)
1	tomato, chopped
1/4	cup diced canned green chiles
1/4	cup onions, diced
1	teaspoon vinegar
	fresh chopped parsley or cilantro, as desired
	seasoned pepper, to taste

Chop the stewed tomatoes. Mix all ingredients, refrigerate to let flavors blend. If you like hotter salsa, add more chiles.

Option: Instead of canned chiles, use fresh chopped jalepeno peppers.

Nutrition: (per serving): 26 calories

Saturated fat . . . . 0 g			
Total Fat . . . . 0 g	(6% of calories)		
Protein . . . . 1 g	(12% of calories)		
Carbohydrates . . . . 5 g	(82% of calories)		
Cholesterol . . . . 0 mg	Sodium . . . . 127 mg		
Fiber . . . . 0 g	Iron . . . . 1 mg		
Vitamin A . . . . 458 IU	Vitamin C . . . . 17 mg		

Source: Gerry Krag is the consulting nutritionist and group facilitator for the Downriver Reversal Team.

Salads

Salads

Picnic Potato Salad 37

Vichyssoise Potato Salad 38

Mixed Bean Salad 39

Babsi's Famous Rice Salad 40

Mock Tuna Salad 41

Broccoli Dressing 42

Egg Salad 43

Apple Coleslaw 44

Classic Molded Salad 45

Oriental Spinach Salad 46

Vegetable Pasta Salad 47

Taco Salad 48

Raspberry Fruit Salad 50

Blueberry Spice Vinegar 52

Easy Trio Pasta Salad 53

Lemon Dill Garlic Vinegar 54

Raspberry Vinegar 55

♥ ♥ ♥

Picnic Potato Salad

Don't wait for a picnic to try this tasty salad

Serves 12 — a serving is about 3/4 cup

Preparation: :30   Cook :25   Stand 1:00   Total 1:55

Ingredients:

2	pounds small new red potatoes
12	hard boiled egg whites
1	green bell pepper
3	stalks celery
3	bunches green onions
1/2	cup skim milk
1	pint fat free mayonnaise
1	tablespoon McCormicks Salt Free Table Seasoning

Boil potatoes until tender, about 25-35 minutes. Cool potatoes, but do not peel. Cut them into quarters. Remove yolks from the eggs and chop the whites. Chop the pepper, celery, and onion as finely as possible. Mix the potatoes, egg whites, and the chopped vegetables together in a large bowl. In a smaller bowl, mix the mayonnaise, milk, and seasoning until smooth. Add to the potatoes and gently stir all the ingredients together. Chill at least an hour before serving. Can be made the day before.

Nutrition: (per serving): 129 calories

Saturated fat . . . . 0 g		
Total Fat . . . . 0 g	(3% of calories)	
Protein. . . . . 4 g	(12% of calories)	
Carbohydrates . . . . . . 27 g	(85% of calories)	
Cholesterol. . . . . 0 mg	Sodium . . . . 210 mg	
Fiber . . . . 2 g	Iron . . . . 2 mg	
Vitamin A. . . . . 364 IU	Vitamin C . . . . 33 mg	

Source: Sally Roulinson, 58, is a seamstress and artist who had a heart attack in 1990, angioplasty in 1993 and bypass in 1995.

♥ ♥ ♥

Vichyssoise Potato Salad

Elegant but easy – with excellent taste

Serves 4 — a serving is about 1 cup

Preparation: :40   Cook :30   Stand 1:00   Total 2:10

Ingredients:

10	new potatoes	3	tablespoons white wine vinegar
3	tablespoons fat free broth	1	tablespoon Dijon mustard
2	cups leeks, chopped	1/4	teaspoon tarragon
3/4	cup green onions		salt and pepper to taste
1/2	cup fresh parsley, chopped		
1/2	cup fat free yogurt		

Cook potatoes until tender. Cool. Chop the leeks and measure two cups. Heat broth in saucepan and add the leeks. Saute for five minutes. Slice potatoes. Chop parsley and measure 1/2 cup. Chop onion and measure 3/4 cup. Mix the yogurt, vinegar and mustard in a small dish until well blended. In a large bowl, mix all the ingredients and toss gently. Cover and chill well before serving.

Nutrition: (per serving): 200 calories

Saturated fat . . . . 0 g		
Total Fat . . . . 1 g	(3% of calories)	
Protein. . . . . 6 g	(12% of calories)	
Carbohydrates . . . . . . 42 g	(85% of calories)	
Cholesterol . . . . 1 mg	Sodium . . . . 143 mg	
Fiber . . . . 2 g	Iron . . . . 4 mg	
Vitamin A. . . . . 524 IU	Vitamin C . . . . 36 mg	

Source: Doris Ferenczi. Doris is married to Jim, 73, a retiree who enjoys gardening and grandchildren. Jim had angioplasty in 1989 and 1993.

♥ ♥ ♥

Mixed Bean Salad

A simple but good vegetarian protein source

Serves 12 — a serving is about 3/4 cup

Preparation: :15   Cook :00   Stand 2:00   Total 2:15

Ingredients:

1	16 ounce can kidney beans, drained
1	16 ounce can green beans, drained
1	16 ounce can wax beans, drained
1	16 ounce can garbanzo beans, drained
1/2	green bell pepper, diced
1/2	cup celery, diced
1/4	cup sweet pickle relish
1/2	cup onions, chopped
	fat free Italian salad dressing, as needed

Rinse all beans. Mix together beans, bell pepper, celery, relish and onion. Add enough fat free dressing to coat the vegetables; mix and let stand for several hours.

Nutrition: (per serving): 225 calories

Saturated fat . . . . 0 g		
Total Fat . . . . 1 g	(5% of calories)	
Protein. . . . . 14 g	(24% of calories)	
Carbohydrates . . . . . . 40 g	(71% of calories)	
Cholesterol . . . . 0 mg	Sodium . . . . 280 mg	
Fiber . . . . 4 g	Iron . . . . 5 mg	
Vitamin A. . . . . 321 IU	Vitamin C . . . . 14 mg	

Source: Paul Bodrie is a Catholic lay pastoral assistant and university instructor who had heart attacks in 1989 and 1992 and angioplasty in 1989.

♥ ♥ ♥

Babsi's Famous Rice Salad

Looks as good as it tastes

Serves 6 — a serving is 2/3 cup

Preparation: :20   Cook :45   Stand :00   Total 1:05

Ingredients:

3   cups cooked brown rice
1   10 ounce package frozen green peas, thawed
1 1/2 red bell peppers, finely chopped
1/4   cup scallions, chopped
1   tablespoon fresh ginger root, grated, or 1 tsp. ginger powder
1   teaspoon powdered mustard
      black pepper, to taste
      cayenne pepper, to taste, optional
      fat free Italian salad dressing, as needed

Allow rice to cool. Then combine rice and vegetables. Add spices and dressing.

Option: Add 1 cup canned drained and rinsed garbanzo beans.

Nutrition: (per serving): 156 calories

Saturated fat . . . . 0 g		
Total Fat . . . . 1 g	(5% of calories)	
Protein. . . . . 5 g	(13% of calories)	
Carbohydrates . . . . . . 32 g	(81% of calories)	
Cholesterol . . . . 0 mg	Sodium . . . . 60 mg	
Fiber . . . . 2 g	Iron . . . . 1 mg	
Vitamin A . . . . 1415 IU	Vitamin C . . . . 44 mg	

Source: Babsi Riegler is a yoga instructor for the Reversal Team. She also has a degree in psychology.

♥ ♥ ♥

Mock Tuna Salad

Has the texture and appearance of tuna; makes a great sandwich

Serves 2

Preparation: :10   Cook :00   Stand :00   Total :10

Ingredients:

6	ounces canned chickpeas
1/4	cup fat free mayonnaise
1	tablespoon mustard
1	tablespoon sweet pickle relish
2	green onions

Use about half of a can of chickpeas. Rinse well and put in a small bowl; mash with a fork. Mix in mayonnaise, mustard and relish. Finely chop the onions and mix in.

Options: spread on toast for a sandwich. Good with sliced tomato and lettuce. Can be made without mayonnaise. Vary the ingredients and seasonings according to your own preferences.

Nutrition: (per serving): 120 calories

Saturated fat . . . . 0 g		
Total Fat . . . . 1 g	(10% of calories)	
Protein . . . . 5 g	(15% of calories)	
Carbohydrates . . . . 22 g	(75% of calories)	

Cholesterol . . . . 0 mg	Sodium . . . . 406 mg
Fiber . . . . 1 g	Iron . . . . 1 mg
Vitamin A . . . . 30 IU	Vitamin C . . . . 4 mg

Source: Alta Prince is a homemaker who had a heart attack in 1987 and bypass surgery in 1995.

♥ ♥ ♥

Broccoli Dressing

Tastes great over rice, baked potatoes or salad

Serves 8 — a serving is about 1/2 cup

Preparation: :15   Cook :00   Stand :30   Total :45

Ingredients:

1/4   cup tomato paste
1   cup water
2 to 3   tablespoons lemon juice
        soy sauce, to taste
1   teaspoon basil, fresh or dried
1   teaspoon dill
        salt, to taste
        black pepper, to taste
4   cups broccoli, cooked, drained and cooled

Blend tomato paste and water until smooth. Then blend with all of the rest of the ingredients until creamy. Toss with broccoli. Soy sauce will increase the sodium level.

Nutrition: (per serving): 26 calories

Saturated fat . . . . 0 g		
Total Fat . . . . 0 g	(8% of calories)	
Protein . . . . 2 g	(26% of calories)	
Carbohydrates . . . . 4 g	(66% of calories)	

Cholesterol . . . . 0 mg	Sodium . . . . 73 mg
Fiber . . . . 1 g	Iron . . . . 1 mg
Vitamin A . . . . 866 IU	Vitamin C . . . . 46 mg

Source: Babsi Riegler is a yoga instructor for the Reversal Team. She also has a degree in psychology.

♥ ♥ ♥

Egg Salad

A delicious alternative to traditional egg salad

Serves 1

Preparation: :15   Cook :00   Stand :00   Total :15

Ingredients:

2	egg whites
4	ounces fat free egg substitute
2	tablespoons fat free mayonnaise
	mustard
	salt and pepper to taste

Hard boil two whole eggs. When cooled, remove the yolks and chop the whites. (Put the yolks in your compost bin!) Cook a one-egg portion of the egg substitute according to the instructions on the label. Do not add fat. Chop the egg substitute and add to whites. Mix in the mayonnaise and mustard as desired. Spread on whole grain bread and enjoy!

Options: chopped onion, celery, Romaine lettuce, or pickle relish will add zest to your sandwich.

Nutrition: (per serving): 83 calories

Saturated fat . . . . 0 g		
Total Fat . . . . 0 g	(0% of calories)	
Protein . . . . 18 g	(85% of calories)	
Carbohydrates . . . . 3 g	(14% of calories)	
Cholesterol . . . . 0 mg	Sodium . . . . 303 mg	
Fiber . . . . 0 g	Iron . . . . 2 mg	
Vitamin A . . . . 113 IU	Vitamin C . . . . 0 mg	

Source: Kathy Williams is a homemaker who had bypass surgery in 1990.

Apple Coleslaw

Crunchy, with a pleasing flavor

Serves 4 — a serving is 1 cup

Preparation: :25   Cook :00   Stand 1:30   Total 1:55

Ingredients:

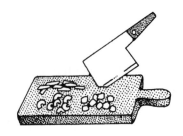

1/2	cup plain fat free yogurt
2	teaspoons sugar
1	teaspoon prepared mustard
1/8	teaspoon salt, optional
1	dash pepper
1	apple, cored and chopped
1/2	small carrot, shredded
1/2	stalk celery, thinly sliced
1-1/2	cups shredded cabbage
3	green onions, chopped

In a medium bowl, stir together yogurt, sugar, mustard, salt and pepper. Add apple and stir to coat. Add all other vegetables; toss lightly until all vegetables are coated. Chill 1-1/2 hours.

Nutrition: (per serving): 73 calories

Saturated fat . . . . 0 g		
Total Fat . . . . 0 g	(6% of calories)	
Protein . . . . 1 g	(8% of calories)	
Carbohydrates . . . . 16 g	(87% of calories)	
Cholesterol . . . . 0 mg	Sodium . . . . 121 mg	
Fiber . . . . 2 g	Iron . . . . 1 mg	
Vitamin A . . . . 1268 IU	Vitamin C . . . . 24 mg	

Source: Helen Moses is a homemaker who keeps busy babysitting her grand-children. Helen has coronary artery disease.

♥ ♥ ♥

Classic Molded Salad

An old family favorite, revisited

Serves 9

Preparation: :15   Cook :00   Stand 1:00   Total 1:15

Ingredients:

1	cup boiling water
1	package lime jello
2	cups miniature marshmallows
16	ounces fat free cottage cheese
1	16 ounce can pineapple, well drained

Boil water and place in a bowl. Sprinkle the gelatin on top and mix well. Add the marshmallows and mix well. Mix in the rest of the ingredients. Pour into an 8 inch square pan or into your favorite mold. Refrigerate until firm.

Note: this salad sets up in about an hour, making it convenient to prepare.

Option: Use sugar free jello.

Nutrition: (per serving): 97 calories

Saturated fat . . . . 0 g		
Total Fat . . . . 0 g	(2% of calories)	
Protein . . . . 7 g	(29% of calories)	
Carbohydrates . . . . 17 g	(69% of calories)	
Cholesterol . . . . 4 mg	Sodium . . . . 211 mg
Fiber . . . . 0 g	Iron . . . . 0 mg
Vitamin A . . . . 94 IU	Vitamin C . . . . 8 mg

Source: Patricia McKenna, 61, is a homemaker with diabetes who had heart bypass surgery in 1991. She also had a kidney bypass in 1991.

♥ ♥ ♥

Oriental Spinach Salad

Great with stir fry

Serves 8 — a serving is 1-3/4 cups

Preparation: :30   Cook :05   Stand :00   Total :35

Ingredients:

1	cup water, cold	3	cups mung bean sprouts, fresh
1	tablespoon cornstarch		
1/2	teaspoon dry mustard	2	cups carrots, thinly sliced or julienned
1/2	cup maple syrup		
1/4	teaspoon dry ginger	1	16 ounce can mandarin orange sections, drained
2	tablespoons low sodium soy sauce		
		1/2	cup chopped red onions
1/2	cup apple cider vinegar	1	6 ounce can water chest-
6	cups spinach, tightly packed		nuts, chopped

Blend the cornstarch and water in a small saucepan. Heat over medium heat, stirring constantly, until liquid bubbles and thickens. Cool. In a salad dressing shaker, mix the cooled liquid, the mustard, maple syrup, ginger, soy sauce and vinegar. Mix well and refrigerate. Mix the remaining salad ingredients together. Taste dressing. If it is too strong, dilute with a little cool water. Pour enough of the dressing to coat the spinach. Toss well and serve.

Nutrition: (per serving): 153 calories

Saturated fat . . . . 0 g		
Total Fat . . . . 1 g	(3% of calories)	
Protein . . . . 3 g	(9% of calories)	
Carbohydrates . . . . 34 g	(88% of calories)	
Cholesterol . . . . 0 mg	Sodium . . . . 311 mg	
Fiber . . . . 1 g	Iron . . . . 2 mg	
Vitamin A . . . . 11087 IU	Vitamin C . . . . 38 mg	

Source: Gerry Krag is the consulting nutritionist and group facilitator for the Downriver Reversal Team.

♥ ♥ ♥

Vegetable Pasta Salad

Quick and easy

Serves 8 — a serving is about 1-1/2 cups

Preparation: :10   Cook :20   Stand :30   Total :60

Ingredients:

1   pound pasta
12   ounces frozen vegetables, California blend
        fat free dressing

Cook pasta according to box. Thaw vegetables. Use either thawed or slightly cooked vegetables. Mix cooled pasta and vegetables together and season with your favorite fat free dressing.

Nutrition: (per serving): 242 calories

Saturated fat . . . . 0 g
Total Fat . . . . 1 g   (7% of calories)
Protein . . . . 8 g   (16% of calories)
Carbohydrates . . . . 50 g   (77% of calories)

Cholesterol . . . . 0 mg   Sodium . . . . 309 mg
Fiber . . . . 1 g   Iron . . . . 3 mg
Vitamin A . . . . 1819 IU   Vitamin C . . . . 1 mg

Source: Betty Gerlach's husband Chuck is a pharmacist who had a valve replacement and bypass surgery in 1995.

"This is not an impossible diet. I have benefitted as well as Chuck, as we journey together toward a healthier lifestyle."

♥ ♥ ♥

Taco Salad

A meal in itself

Serves 10 — a serving is about 1-1/2 cups

Preparation: :20   Cook :00   Stand :00   Total :20

Ingredients:

2	cups fat free textured soy protein
2	cups water
1	packet fat free taco seasoning mix, (1/2 cup)
1	cup fat free refried beans
4	tablespoons green onions, chopped
4	tablespoons green or red bell peppers, chopped
1	tomato, diced
2	cups shredded lettuce
2	cups fat free sour cream
3	cups grated fat free cheddar cheese
2	cups salsa
1	8 ounce package corn chips made without fat

Mix water and soy protein in a skillet. Let stand for five minutes. Stir in the taco seasoning and heat until warm. Add the refried beans and continue to cook. If mixture thickens too much, add a little water. Keep pan on a warm burner while chopping the onion, pepper, lettuce and tomato. Use a large salad bowl and make several layers of the corn chips, the seasoned soy protein, onion, green pepper, tomato, sour cream, lettuce and cheese. Top with cheddar cheese. Toss gently and top each serving with salsa.

♥ ♥ ♥

Nutrition: (per serving): 246 calories

Saturated fat . . . . 0 g	
Total Fat . . . . 1 g	(3% of calories)
Protein . . . . 27 g	(43% of calories)
Carbohydrates . . . . 33 g	(54% of calories)

Cholesterol . . . . 0 mg	Sodium . . . . 462 mg
Fiber . . . . 5 g	Iron . . . . 3 mg
Vitamin A . . . . 282 IU	Vitamin C . . . . 10 mg

Source: Kathryn M. Peters is a homemaker with blocked arteries.

". . . this threw me for a loop. I really believed that my chest pain was from a hiatal hernia. When I was told it was heart disease, all I did was cry. Then I started the program and soon I knew that I could get better. When I first started the program, I could not go up stairs, could not walk to my corner. could not do the dishes or even hang up clothes without my chest hurting. I had little stamina and felt tired all the time. I listened and learned and exercised and followed the eating plan and now I can walk up 2-1/2 flights of stairs without a problem. I can walk all over without getting tired. My exercise tolerance on the treadmill and stationary bike has improved dramatically. My 10 year old goes right along with me and she is proud of what I've done and she plans to stay healthy, too. If you are thinking about following a reversal program, give yourself a break and do it — trust and you will get better every week."

Kathryn M. Peters

♥ ♥ ♥

Raspberry Fruit Salad

Makes a hearty lunch

Serves 4 — a serving is 2 cups

Preparation: :20   Cook :00   Stand :00   Total :20

Ingredients:

2	cups fresh spinach, chopped
2	cups red leaf lettuce, chopped
1	4 ounce can mandarin orange sections
1	cup kidney beans, rinsed
1	cup canned chickpeas, rinsed
1	apple, diced
1	finely sliced red onion
1	cup fat free sour cream
3	tablespoons raspberry vinegar
3	tablespoons honey, or sugar substitute
1	tablespoon raspberry jam

Put first seven ingredients in a salad bowl and gently toss. Set aside. Mix sour cream, vinegar, honey and jam in a small bowl until well blended. Pour over salad and toss.

Optional Dressing: Instead of a sour cream based dressing, use arrowroot thickened dressing. Ingredients: 1/2 cup water, 1/2 cup raspberry vinegar, 1-2 tablespoons arrowroot, several packages of artificial sweetener. Boil water and remove from heat. Stir in arrowroot until thickened. Mix in the rest of the ingredients. Pour over salad and toss.

♥ ♥ ♥

Nutrition: (per serving): 374 calories

Saturated fat . . . . 0 g		
Total Fat . . . . 1 g	(3% of calories)	
Protein . . . . 16 g	(17% of calories)	
Carbohydrates . . . . 75 g	(80% of calories)	

Cholesterol . . . . 0 mg	Sodium . . . . 185 mg
Fiber . . . . 5 g	Iron . . . . 6 mg
Vitamin A . . . . 2717 IU	Vitamin C . . . . 33 mg

Source: Jeanne M. Eckert, 62, is a homemaker and gardening expert who grows her own herbs. In addition to having coronary artery disease, she has blockages in her legs.

"I believe that if I had not joined this reversal program a year ago, I would have had a heart attack by now. I would recommend it for anyone, even those in good health, as a preventative to heart disease"

Jeanne M. Eckert

♥ ♥ ♥

Blueberry Spice Vinegar

Use on tossed salads, fruit salads or steamed vegetables

Serves 32 — a serving is 1 ounce

Preparation: :30   Cook :00   Stand :00   Total :30

Ingredients:

3	cups blueberries, fresh or frozen
2	cinnamon sticks, crushed in half
1/2	whole nutmeg, cracked
4	cups white vinegar
3	tablespoons sugar, or substitute such as Sweet and Low™

Put blueberries, cinnamon and nutmeg in a half gallon glass container, such as a mayonnaise jar. In a medium saucepan, combine vinegar and sugar. Bring to a boil, *but remove from heat immediately. Do not continue boiling.* Stir to dissolve sugar. Pour hot mixture over berries. Cover jar with waxed paper or plastic wrap; then put on lid. Let stand 4 days to one week. Pour through a strainer and a second time with a coffee filter inserted in the strainer. Rebottle and use to season foods and make salad dressings.

Nutrition: (per serving): 19 calories

Saturated fat . . . . 0 g		
Total Fat . . . . 0 g	(2% of calories)	
Protein . . . . 0 g	(2% of calories)	
Carbohydrates . . . . 5 g	(96% of calories)	
Cholesterol . . . . 0 mg	Sodium . . . . 1 mg	
Fiber . . . . 0 g	Iron . . . . 0 mg	
Vitamin A . . . . 14 IU	Vitamin C . . . . 2 mg	

Source: Jeanne M. Eckert is a homemaker and gardening expert who grows her own herbs. She has blockages in her coronary arteries as well as in her legs.

♥ ♥ ♥

Easy Trio Pasta Salad

The pasta and vegetables are appealing and colorful

Serves 10 — a serving is about 1-1/4 cups

Preparation: :30   Cook :00   Stand :30   Total 1:00

Ingredients:

8	ounces pasta, tricolor twists	1	cup frozen green peas
1	green bell pepper	2	stalks celery
1	yellow bell pepper	2	tomatoes
1	red bell pepper	1	cup corn
1/2	sweet red onion		fresh ground black pepper
1/2	white onion		fat free Italian dressing, to
2	carrots		taste
2	cloves garlic, minced		salad seasoning, to taste

Cook the pasta as directed on package. Meanwhile, cut vegetables in bite-size pieces. When pasta is cooled, add all ingredients in a large salad bowl, mixing well. Use your favorite dressings and seasonings.

Nutrition: (per serving): 184 calories

Saturated fat . . . . 0 g		
Total Fat . . . . 1 g	(5% of calories)	
Protein . . . . 6 g	(14% of calories)	
Carbohydrates . . . . 36 g	(81% of calories)	
Cholesterol . . . . 0 mg	Sodium . . . . 417 mg	
Fiber . . . . 3 g	Iron . . . . 2 mg	
Vitamin A . . . . 5499 IU	Vitamin C . . . . 61 mg	

Source: Ronald Konopka, 52, is an auto stylist who had angioplasty in 1988 and 1990 and bypass in 1994.

". . . Since joining the program, my health has improved dramatically."

♥ ♥ ♥

Lemon Garlic Dill Vinegar

To be enjoyed and shared with others

Serves 16 — a serving is about 1 tablespoon

Preparation: :20   Cook :00   Stand :00   Total :20

Ingredients:

1	lemon
1	pint vinegar

4 to 5 sprigs fresh dill
1 clove garlic

Peel lemon without the white pith, in one continuous strip from top to bottom. Place lemon peel and dill in a glass quart jar with lid. Pour vinegar into jar until it is full. Cover jar. If lid is metal, place a piece of plastic wrap or waxed paper over jar before covering with lid. Place in a sunny window for 2-3 weeks, shaking occasionally. Strain through cheese cloth. Strain again through a coffee filter. Pour into sterilized bottles. Cap or cork tightly. Fresh dill, lemon peel or garlic may be added for show. Makes 1 pint. If using for gifts, you may want to cork bottles and then seal them with paraffin wax.

Options: this recipe can be prepared with other herbs such as tarragon or mint. Fresh herbs are best, but dried can be used. May also be thickened with cornstarch or arrowroot.

Nutrition: (per serving): 8 calories

Saturated fat . . . . 0 g		
Total Fat . . . . 0 g	(2% of calories)	
Protein . . . . 0 g	(3% of calories)	
Carbohydrates . . . . 2 g	(96% of calories)	
Cholesterol . . . . 0 mg	Sodium . . . . 1 mg	
Fiber . . . . 0 g	Iron . . . . 0 mg	
Vitamin A . . . . 1 IU	Vitamin C . . . . 2 mg	

Source: Jeanne M. Eckert, 62, is a homemaker and gardening expert with blocked arteries.

♥ ♥ ♥

Raspberry Vinegar

Fat free and flavorful

Serves 16 — a serving is about 1 tablespoon

Preparation: :15   Cook :00   Stand :00   Total :15

Ingredients:

1	cup fresh raspberries
1	cup white vinegar, or white wine vinegar
	sugar or substitute to taste

Rinse raspberries in cold water. Drain and pat dry with paper towels. Place in non-metal container such as a 2 quart glass jar or bowl. Crush berries slightly with a wooden spoon. Add vinegar and cover. If using a metal lid, be sure to place plastic wrap or waxed paper on jar before covering, so that metal lid does not touch contents. Place in a sunny window for two or three weeks, shaking occasionally. Strain through cheese cloth into a non-metal container. Strain a second time through a coffee filter. Add sugar or sugar substitute to taste. Pour into a sterilized bottle. Three or four raspberries may be added for decoration. Makes one pint.

Options: If the vinegar tastes too strong, dilute with a little water. May be mixed with Dijon-style mustard (to taste) and used as a dressing. Add to fat free sour cream to make a creamy dressing. Experiment and have fun!

Nutrition: (per serving): 7 calories (analysis does not include sugar)

Saturated fat . . . . 0 g		
Total Fat . . . . 0 g	(5% of calories)	
Protein . . . . 0 g	(4% of calories)	
Carbohydrates . . . . 2 g	(91% of calories)	
Cholesterol . . . . 0 mg	Sodium . . . . 0 mg	
Fiber . . . . 0 g	Iron . . . . 0 mg	
Vitamin A . . . . 10 IU	Vitamin C . . . . 2 mg	

Source: Jeanne M. Eckert, 62, is a homemaker with blocked arteries.

Soups

Soups

Donna's Potato Soup 59

Vegetable Soup 60

Soup au Pistou 62

Ruby's Potato Soup 64

Mushroom Soup 65

Mildred's Minestrone 66

Cabbage and Beer Soup 68

Greek Lemon Rice Soup 70

Key West Ten Can Soup 71

Beet Soup 72

Hermit's Soup 73

Babsi's Navy Bean Soup 74

Fifteen Minute Bean Soup 75

Babsi's Potato Soup 76

Beet Soup a la Doris 77

Butternut Squash Soup 78

Sharon's Broccoli and
     Cheese Soup 79

Cabbage Soup 80

♥ ♥ ♥

Donna's Potato Soup

Chunky with mild seasoning

Serves 6

Preparation: :20   Cook :30   Stand :00   Total :50

Ingredients:

1	medium onion, chopped
1	finely chopped carrot
4	cups peeled, diced potatoes
4	cups fat free broth, low sodium
1/4	teaspoon dried thyme
1	teaspoon fresh or dried parsley
1/4	teaspoon black pepper

Add ingredients to pot. Bring to a boil. Reduce heat and simmer for 20 minutes or until tender. Mash potatoes with hand potato masher. Serve soup chunky.

Nutrition: (per serving): 134 calories

Saturated fat	0 g	
Total Fat	0 g	(1% of calories)
Protein	4 g	(11% of calories)
Carbohydrates	28 g	(87% of calories)

Cholesterol	0 mg	Sodium	14 mg
Fiber	1 g	Iron	1 mg
Vitamin A	3397 IU	Vitamin C	18 mg

Source: Donna Hardin, whose husband Larry is a tool and die maker, cross country biker and was a bypass surgery candidate in 1993.

"Since entering the program, I have not had any angina attacks. I have more energy and have lost 15 pounds. I don't find the diet hard at all except when I travel."

Vegetable Soup

A hearty soup that's even better the second day

Serves 16 — a serving is a generous cup

Preparation: :25   Cook 2:00   Stand :00   Total 2:25

Ingredients:

1/2	cup fat free broth
1	large onion, diced
1	cup cabbage, diced
1/2	cup celery, diced
2	potatoes, diced
2	cups green beans, fresh or frozen
2	cups peas, fresh or frozen
2	cups carrots, fresh or frozen
1/2	green pepper, diced
1	8 ounce can tomato sauce
29	ounces canned stewed tomatoes (or two 14-1/2 ounce cans)
1	10-3/4 ounce can tomato soup (use Pritikin low-fat soup)
1	16 ounce can kidney beans
1	pinch garlic powder
1	tablespoon parsley
1	teaspoon sugar
	salt and pepper, and Mrs. Dash, to taste
	bottled hot pepper sauce, if you like it spicy (optional)
1	cup rotini noodles, uncooked

Saute onion in 1/2 cup fat free broth. Add cabbage, salt and pepper. Cook until cabbage and onion are soft. Dice vegetables. Add tomato sauce, stewed tomatoes, tomato soup, spices, parsley and vegetables. Add enough water to cover the vegetables. Simmer on low heat for about 1-1/2 hours. Cook noodles; drain and add to soup. Add water if needed.

♥ ♥ ♥

Nutrition: (per serving): 190 calories

Saturated fat . . . . 0 g		
Total Fat . . . . 1 g	(2% of calories)	
Protein . . . . 10 g	(21% of calories)	
Carbohydrates . . . . 36 g	(76% of calories)	

Cholesterol . . . . 0 mg	Sodium . . . . 314 mg
Fiber . . . . 3 g	Iron . . . . 4 mg
Vitamin A . . . . 4545 IU	Vitamin C . . . . 30 mg

Source: Clyde Whitehead is an elementary school teacher who had a heart attack and bypass surgery in 1990.

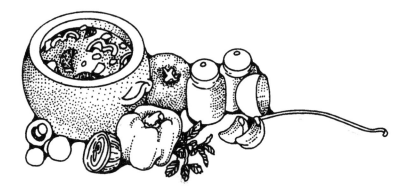

♥ ♥ ♥

Soup au Pistou

Easy, fast and delicious—good to eat anytime

Serves 10 — a serving is about 2 cups

Preparation: :45   Cook :00   Stand :00   Total :45

Ingredients:

3	quarts water
8-10	low sodium fat free bouillon cubes
3	potatoes, peeled and diced
1/2	pound green beans, fresh or a one pound can
2	carrots, sliced or diced
1	onion, sliced in thin circles
2	teaspoons salt, optional
1/4	teaspoon pepper
1/2	pound zucchini, sliced in circles
1/2	pound summer squash, sliced in circles
1	16 ounce can kidney beans, rinsed
1/4	pound macaroni, such as elbow

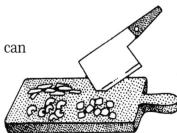

Sauce:

4	cloves garlic, minced
1	6 ounce can tomato paste
1	tablespoon basil
1/2	cup parsley

Combine soup ingredients in a large pot and bring to boil. Reduce heat and simmer until vegetables are tender. Mix the sauce ingredients together and add to soup. Continue cooking for about 10 minutes.

If spicier soup is desired, add 1-1/2 cups fat free pizza sauce.

♥ ♥ ♥

Nutrition: (per serving): 201 calories (analyzed without salt)

Saturated fat . . . . 0 g		
Total Fat . . . . 1 g	(3% of calories)	
Protein . . . . 8 g	(16% of calories)	
Carbohydrates . . . . 41 g	(81% of calories)	

Cholesterol . . . . 0 mg	Sodium . . . . 185 mg
Fiber . . . . 5 g	Iron . . . . 4 mg
Vitamin A . . . . 4986 IU	Vitamin C . . . . 30 mg

Source: Judith Caplan Phillips is the general manager of an ad specialty supplier. She had a bypass in 1992 and has diabetes.

"Becoming a vegetarian was easy. I was determined not to repeat my medical history. The best benefit of the program is the weight loss and the new energy I feel. The unexpected benefit was my husband joining me as a vegetarian — he has lost over 30 pounds without trying. My daughters were so impressed they started an exercise and veggie program on their own!"

Judith Caplan Phillips

♥ ♥ ♥

Ruby's Potato Soup

Warm your tummy with this on a cool day

Serves 6 — a serving is about 1 cup

Preparation: :15   Cook :50   Stand :00   Total 1:05

Ingredients:

8	potatoes, peeled and diced	2	cups skim milk
1	large onion, chopped	2	tablespoons fat free
1	large carrot, shredded		margarine
1	teaspoon cilantro		seasonings of your choice
	salt and pepper, to taste		

Boil potatoes, onions and carrots until tender; drain. Add milk, cilantro, salt and pepper. Mash the potatoes in mixture until lumpy. Add your favorite seasonings, such as rosemary. Simmer 15 minutes longer. Add margarine about 5 minutes before serving. Serve hot.

Nutrition: (per serving): 344 calories

Saturated fat	0 g	
Total Fat	1 g	(1% of calories)
Protein	10 g	(12% of calories)
Carbohydrates	75 g	(87% of calories)

Cholesterol	1 mg	Sodium	136 mg
Fiber	3 g	Iron	4 mg
Vitamin A	4390 IU	Vitamin C	46 mg

Source: Ruby Dedenbach is a homemaker who had bypasses in 1988 and 1992 and stent surgery in 1995.

"Because of low-fat eating, I was taken off Mevacor."

♥ ♥ ♥

Mushroom Soup

Wonderful as a soup or use it as a sauce for pasta and rice

Serves 4 — a serving is one cup

Preparation: :30   Cook :00   Stand :00   Total :30

Ingredients:

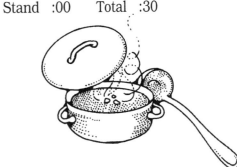

1	pound mushrooms
3	cups fat free broth
8	ounces fat free cream cheese
1	tablespoon chopped chives

Wash mushrooms and cut into chunks. In a medium saucepan, simmer mushrooms in the broth until tender. Cut the cream cheese into eight pieces and add to mushrooms. Stir well to blend the cheese into the liquid. Do not overcook. Place the soup in a food processor or blender and process until the mushrooms are coarse. Pour into bowls and serve garnished with chives.

Nutrition: (per serving): 87 calories

Saturated fat . . . . 0 g		
Total Fat . . . . 0 g	(5% of calories)	
Protein . . . . 11 g	(50% of calories)	
Carbohydrates . . . . 9 g	(45% of calories)	

Cholesterol . . . . 0 mg	Sodium . . . . 278 mg
Fiber . . . . 1 g	Iron . . . . 4 mg
Vitamin A . . . . 16 IU	Vitamin C . . . . 4 mg

Source: Wendy Krag is the sister-in-law of Gerry Krag, dietitian for the Reversal Team.

♥ ♥ ♥

Mildred's Minestrone

A mellow soup with a hint of garlic

Serves 10 — a serving is one cup

Preparation: :45   Cook 2:25   Stand :00   Total 3:10

Ingredients:

1/2	cup dried beans
1/2	cup elbow macaroni
1	onion, chopped
2	cloves garlic
7	cups fat free broth
1	carrot
2	potatoes
1	tomato
1/2	cup green beans
1	teaspoon sage
1	teaspoon parsley
1	teaspoon oregano
1/2	cup fresh spinach

Select your favorite dried beans and cook them according to package until beans are tender. Set aside. Cook the pasta according to package, but cook only until firm (al dente) and set aside. Chop the onion, garlic, carrot, potatoes, tomato, green beans and spinach. In a large soup pot, saute the onion and garlic in a small amount of the broth for about five minutes. Add the rest of the broth, bring to a rolling boil and add all the chopped vegetables except the spinach. Add the herbs. Simmer until vegetables are tender. Add the cooked beans, pasta, and spinach. Simmer until pasta is soft. If desired, add salt and seasonings to taste. Try a little basil and seasoned pepper.

Option: Add a few tablespoons of tomato paste for additional flavor.

♥ ♥ ♥

Nutrition: (per serving): 74 calories

Saturated fat . . . . 0 g		
Total Fat . . . . 0 g	(3% of calories)	
Protein . . . . 2 g	(11% of calories)	
Carbohydrates . . . . 16 g	(86% of calories)	

Cholesterol . . . . 0 mg	Sodium . . . . 10 mg
Fiber . . . . 1 g	Iron . . . . 1 mg
Vitamin A . . . . 2354 IU	Vitamin C . . . . 12 mg

Source: Mildred F. Conley is a homemaker who had a heart attack and bypass in 1983. In 1991 she had angioplasty.

"I have been earnest in changing my diet and am a regular 'mall walker.'"

Mildred F. Conley

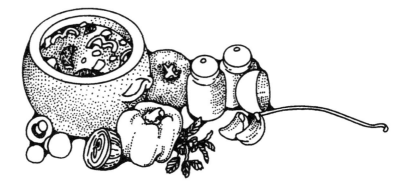

♥ ♥ ♥

Cabbage and Beer Soup

Taste the wonderful flavor of Denmark in this unique soup

Serves 10 — a serving is about 1 cup

Preparation: :45   Cook 4:25   Stand :00   Total 5:10

Ingredients:

1	28 ounce can tomatoes, chopped or stewed
2	cups tomato juice
1	cup water
3	cups fat free broth
2	lemons, juiced
3	tablespoons Worcestershire sauce
1	tablespoon basil, dried
1	tablespoon dry mustard
1/4	cup brown sugar, packed
1	tablespoon salt, optional
1	teaspoon ground pepper
1	cabbage, small white head, cored and coarsely chopped
2	Spanish onions, chopped
1	rutabaga, medium sized, peeled and chopped
2	celery stalks, chopped with leaves
12	fluid ounces beer, preferably dark

In large pot, combine the first eleven ingredients. Bring to a boil and then add cabbage, onions, rutabaga, celery and beer. Return to a boil and reduce heat and simmer for four hours.

Serve hot with pumpernickel bread. A can of northern beans can be added at the end and heated up.

♥ ♥ ♥

Nutrition: (per serving): 115 calories

Saturated fat . . . . 0 g		
Total Fat . . . . 1 g	(8% of calories)	
Protein . . . . 3 g	(12% of calories)	
Carbohydrates . . . . 21 g	(72% of calories)	
Alcohol . . . . 1 g	(8% of calories)	

Cholesterol . . . . 0 mg	Sodium . . . . 219 mg
Fiber . . . . 2 g	Iron . . . . 2 mg
Vitamin A . . . . 896 IU	Vitamin C . . . . 83 mg

Source: Judith Caplan Phillips is the general manager of an ad specialty supplier who had a bypass in 1992 and diabetes.

"Dr. Dean Ornish should be proud of this grassroots movement that has grown as a result of his book, Dr. Dean Ornish's Program for Reversing Heart Disease.*"*

Judith Caplan Phillips

♥ ♥ ♥

Greek Lemon Rice Soup

A fat free version of this ethnic favorite

Serves 6 — a serving is 3/4 cup

Preparation: :10   Cook :30   Stand :00   Total :40

Ingredients:

4   cups fat free broth, low sodium
1/4   cup rice, uncooked
6   egg whites
        juice of 1 lemon
        salt and pepper, to taste

Heat broth, add rice. Cover and simmer until rice is tender (approximately 30 minutes). Beat egg whites and lemon juice; add 1/2 cup broth to egg mixture (a tablespoon at a time to prevent eggs from scrambling) stirring constantly. Add egg mixture to remaining hot soup. Season to taste. Serve at once.

Nutrition: (per serving): 62 calories

Saturated fat . . . . 0 g		
Total Fat . . . . 0 g	(1% of calories)	
Protein . . . . 5 g	(38% of calories)	
Carbohydrates . . . . 8 g	(61% of calories)	

Cholesterol . . . . 0 mg	Sodium . . . . 55 mg
Fiber . . . . 0 g	Iron . . . . 1 mg
Vitamin A . . . . 2 IU	Vitamin C . . . . 5 mg

Source: Gerald Nagle, 63, is a retiree who enjoys traveling. He had bypass surgery and aortic valve replacement in 1988. He also has diabetes.

♥ ♥ ♥

Key West Ten Can Soup

Nice taste—use this base to develop other recipes

Serves 12 — a serving is about 1-1/2 cups

Preparation: :05   Cook :20   Stand :00   Total :25

Ingredients:

1	16 ounce can kidney beans	1	14 ounce can potatoes,
1	16 ounce can corn		sliced
1	16 ounce can creamed corn	4	cups broth
1	16 ounce cans butter beans	6	ounces bow tie or
2	4 ounce cans commercial mushrooms		farfalle pasta (optional)
2	14 ounce cans tomatoes, no salt added		garlic powder and
1	14 ounce can carrots		cajun seasonings

Combine all ingredients except pasta in a large saucepan. Cook over medium heat until liquid boils. Season with garlic powder and cajun seasonings to suit your taste. Cook about 15 minutes. If using pasta, cook separately and add to sauce. Serve with Crystal or Red Hot Cayenne Pepper Sauce. This will warm you up on a cold night! Those watching sodium should: 1) Use fresh or frozen corn, mushrooms and carrots. 2) Use reduced sodium broth and canned tomatoes with "no added salt." 3) Rinse beans, or cook dried beans from scratch.

Nutrition: (per serving): 362 calories

Saturated fat . . . . 0 g		
Total Fat . . . . 1 g	(4% of calories)	
Protein . . . . 18 g	(20% of calories)	
Carbohydrates . . . . 69 g	(77% of calories)	
Cholesterol . . . . 0 mg	Sodium . . . . 751 mg	
Fiber . . . . 4 g	Iron . . . . 6 mg	
Vitamin A . . . . 9901 IU	Vitamin C . . . . 25 mg	

Source: Cheryl Taylor and Richard Mills; Richard had a heart attack in 1985 and angioplasty in 1985 and 1986.

♥ ♥ ♥

Beet Soup

So easy, so delicious

Serves 8 — a serving is about 2 cups

Preparation: :10   Cook 1:30   Stand :45   Total 2:25

Ingredients:

16	cups fat free broth
1/2	cup celery
1/2	cup onions
3	16 ounce cans beets
1	cup vinegar
16	ounces fat free sour cream

Put the broth in a large pot. Chop the celery and onions and add to the broth. Simmer until vegetables are very soft. Strain off vegetables. If desired, puree and return to broth. Add beets to the broth with their own juice. Add the vinegar and simmer for 45 minutes. Let cool for 45 minutes and slowly blend in the fat free sour cream.

Options: Look for julienned cut beets. This soup is delicious when made with fresh beets.

Nutrition: (per serving): 99 calories

Saturated fat	0 g	
Total Fat	0 g	(2% of calories)
Protein	4 g	(18% of calories)
Carbohydrates	20 g	(80% of calories)

Cholesterol	3 mg	Sodium	153 mg
Fiber	1 g	Iron	2 mg
Vitamin A	300 IU	Vitamin C	20 mg

Source: Judy and Joe Borawski; Joe is a retired mail carrier who had bypass surgery in 1988.

♥ ♥ ♥

Hermit's Soup

A simple but flavorful soup to enjoy on chilly nights

Serves 8 — a serving is about 1 cup

Preparation: :30   Cook 1:10   Stand :00   Total 1:40

Ingredients:

1	turnip
2	carrots
1/2	cabbage
1	onion
1/4	cup apple juice
1/3	cup brown rice
8	cups fat free broth, low sodium
	salt and pepper to taste

Wash and trim the vegetables. Slice thinly and saute in the apple juice until heated through. Add the rice and broth. Stir well, cover the pan, and simmer slowly for one hour. Add the salt and pepper just before serving.

Nutrition: (per serving): 69 calories (analyzed without adding salt)

Saturated fat . . . . 0 g		
Total Fat . . . . 0 g	(5% of calories)	
Protein . . . . 2 g	(11% of calories)	
Carbohydrates . . . . 14 g	(84% of calories)	
Cholesterol . . . . 0 mg	Sodium . . . . 24 mg	
Fiber . . . . 1 g	Iron . . . . 1 mg	
Vitamin A . . . . 5142 IU	Vitamin C . . . . 35 mg	

Source: Bob Shank is a retired Episcopal priest with multiple risk factors for coronary artery disease. He is currently the executive director of the Cranbrook Peace Foundation.

Babsi's Navy Bean Soup

Satisfying and easy to prepare

Serves 8 — a serving is about one cup

Preparation: :25   Cook 2:00   Stand :00   Total 2:25

Ingredients:

1	pound navy beans, soaked overnight
1	large onion, chopped
2	cloves garlic, minced
1/2	teaspoon caraway seeds
1/2	teaspoon rosemary
2	tablespoons tomato paste
2	bay leaves
1/4	cup vinegar
	salt and pepper to taste

Rinse beans, place in pot and cover with water. Bring to boil, then add the rest of the ingredients. Simmer for two hours. Add salt and pepper. Remove bay leaves before serving. If you like it creamy, puree the cooked soup.

Option: Add more tomato sauce and vinegar as desired.

Nutrition: (per serving): 219 calories

Saturated fat	0 g	
Total Fat	1 g	(4% of calories)
Protein	13 g	(24% of calories)
Carbohydrates	39 g	(72% of calories)

Cholesterol	0 mg	Sodium	60 mg
Fiber	4 g	Iron	4 mg
Vitamin A	128 IU	Vitamin C	6 mg

Source: Babsi Riegler is a yoga instructor for the Downriver Reversal Team. She also has a degree in psychology.

♥ ♥ ♥

Fifteen Minute Bean Soup

No excuses for not making this easy, fast soup

Serves 8 — a serving is 1 cup

Preparation: :15   Cook :00   Stand :00   Total :15

Ingredients:

2	carrots
1/2	onion
2	tablespoons water
1	cup fat free broth, low sodium
32	ounces canned pinto beans, or other beans
16	ounces tomato sauce, low sodium
1	cup water
2	tablespoons fresh parsley
	salt and pepper to taste

Chop the carrots and onion. In a medium soup pot, cook the onion in the water until translucent, about 3-4 minutes. Add broth and bring to a boil. Add carrots, reduce heat and simmer for ten minutes. Add beans, tomato sauce and water. Simmer until heated through. Add parsley, salt and pepper to taste.

Nutrition: (per serving): 124 calories

Saturated fat . . . . 0 g		
Total Fat . . . . 1 g	(4% of calories)	
Protein . . . . 6 g	(20% of calories)	
Carbohydrates . . . . 24 g	(76% of calories)	
Cholesterol . . . . 0 mg	Sodium . . . . 489 mg	
Fiber . . . . 2 g	Iron . . . . 2 mg	
Vitamin A . . . . 5676 IU	Vitamin C . . . . 12 mg	

Source: Barbara Popyk, whose husband Marv had a heart attack in 1981.

♥ ♥ ♥

Babsi's Potato Soup

If you love potatoes, you'll enjoy this soup

Serves 8 — a serving is about 1 cup

Preparation: :25   Cook 2:00   Stand :00   Total 2:25

Ingredients:

5	large potatoes, sliced and peeled
6	cups water
2	onions, sliced
1	carrot, chopped
1/2	teaspoon ground thyme
1/2	bay leaf
1/4	teaspoon ground cloves
1	cut skim milk
	salt and pepper, to taste

Simmer potatoes, onions, carrots and spices in water for 50 minutes. Puree in blender or food processor, then add milk, salt and pepper, reheat but do not boil. Serve at once and enjoy.

Nutrition: (per serving): 251 calories

Saturated fat	0 g	
Total Fat	0 g	(1% of calories)
Protein	7 g	(11% of calories)
Carbohydrates	55 g	(88% of calories)

Cholesterol	1 mg	Sodium	85 mg
Fiber	2 g	Iron	3 mg
Vitamin A	2609 IU	Vitamin C	35 mg

Source: Babsi Riegler is a yoga instructor for the Downriver Reversal Team. She also has a degree in psychology.

♥ ♥ ♥

Beet Soup a la Doris

Creamy with a hint of tartness

Serves 6 — a serving is about 2 cups

Preparation: :20   Cook 1:15   Stand :00   Total 1:35

Ingredients:

2	cups fat free broth	3	tablespoons concentrated
6	cups water		lemon juice
4	potatoes, peeled and grated		pepper, to taste
8	beets, peeled and grated	3	tablespoons flour
	beet tops, chopped	1	cup fat free sour cream
3	tablespoons white vinegar		

In a large soup pot, cook the potatoes, beets and chopped beet tops in the broth and water until very tender, about one hour. Then add vinegar and lemon juice and pepper, as desired. Remove one cup of the soup and put in small saucepan. Allow it to cool. Add the flour and the sour cream. Blend well and then add to soup. Stir well but do not overheat.

Nutrition: (per serving): 243 calories

Saturated fat . . . . 0 g		
Total Fat . . . . 0 g	(2% of calories)	
Protein . . . . 7 g	(12% of calories)	
Carbohydrates . . . . 52 g	(86% of calories)	
Cholesterol . . . . 0 mg	Sodium . . . . 222 mg	
Fiber . . . . 2 g	Iron . . . . 3 mg	
Vitamin A . . . . 2477 IU	Vitamin C . . . . 51 mg	

Source: Doris Ferenczi, who is married to Jim, 73, a retiree who enjoys gardening and grandchildren. Jim had angioplasty in 1989 and 1993.

♥ ♥ ♥

Butternut Squash Soup

Sweet and yummy

Serves 6 — a serving is 1-1/2 cups

Preparation: :20   Cook 2:20   Stand :00   Total 2:40

Ingredients:

1	butternut squash
1/2	cup fat free broth
3	medium leeks
1	tablespoon dried thyme
6	cups fat free broth, low sodium
	salt and pepper, to taste

Bake or microwave whole squash until tender. Cool well and scoop out seeds and membranes. Mash squash well. Chop leeks. In large soup pot, cook leeks in the 1/2 cup broth until soft. Add the thyme. Add the 6 cups of broth and bring to a boil. Add the mashed squash and simmer an additional 15-20 minutes.

Options: Add chopped broccoli or potatoes

Nutrition: (per serving): 165 calories

Saturated fat . . . . 0 g		
Total Fat . . . . 0 g	(3% of calories)	
Protein . . . . 4 g	(11% of calories)	
Carbohydrates . . . . 36 g	(87% of calories)	
Cholesterol . . . . 0 mg	Sodium . . . . 22 mg	
Fiber . . . . 4 g	Iron . . . . 4 mg	
Vitamin A . . . . 17792 IU	Vitamin C . . . . 55 mg	

Source: Doris Ferenczi, who is married to Jim, 73, a retiree who enjoys gardening and grandchildren. Jim had angioplasty in 1989 and 1993.

♥ ♥ ♥

Sharon's Broccoli and Cheese Soup

In a word: Excellent

Serves 8 — a serving is about 2 cups

Preparation: :15   Cook :20   Stand :00   Total :35

Ingredients:

4	cups fat free broth, low sodium	4	cups broccoli, chopped
12	ounces frozen shredded hash brown potatoes, about 2 cups	3	tablespoons flour
		2	cups skim milk
1	cup celery, chopped	8	ounces fat free pasteur-
1	cup onions, chopped		ized cheese, cubed
1	cup carrots, chopped		salt and pepper to taste

Put broth and vegetables in a large stock pot and bring to boil. Simmer until vegetables are tender, about 15 minutes. Blend flour with milk and add to vegetables, stirring constantly until soup thickens. Remove from heat. Add cheese cubes and stir until cheese is melted and smooth. Season to taste.

Options: Use more cheese, if you prefer a cheesier flavor. Sprinkle a bit of paprika on each bowl before serving. If you want your broccoli to remain bright green, put it in the soup about five minutes after the other vegetables.

Nutrition: (per serving): 144 calories

Saturated fat . . . . 0 g		
Total Fat . . . . 1 g	(4% of calories)	
Protein . . . . 13 g	(36% of calories)	
Carbohydrates . . . . 22 g	(60% of calories)	
Cholesterol . . . . 6 mg	Sodium . . . . 440 mg	
Fiber . . . . 1 g	Iron . . . . 1 mg	
Vitamin A . . . . 4691 IU	Vitamin C . . . . 49 mg	

Source: Sharon Hodge is married to Charles Hodge who has coronary artery disease.

♥ ♥ ♥

Cabbage Soup

A family favorite

Serves 8 — a serving is about 2 cups

Preparation: :10   Cook :45   Stand :00   Total :55

Ingredients:

1	head cabbage, chopped
2	cups chopped celery
1	cup onions, chopped
1	tablespoon lemon juice
46	ounces tomato juice
1	dash liquid hot pepper sauce, optional
2	cups fat free broth
12	ounces club soda
	salt and pepper to taste

Combine all ingredients in a large pot. Cook approximately 45 minutes or until desired tenderness. Soup is better on the second day.

Option: Use reduced sodium tomato juice.

Nutrition: (per serving): 80 calories

Saturated fat . . . . 0 g		
Total Fat . . . . 0 g	(4% of calories)	
Protein . . . . 3 g	(16% of calories)	
Carbohydrates . . . . 16 g	(80% of calories)	
Cholesterol . . . . 0 mg	Sodium . . . . 693 mg	
Fiber . . . . 2 g	Iron . . . . 2 mg	
Vitamin A . . . . 1090 IU	Vitamin C . . . . 88 mg	

Source: Charles Hodge is a journeyman millwright and volunteer firefighter, who has blocked arteries.

Breads

Breads

Gene's Dill Bread 83

Honey Whole Wheat Bread 84

Sweet Potato Rolls 86

Basic White Bread 88

Estella's Fat Free Dinner Rolls . .90

Bran Muffins 91

Raisin Bread 92

Apple Muffins 93

Al's Carrot Muffins 94

Yummy Morning Cereal 96

Edie's Granola 97

Estella's Dark Pumpernickel
    Batter Bread 98

Fran's Bran Muffins 100

Zesty Corn Muffins 101

Shaun's Carrot Raisin
    Muffins 102

Zucchini Bread 104

♥ ♥ ♥

Gene's Dill Bread

Makes two round loaves

Serves 36

Preparation: :25   Cook :35   Stand 1:00   Total 2:00

Ingredients:

3	cups multi grain bread flour	1/2	cup fat free yogurt
3-1/2	cups all-purpose flour 1/2	4	ounces fat free egg substitute
	cup sugar	1	egg white
2	teaspoons salt	1	teaspoon dried dill weed, divided
2	packets active dry yeast	1/2	teaspoon basil
1	cup water	3/4	teaspoon dried onion flakes
1	cup skim milk		vegetable oil cooking spray

In a large bowl, combine one cup multi grain bread flour and one cup of all purpose flour with the sugar, salt, yeast and 1/2 teaspoon dill. Blend well. In a small container, heat the water and milk in the microwave to 120° to 130°F. Add hot liquid to mix and blend well. Mix in the yogurt, egg substitute and beat well until moistened and lump free. Stir remaining flour into dough until dough pulls away from bowl. On floured surface, knead dough until smooth and elastic, 5-10 minutes. If dough is sticky, add additional flour as needed. Place dough in a bowl sprayed with vegetable oil cooking spray. Cover with towel and let rise until doubled, about 60 minutes. Punch down and make into two round loaves. Place on a baking sheet. In a small container, beat egg white until frothy. Add the remaining dill, the basil and the onion flakes. Blend well with a fork. Brush the top of each loaf with the egg white mixture. Bake loaves at 350°F for 35-40 minutes.

Nutrition: (per serving): 102 calories

Saturated fat . . . . 0 g		
Total Fat . . . . 0 g	(3% of calories)	
Protein . . . . 4 g	(14% of calories)	
Carbohydrates . . . . 21 g	(83% of calories)	
Cholesterol . . . . 0 mg	Sodium . . . . 144 mg
Fiber . . . . 0 g	Iron . . . . 1 mg
Vitamin A . . . . 17 IU	Vitamin C . . . . 0 mg

Source: Gene Pluhar, 52, is a high school teacher who had heart attacks in 1992 and 1995.

♥ ♥ ♥

Honey Whole Wheat Bread

Makes two wonderful loaves

Serves 36

Preparation: :25   Cook :40   Stand 1:15   Total 2:20

Ingredients:

6 to 7   cups whole wheat flour
2   envelopes quick-rise active dry yeast
1   tablespoon salt
2-1/4   cups warm water (125-130°F)
1/3   cup honey
1/4   cup applesauce
          vegetable oil cooking spray

Mix 3-1/2 cups flour, the yeast and salt in a large bowl. Water should be 125-130°F. Stir in water, honey and applesauce. Beat until smooth. Mix in enough remaining flour to make dough easy to handle. Turn onto lightly floured surface and knead about ten minutes or until smooth and elastic. Cover and let rest for ten minutes.

Lightly spray two loaf pans, either 8 or 9 inches. Punch down dough and divide in half. Roll each half into a rectangle 18 x 9 inches. Roll up each rectangle beginning at the short side. With the side of hand, press ends to seal. Fold ends under loaves. Place each with seam side down in loaf pan. Cover and let rise 45-60 minutes, or until double.

Heat oven to 375°F. Place pans on low rack so that tops are in center of oven. Pans should not touch each other or sides of oven. Bake 35-40 minutes or until deep golden brown and loaves sound hollow when tapped. Remove from pans. Cool on wire rack.

♥ ♥ ♥

Nutrition: (per serving): 85 calories

Saturated fat . . . . 0 g		
Total Fat . . . . 0 g	(4% of calories)	
Protein . . . . 3 g	(14% of calories)	
Carbohydrates . . . . 18 g	(82% of calories)	

Cholesterol . . . . 0 mg	Sodium . . . . 197 mg
Fiber . . . . 0 g	Iron . . . . 1 mg
Vitamin A . . . . 0 IU	Vitamin C . . . . 0 mg

Source: Patrick Beaudrie, 59, is a retiree who had a heart attack and bypass surgery in 1989.

"With a dedicated staff and the help of the support group, you can't go wrong. I've lost 28 pounds and my cholesterol numbers are right where they should be. My latest thallium stress test showed significant improvement. I plan on being around for a long time! A big part of the program's success is the support group and of course Dr. Rogers. Without him, there would be no program."

Patrick Beaudrie

♥ ♥ ♥

Sweet Potato Rolls

Sweet potatoes add a southern twist to these wonderful dinner rolls

Serves 18

Preparation: :40   Cook :20   Stand 1:30   Total 2:30

Ingredients:

3-3/4 to 4 cups flour, or bread flour
1/4   cup sugar
1   teaspoon salt
1   package or 2-1/4 teaspoons active dry yeast
1   cup skim milk
1/4   cup applesauce
3/4   cup mashed canned sweet potatoes
1/4   cup fat free egg substitute

In a large bowl, combine 1 cup flour, sugar, salt and yeast; blend well. In a small saucepan, heat milk and applesauce until very warm (120-130°F). Add warm liquid, sweet potatoes and egg substitute to flour mixture. Blend at low speed until moistened; beat 2 minutes at medium speed. By hand, stir in remaining 2-3/4 to 3 cups flour to form a soft dough (dough will be somewhat sticky). On a floured surface, knead dough until smooth and elastic, about 2 minutes. Place dough in bowl sprayed with non-stick cooking spray; cover loosely with plastic wrap and cloth towel. Let rise in a warm place (80 to 85°F) until light and dough has doubled in size, about 45 to 55 minutes. Spray 2 large cookie sheets with non-stick cooking spray. Punch down dough several times. On floured surface, toss dough lightly until it is no longer sticky. Divide dough into 18 pieces; shape into long rolls (6 to 8 inches) then tie into knots. Cover and let rise in a warm place until double in size (35 to 40 minutes). Bake in 325°F oven for 15 to 20 minutes.

Option: Makes 24 smaller rolls.

♥ ♥ ♥

Nutrition: (per serving): 121 calories

Saturated fat . . . . 0 g		
Total Fat . . . . 0 g	(2% of calories)	
Protein . . . . 3 g	(11% of calories)	
Carbohydrates . . . . 26 g	(86% of calories)	

Cholesterol . . . . 0 mg	Sodium . . . . 142 mg
Fiber . . . . 0 g	Iron . . . . 0 mg
Vitamin A . . . . 612 IU	Vitamin C . . . . 1 mg

Source: Estella Johnson, who helped with our food service during the first years of our program, developed many bread and dessert recipes that have become team favorites.

♥ ♥ ♥

Basic White Bread

Fresh from the oven, this is a warm and comforting bread

Serves 20

Preparation: :20   Cook :30   Stand 2:00   Total 2:50

Ingredients:

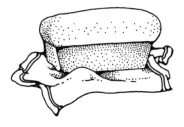

1/2   cup skim milk
3   tablespoons sugar
3   tablespoons applesauce
2   packages active dry yeast
1-1/2   cups warm water (105-115°F)
2   teaspoons salt
5 to 6 cups all-purpose flour
        vegetable oil cooking spray

Combine milk, sugar, salt and applesauce in small saucepan. Heat over low heat until sugar dissolves. Cool to lukewarm. Dissolve yeast in warm water in warmed bowl. Add lukewarm milk mixture and 4-1/2 cups flour along with salt. Mix well on medium speed for several minutes until well blended. Add remaining flour, 1/2 cup at a time, blending by hand, or use an electric mixer that is designed to handle yeast dough. Knead until dough is smooth and elastic. If kneading by hand, this will take a while. Dough will be slightly sticky to the touch. Place dough in a bowl sprayed with non-stick cooking spray, turning to coat top of dough. Cover and let rise in a warm place, free from drafts, until double in size (about 1 hour). Punch dough down and divide in half. Shape each half into a loaf and place in a sprayed loaf pan. Cover and let rise again until double in size (about 1 hour). Bake at 400°F for 30 minutes. Remove from pan immediately and cool on wire racks. Yield: 2 loaves.

♥ ♥ ♥

Nutrition: (per serving): 125 calories

Saturated fat . . . . 0 g		
Total Fat . . . . 0 g	(3% of calories)	
Protein . . . . 4 g	(12% of calories)	
Carbohydrates . . . . 27 g	(85% of calories)	

Cholesterol . . . . 0 mg	Sodium . . . . 239 mg
Fiber . . . . 0 g	Iron . . . . 0 mg
Vitamin A . . . . 13 IU	Vitamin C . . . . 0 mg

Source: Patrick Beaudrie, 59, is a retiree who had a heart attack and bypass surgery in 1989.

"With a dedicated staff and the help of the support group, you can't go wrong. I've lost 28 pounds and my cholesterol numbers are right where they should be. My latest thallium stress test showed significant improvement. I plan on being around for a long time! A big part of the program's success is the support group and of course Dr. Rogers. Without him, there would be no program."

Patrick Beaudrie

♥ ♥ ♥

Estella's Fat Free Dinner Rolls

A hearty dinner roll that's good with any meal

Serves 24

Preparation: :20   Cook :12   Stand 1:00   Total 1:32

Ingredients:

5-3/4 to 6-3/4 cups flour		1	cup water
1/2	cup sugar	1	cup skim milk
2	teaspoons salt	1/2	cup applesauce
2	packages active dry yeast	4	ounces fat free egg substitute

In a large bowl, combine 2 cups flour, sugar, salt and yeast; blend well. Heat water and milk until very warm. Add warm liquid to flour and blend well. Add applesauce and egg substitute. Blend at low speed until moistened; beat three minutes at medium speed. By hand, stir in an additional 2-1/2 to 3 cups flour until the dough pulls cleanly away from the sides of the bowl. On a floured surface, knead in 1-1/4 to 1-3/4 cups flour until dough is smooth and elastic, about 8-10 minutes. Place dough in a bowl sprayed with non-stick cooking spray; cover loosely with plastic wrap and cover with a cloth towel. Let rise in a warm place (80 to 85°F) until light and double in size, about 45-60 minutes. Punch down and make into 24 rolls. Bake in a 325°F oven for 10 to 12 minutes or until golden.

Nutrition: (per serving): 135 calories

Saturated fat . . . . 0 g		
Total Fat . . . . 0 g	(2% of calories)	
Protein . . . . 4 g	(12% of calories)	
Carbohydrates . . . . 29 g	(86% of calories)	
Cholesterol . . . . 0 mg	Sodium . . . . 208 mg	
Fiber . . . . 0 g	Iron . . . . 1 mg	
Vitamin A . . . . 26 IU	Vitamin C . . . . 0 mg	

Source: Estella Johnson, who helped with our food service during the first years of our program, developed many bread and dessert recipes.

♥ ♥ ♥

Bran Muffins

Bake ahead and freeze—great for busy mornings

Serves 24

Preparation: :10 Cook :25 Stand :00 Total :35

Ingredients:

1-1/2	cups bran or oatmeal	1-1/4	teaspoons baking soda
2	cups whole wheat flour	2	cups fat free buttermilk
2	tablespoons honey	1	egg white
1/2	teaspoon salt	1/2	cup dark molasses

Combine all ingredients and stir until mixed. Line muffin tins with paper liners, fill approximately 2/3 full. Bake at 350 degrees for 20-25 minutes. If you cannot find fat free buttermilk, use skim milk and add two teaspoons of vinegar to sour it. Then put it in the recipe.

For variety, add raisins, diced apples, well drained pineapple or substitute two cups applesauce for the buttermilk.

Nutrition: (per serving): 71 calories

Saturated fat . . . . 0 g		
Total Fat . . . . 0 g	(4% of calories)	
Protein . . . . 2 g	(12% of calories)	
Carbohydrates . . . . 15 g	(84% of calories)	
Cholesterol . . . . 0 mg	Sodium . . . . 101 mg	
Fiber . . . . 0 g	Iron . . . . 2 mg	
Vitamin A . . . . 0 IU	Vitamin C . . . . 0 mg	

Source: Carol Rhora is a neurodiagnostic technician who had a heart attack in 1992 and has hypertension.

"If not for this program, I feel that I would have had another heart attack."

♥ ♥ ♥

Raisin Bread

A special bread that's slightly sweet

Serves 20

Preparation: :20   Cook :30   Stand 1:45   Total 2:35

Ingredients:

1-1/2	cups raisins	2	packages active dry yeast
1	tablespoon cinnamon	1/4	cup fat free egg substitute
1-1/3	cups warm water	1/4	cup sugar
1	teaspoon salt	4 to 4-1/2 cups whole wheat flour (white	
2	tablespoons applesauce		flour may be substituted if you like)
1/4	cup water	cooking spray	

Heat raisins, 1/4 cup water and cinnamon until water is absorbed; cool. Dissolve yeast in 1-1/3 cups warm water (105 to 115 degrees). Stir in egg substitute, salt, sugar, applesauce and raisins. Mix in 4 to 4-1/2 cups flour. Knead on lightly floured surface at least 5 minutes. Let rise in bowl sprayed with nonstick cooking spray, until double in size. Punch down and form two loaves. Place dough in bread pans sprayed with fat free cooking spray. Let rise until double in size and bake in 350°F oven until brown (about 30 minutes). Turn onto wire racks to cool.

Nutrition: (per serving): 140 calories

Saturated fat . . . . 0 g			
Total Fat . . . . 1 g	(3% of calories)		
Protein . . . . 4 g	(11% of calories)		
Carbohydrates . . . . 30 g	(85% of calories)		
Cholesterol . . . . 0 mg	Sodium . . . . 121 mg		
Fiber . . . . 1 g	Iron . . . . 2 mg		
Vitamin A . . . . 2 IU	Vitamin C . . . . 1 mg		

Source: Patrick Beaudrie, 59, is a retiree who had a heart attack and bypass surgery in 1989.

"My latest thallium stress test showed significant improvement."

♥ ♥ ♥

Apple Muffins

Bake a batch for the favorite people in your life

Serves 12

Preparation: :20   Cook :25   Stand :10   Total :55

Ingredients:

1-3/4	cups sifted flour	3/4	cup brown sugar
2-1/2	teaspoons baking powder	1/4	cup sugar
1/2	teaspoon salt	1/4	cup applesauce
1	teaspoon cinnamon	4	golden delicious apples,
1	cup skim milk		peeled, cored and sliced
1/4	cup fat free egg substitute		

Sift flour, baking powder, salt and cinnamon. Place egg substitute in cup and add enough milk to equal 1 cup. Mix sugars and applesauce. Beat in egg mixture. Stir in dry ingredients. Stir in apples. Line muffin tin with cupcake liners. Fill cups to 2/3 full. Bake at 400°F for 20-25 minutes.

Nutrition: (per serving): 168 calories

Saturated fat . . . . 0 g	
Total Fat . . . . 0 g	(3% of calories)
Protein . . . . 3 g	(6% of calories)
Carbohydrates . . . . 38 g	(91% of calories)
Cholesterol . . . . 0 mg	Sodium . . . . 190 mg
Fiber . . . . 1 g	Iron . . . . 1 mg
Vitamin A . . . . 78 IU	Vitamin C . . . . 4 mg

Source: Patricia Fecker, R.N., is a nurse at Downriver Cardiology who enjoys cooking healthy food and adapting recipes.

♥ ♥ ♥

Al's Carrot Muffins

A terrific way to start the day

Serves 8

Preparation: :20   Cook :30   Stand :10   Total 1:00

Ingredients:

	vegetable oil cooking spray
1	cup oat bran
1-1/4	cups whole wheat flour
1	teaspoon baking soda
1/2	teaspoon baking powder
1	teaspoon ground cinnamon
1/4	teaspoon ground ginger
3	carrots
8	ounces fat free yogurt
1/2	cup fat free egg substitute
1/2	cup unsweetened applesauce
1/2	cup seedless raisins
1/3	cup brown sugar
1	teaspoon vanilla

Preheat oven to 350°F. Spray eight jumbo muffin cups with vegetable oil cooking spray or use a regular size muffin pan, but fill eight cups to the top. Mix all the dry ingredients into a medium size bowl. Shred the carrots. In a larger bowl, mix the shredded carrots, yogurt, egg substitute, applesauce, raisins, brown sugar and vanilla until well mixed. With spoon, stir the dry mixture gently into the liquid, stirring until the flour is moistened. Do not overmix.

Spoon into muffin pan. Bake for 30 minutes at 350°F or until a toothpick pushed into center comes out clean. Cool about 10 minutes before removing from pan.

Option: Use brown sugar substitute for the regular brown sugar.

♥ ♥ ♥

Nutrition: (per serving): 205 calories

Saturated fat . . . . 0 g		
Total Fat . . . . 1 g	(6% of calories)	
Protein . . . . 7 g	(13% of calories)	
Carbohydrates . . . . 41 g	(80% of calories)	

Cholesterol . . . . 1 mg	Sodium . . . . 161 mg
Fiber . . . . 3 g	Iron . . . . 2 mg
Vitamin A . . . . 7614 IU	Vitamin C . . . . 3 mg

Source: Al Spiteri, 52, is a journeyman in hydraulic repair. He had a heart attack in 1993.

"I thank God I was informed about this program and I pursued it until I joined the Downriver Reversal Team. Both my weight and my cholesterol are down. I'm avoiding surgery and feeling better than I ever have. In 1995, I was shown reasons why I should stop eating sugar. I thought I felt great before, but now I'm at a whole other level of "feeling great." My weight loss had plateaued, but since giving up sugar, I have lost an additional 20 pounds to the total of 50 lost since joining the program. My cholesterol is almost down to 150 and my triglycerides are now 88. I continue to learn better ways to keep me off the operating table as I continue to participate in the program."

Al Spiteri

♥ ♥ ♥

Yummy Morning Cereal

Start your day with this tasty treat

Serves 2

Preparation: :05   Cook :30   Stand :00   Total :35

Ingredients:

1/2	cup amaranth (or quinoa, oat groats or millet)
1	cup water
1 to 2	tablespoons raisins
1/4	cup pineapple, fresh, cut into small chunks
1	pinch ground cardamom
1	pinch ground cinnamon

Combine amaranth with water. Bring to a boil, reduce heat and simmer 25 minutes. Mix in remaining ingredients and serve.

Nutrition: (per serving): 57 calories

Saturated fat . . . . 0 g		
Total Fat . . . . 1 g	(10% of calories)	
Protein . . . . 1 g	(9% of calories)	
Carbohydrates . . . . 12 g	(81% of calories)	
Cholesterol . . . . 0 mg	Sodium . . . . 2 mg	
Fiber . . . . 1 g	Iron . . . . 1 mg	
Vitamin A . . . . 6 IU	Vitamin C . . . . 4 mg	

Source: Babsi Riegler is a yoga instructor for the Downriver Reversal Team. She also has a degree in psychology.

♥ ♥ ♥

Edie's Granola

Wonderful for breakfast or for a snack

Serves 24 — a serving is 1/2 cup

Preparation: :20   Cook 3:00   Stand :00   Total 3:20

Ingredients:

7	cups rolled oats, not quick	1/4	cup cinnamon, or to taste
1	cup untoasted wheat germ	3	cups Grape Nuts cereal
1	cup oat bran		cooking spray
1	12 ounce can frozen apple juice concentrate, or other flavor, thawed (recommended: raspberry or cherry)		

Lightly spray a 9 x 13 inch pan with vegetable oil cooking spray. In a large bowl, mix the oats, wheat germ, oat bran, the juice concentrate and cinnamon. Put in the pan and bake at 250°F until dry, about 3 hours. Add more cinnamon during baking, if desired. Cool and add Grape Nuts™ cereal. Store in an airtight container.

Nutrition: (per 1/2 cup serving): 152 calories

Saturated fat . . . . 0 g		
Total Fat . . . . 2 g	(9% of calories)	
Protein . . . . 5 g	(13% of calories)	
Carbohydrates . . . . 30 g	(78% of calories)	
Cholesterol . . . . 0 mg	Sodium . . . . 92 mg	
Fiber . . . . 2 g	Iron . . . . 2 mg	
Vitamin A . . . . 567 IU	Vitamin C . . . . 13 mg	

Source: The Reverend Edie Gause, who is married to Ken Miller. Ken had heart attacks in 1987 and 1988 and bypass surgery in 1988.

"Cooking fat free has opened up a whole new world of grains and flavors . . ."

♥ ♥ ♥

Estella's Dark Pumpernickel Batter Bread

A nice variation from traditional wheat bread

Serves 12

Preparation: :45   Cook :30   Stand 1:30   Total 2:45

Ingredients:

1	packet yeast
1-1/4	cups warm water
1	teaspoon salt
4	teaspoons unsweetened cocoa
3/4	teaspoon onion powder
3/4	teaspoon instant coffee, decaffeinated
2	tablespoons unsweetened applesauce
2	tablespoons molasses
4	teaspoons vinegar
1	cup rye flour
2	teaspoons caraway seeds
1/4	teaspoon fennel seeds

2 to 2-1/4 cups bread flour

In a large bowl or mixer, dissolve yeast in warm water (105-115°F). Blend in salt, cocoa, onion powder, instant coffee, applesauce, molasses and vinegar. Add rye flour, caraway and fennel seeds. Blend until well moistened. Stir in remaining flour to form a stiff batter. Cover loosely with plastic wrap and a cloth towel. Let rise in a warm spot (80-85°F) until double.

Punch dough down to remove all air bubbles. Make into 12 or 18 rolls or one 9 x 5 inch loaf. Let rise about 30-45 minutes until dough has doubled in size.

Bake at 325°F 15-20 minutes for rolls, 30-40 minutes for bread.

♥ ♥ ♥

Nutrition: (per serving): 128 calories

Saturated fat	0 g	
Total Fat	1 g	(5% of calories)
Protein	4 g	(13% of calories)
Carbohydrates	26 g	(83% of calories)

Cholesterol	0 mg	Sodium	205 mg
Fiber	0 g	Iron	2 mg
Vitamin A	2 IU	Vitamin C	0 mg

Source: Estella Johnson, who helped with our food service during the first years of our program, developed many bread and dessert recipes that have become team favorites.

♥ ♥ ♥

Fran's Bran Muffins

Delicious and satisfying

Serves 12

Preparation: :10   Cook :25   Stand :00   Total :35

Ingredients:

1-1/2 cups oat bran
1-1/2 cups wheat germ
1-1/2 teaspoons baking powder
1-1/2 cups prune juice
1   tablespoon sweetener
2   tablespoons fat free sour cream
4   ounces fat free egg substitute
1   cup raisins

In a large bowl, mix the oat bran, wheat germ and baking powder. In a small bowl, mix the prune juice, sweetener, sour cream and egg substitute. Add liquid ingredients to dry ingredients and mix well. Fold in the raisins. Line muffin tins with paper liners, fill approximately 2/3 full. Bake at 325°F for 20 to 25 minutes.

Nutrition: (per serving): 170 calories

Saturated fat . . . . 0 g		
Total Fat . . . . 2 g	(11% of calories)	
Protein. . . . . 6 g	(15% of calories)	
Carbohydrates . . . . 31 g	(74% of calories)	
Cholesterol. . . . . 0 mg	Sodium. . . . . 63 mg	
Fiber . . . . 3 g	Iron . . . . 2 mg	
Vitamin A. . . . . 12 IU	Vitamin C. . . . . 2 mg	

Source: Frances Eller, who is married to Lyle Eller, a retiree who enjoys computer work. Lyle had a heart attack in 1991.

♥ ♥ ♥

Zesty Corn Muffins

Ole!

Serves 12

Preparation: :10   Cook :20   Stand :00   Total :30

Ingredients:

1	cup corn meal	1	cup fat free buttermilk or 1 cup
	vegetable oil cooking spray		skim milk with 1 tablespoon
1	cup all-purpose flour		vinegar added
3	tablespoons sugar, or substitute	1/4	cup applesauce
1	tablespoon baking powder	1	4 ounce can green chilies, drained
2	egg whites, lightly whipped	3/4	cup shredded fat free cheese

Preheat oven to 400°F. Spray pan with vegetable oil cooking spray. Use either a 12 muffin pan or a 9 inch square pan. In a large bowl, combine cornmeal, flour, sugar and baking powder until well mixed. Make a well in the center. If fat free buttermilk is not available, put 1 tablespoon of vinegar into a measuring cup. Add skim milk to equal one cup. In a small bowl, mix the egg whites, milk and applesauce. Pour this into the well. Stir until just moistened. Quickly add the chilies and cheese. Spoon into muffin cups or pan. Bake 20-22 minutes until toothpick inserted in center comes out dry. Muffins cool best on a rack out of pan.

Nutrition: (per serving): 120 calories

Saturated fat . . . . 0 g		
Total Fat . . . . 0 g	(3% of calories)	
Protein . . . . 6 g	(19% of calories)	
Carbohydrates . . . . 23 g	(78% of calories)	
Cholesterol . . . . 1 mg	Sodium . . . . 280 mg	
Fiber . . . . 0 g	Iron . . . . 0 mg	
Vitamin A . . . . 112 IU	Vitamin C . . . . 7 mg	

Source: The Reverend Edie Gause, who is married to Ken Miller. Ken had heart attacks in 1987 and 1988 and bypass surgery in 1988.

♥ ♥ ♥

Shaun's Carrot Raisin Muffins

Great for breakfast or a snack

Serves 12

Preparation: :15   Cook :25   Stand 2:02   Total 2:42

Ingredients:

1	cup skim milk
1	cup oatmeal
1/2	cup raisins
	vegetable oil cooking spray
3/4	cup carrots, peeled and grated
1/4	cup brown sugar
1/4	cup white sugar
2	tablespoons applesauce
3	tablespoons fat free yogurt
2	egg whites
1	teaspoon grated orange rind
1/2	cup all-purpose flour
1/2	cup whole wheat flour
1	tablespoon baking powder
1/2	teaspoon baking soda

In a large bowl, pour milk over oats and raisins. Stir to mix and then cover and let stand for at least two hours. Batter can also be refrigerated overnight. Preheat oven to 400°F. Spray muffin tins lightly with vegetable oil cooking spray. In a small bowl, mix carrots, sugars, applesauce, yogurt, egg whites and grated orange rind. Stir into oat mixture. In another bowl, mix together the white and whole wheat flour, baking powder and baking soda. Stir into the batter until mix is barely moistened. Overmixing will cause muffins to be tough and have air tunnels. Spoon batter into prepared muffin tins. Bake for 20-25 minutes or until firm to touch. Remove from oven and let stand at least two minutes before removing from tins.

♥ ♥ ♥

Nutrition: (per serving): 130 calories

Saturated fat . . . . 0 g		
Total Fat . . . . 1 g	(6% of calories)	
Protein . . . . 4 g	(13% of calories)	
Carbohydrates . . . . 26 g	(81% of calories)	

Cholesterol . . . . 0 mg	Sodium . . . . 149 mg
Fiber . . . . 1 g	Iron . . . . 1 mg
Vitamin A . . . . 1982 IU	Vitamin C . . . . 1 mg

Source: Shaun P. Pochik. Shaun is a cardiovascular rehabilitation technician and a licensed paramedic. He also teaches martial arts at his health and fitness training center.

"To achieve good health takes more than a short term goal; it takes a life-long commitment."

Zucchini Bread

A yummy treat any time of the day

Serves 20

Preparation: :30   Cook 1:00   Stand :30   Total 2:00

Ingredients:

3/4	cup fat free egg substitute	1	teaspoon nutmeg
1	cup chunky style applesauce	1/2	teaspoon ginger
2-1/2	cups sugar	1	tablespoon baking soda
2-1/2	cups peeled and grated zucchini	1/2	teaspoon baking powder
3	teaspoons vanilla	3	cups flour
1	teaspoon salt		vegetable oil cooking spray
1-1/2	teaspoons cinnamon		

Preheat oven to 350°F. Beat egg substitute until light and fluffy. Stir in applesauce and sugar, then add vanilla and zucchini. Blend in spices, baking soda and baking powder. Fold in flour. Spray 2 loaf pans with non-stick cooking spray. Divide batter evenly into pans. Bake for 1 hour. Cool before slicing.

Nutrition: (per serving): 182 calories

Saturated fat . . . . 0 g		
Total Fat . . . . 0 g	(1% of calories)	
Protein . . . . 2 g	(5% of calories)	
Carbohydrates . . . . 43 g	(94% of calories)	
Cholesterol . . . . 0 mg	Sodium . . . . 251 mg	
Fiber . . . . 0 g	Iron . . . . 0 mg	
Vitamin A . . . . 58 IU	Vitamin C . . . . 2 mg	

Source: Chuck Hodge is a journeyman millwright and volunteer firefighter, who has blocked arteries.

"Thank God for this life saving program."

♥♥♥

Main Dishes

Main Dishes

Donna's Vegetarian Chili 107

Vegetarian Meatloaf 108

Vic's Baked Beans 110

Jennifer's Spinach Lasagna 112

Pizza Pasta Casserole 113

Jerry's Sweet and Sour Beans . . .114

Betty's Stuffed Peppers
    with Black Beans 116

Best Ever Black-Eyes 118

Kathy's Grilled Cheese
    Sandwich 120

Helen's Barley Casserole 121

Jerry's Vegetarian Chili 122

Southwestern Baked Beans 123

Diane's Kidney Bean Loaf 124

Tomato Relish 126

Dan's Grilled Cheese Sandwich . .127

Helen's Stuffed Peppers 128

Spaghetti Sauce 129

Cabbage Rolls 130

Sauerkraut Casserole 132

Lentil Loaf 133

Lasagna Roll-ups 134

Rice with Black Beans 136

Black Bean Vegetable Chili 138

Festival Couscous 140

Garlic Pepper Sauce 142

Stuffed Shells 143

Red Beans and Rice 144

Broccoli Strata 145

Meatless Sloppy Joe 146

Betty's Sausage Patties 148

Spaghetti Squash Casserole 150

John's Famous Chili 152

Soft Soy Tacos 153

Hearty Stew 154

Carol's Santa Fe Casserole 157

Imqarrun Fil-forn 158

Baked Bean Casserole 159

Vegetarian Stew 160

Bean Burritos 162

Enchilada Pie 164

Mickie's Gingered Asparagus
    Fettuccine 166

Cabbage, White Beans and Rice .168

Basic Burgers 170

Chop Suey 172

Sasaki 174

Barbeque Sandwiches 175

Wild Mushroom and Red Pepper
    Baked Pasta 176

Sandwich Spread 178

Southwest Spaghetti 179

Spaghetti Sauce Calderone 180

Sharon's Lasagna 182

Jeanne's "Chicken" & Dumplings .184

Easy Pot Pie 186

Pasta and Bean Stew 188

Bean Stuffed Spuds 189

Elbow Macaroni Skillet Dinner . .190

Green Goddess Pasta Sauce 191

Chickpea and Rice Casserole 192

♥ ♥ ♥

Donna's Vegetarian Chili

Warms you up on a stormy night

Serves 12 — a serving is about 1 cup

Preparation: :10   Cook :20   Stand :00   Total :30

Ingredients:

46	ounces low-sodium tomato juice
28	ounces diced canned tomatoes, no-salt-added
2	chopped, medium sized onions
2	tablespoons dried parsley
2	tablespoons chili powder, or more for taste
2	20 oz. cans Brook's™ chili beans

Bring first six ingredients to a boil in a large pot. Reduce the heat and simmer until thick. Add the Brook's™ chili beans. Simmer for about 20 minutes. Stir often or beans will stick.

Option: To reduce the sodium further, use plain cooked red beans.

Nutrition: (per serving): 240 calories

Saturated fat . . . . 0 g		
Total Fat . . . . 1 g	(5% of calories)	
Protein . . . . 14 g	(23% of calories)	
Carbohydrates . . . . 43 g	(72% of calories)	
Cholesterol . . . . 0 mg	Sodium . . . . 578 mg	
Fiber . . . . 4 g	Iron . . . . 4 mg	
Vitamin A . . . . 1989 IU	Vitamin C . . . . 34 mg	

Source: Donna Hardin, whose husband Larry is a tool and die maker, cross country biker and was a bypass surgery candidate in 1993.

"Since entering the program, I have not had any angina attacks. I have more energy and have lost 15 pounds. I don't find the diet hard at all except when I travel."

♥ ♥ ♥

Vegetarian Meatloaf

Serve with mashed potatoes and gravy

Serves 6

Preparation: :20   Cook 1:10   Stand :10   Total 1:40

Ingredients:

1-1/2 cups fat free textured soy protein
1-1/3 cups water
10   slices fat free dried bread
1   10-3/4 ounce can fat free broth
1   cup chopped onions
1   cup chopped carrots
1   cup chopped celery
1/4   cup fat free egg substitute
           black pepper, to taste
           vegetable oil cooking spray

Mix the soy protein with water until soy is soft and similar to hamburger. Soak bread in broth to soften. Squeeze out the extra broth, then mix all the above ingredients together. Mix should be the consistency of uncooked meatloaf. If it seems too moist, add bread crumbs or a little oatmeal. Spray a small loaf pan with non-stick cooking spray and place mixture into pan. Cover pan with foil and bake at 350°F for 1 hour. Remove foil and bake for 10 minutes more. Let sit 10 minutes before slicing.

Options: serve with tomato sauce or fat free gravy. Add minced garlic or other herbs to recipe. Poultry seasoning gives this recipe a mellow flavor.

♥ ♥ ♥

Nutrition: (per serving): 175 calories

Saturated fat . . . . 0 g	
Total Fat . . . . 1 g	(8% of calories)
Protein . . . . 20 g	(25% of calories)
Carbohydrates . . . . 29 g	(67% of calories)

Cholesterol . . . . 1 mg	Sodium . . . . 266 mg
Fiber . . . . 1 g	Iron . . . . 4 mg
Vitamin A . . . . 5184 IU	Vitamin C . . . . 3 mg

Source: Betty Verdone is married to Carmine Verdone who is retired. Carmine has had five heart attacks, bypass surgery in 1983, and stent surgery in 1994. He also has diabetes.

"I've been a strict vegetarian since 1992. If I had been a strict vegetarian for the past twenty years, I would have alleviated my heart disease and stabilized my diabetes, eliminating all its collateral complications. Being a strict vegetarian, I find I have stabilized my heart disease and diabetes. I believe being a strict vegetarian has improved my chances for a longer and better quality life."

Carmine Verdone

♥ ♥ ♥

Vic's Baked Beans

A mouth-watering favorite

Serves 12 — a serving is 1 cup

Preparation: :15   Cook 2:35   Stand 1:00   Total 3:50

Ingredients:

1-1/2   pounds dried great northern white beans, abut 3-1/2 to 4 cups
2   cups finely chopped onions
1-1/4   cups tomato based barbecue sauce
12   ounces hot, tomato based salsa
1/3   cup firmly packed brown sugar
1/4   cup Dijon mustard
1/4   cup molasses
2   teaspoons salt

Place white beans in heavy large Dutch oven. Cover with cold water. Bring to boil over medium-high heat. Remove from heat and let beans stand until cool, about one hour.

Drain beans. Return to same pot. Cover with cold water. Bring to boil over medium-high heat. Reduce heat to low and simmer about 20 minutes. Add two teaspoons salt and simmer 20 minutes longer. Drain beans, reserving 1-1/2 cups liquid.

Position rack in center of oven and preheat to 350°F. Combine cooked beans, reserved liquid, chopped onion, barbecue sauce, salsa, brown sugar, mustard, molasses and additional salt to taste in same large pot. Cover pot and bake bean mixture 1 hour. Uncover and bake until bean mixture is very thick, stirring occasionally, about 40 minutes longer.

Note: recipe can be prepared day ahead. Cover tightly and refrigerate. Before serving, warm over low heat, stirring frequently.

♥ ♥ ♥

Nutrition: (per serving): 269 calories

Saturated fat	0 g	
Total Fat	1 g	(3% of calories)
Protein	15 g	(22% of calories)
Carbohydrates	51 g	(75% of calories)

Cholesterol	0 mg	Sodium	868 mg	
Fiber	20 g	Iron	2 mg	
Vitamin A	384 IU	Vitamin C	7 mg	

Source: Victor R. Le Veque works in the flooring business and has multiple risk factors for coronary artery disease.

♥♥♥

Jennifer's Spinach Lasagna

No need to pre-cook the noodles; this is a delicious time-saver!

Serves 8

Preparation: :40   Cook 1:00   Stand :10   Total 1:50

Ingredients:

25-1/2 ounce jar of fat free spaghetti sauce
4   ounce carton fat free egg substitute
2   cups fat free ricotta or cottage cheese
1   10 ounce package frozen chopped spinach, thawed and drained
1   16 ounce package shredded fat free mozzarella cheese
1/4   cup fat free parmesan cheese
1   8 ounce box of lasagna noodles

Combine egg substitute, cottage cheese and spinach. Spread 3/4 cup spaghetti sauce in lightly sprayed 13 x 9 x 2 baking dish. Layer 1/2 each: uncooked lasagna noodles, spinach mixture, mozzarella cheese and parmesan cheese. Spread spaghetti sauce over top. Repeat for second layer. Cover with remaining spaghetti sauce. Cover dish securely with aluminum foil and bake at 350°F for 1 hour. Let stand 10 minutes before serving. To reduce sodium, look for low sodium spaghetti sauce.

Nutrition: (per serving): 265 calories

Saturated fat . . . . 0 g		
Total Fat . . . . 1 g	(3% of calories)	
Protein . . . . 32 g	(49% of calories)	
Carbohydrates . . . . 32 g	(48% of calories)	
Cholesterol . . . . 15 mg	Sodium . . . . 691 mg	
Fiber . . . . 0 g	Iron . . . . 2 mg	
Vitamin A . . . . 3009 IU	Vitamin C . . . . 9 mg	

Source: Paul Bodrie's daughter-in-law, Jennifer, developed this recipe. Paul had heart attacks in 1989 and 1992 and had angioplasty in 1989.

♥ ♥ ♥

Pizza Pasta Casserole

A family favorite

Serves 4

Preparation: :25   Cook :40   Stand :05   Total 1:10

Ingredients:

8   ounces elbow macaroni
32   ounces fat free spaghetti sauce
2   cups fat free mozzarella
      favorite toppings such as mushrooms

Prepare macaroni according to package. Drain. In an 8 or 9 inch square pan, spoon half of the sauce. Add the macaroni and spread evenly in the pan. Spread the remaining sauce over the noodles. Add toppings and cover with cheese. Bake in a 350°F oven until the mixture is set, about 40 minutes. Do not overcook or the cheese will get tough. Let set five minutes before cutting.

Options: Toppings can include broccoli, cauliflower, onion, green pepper, soy protein, "Lightlife™" ham substitute, or other fat free meat substitutes. Those watching sodium should look for reduced sodium spaghetti sauce and mozzarella.

Nutrition: (per serving): 286 calories

Saturated fat	0 g	
Total Fat	1 g	(3% of calories)
Protein	11 g	(15% of calories)
Carbohydrates	59 g	(82% of calories)

Cholesterol	0 mg	Sodium	712 mg
Fiber	1 g	Iron	4 mg
Vitamin A	1744 IU	Vitamin C	29 mg

Source: Barbara Popyk is married to Marv Popyk, a stock broker who had a heart attack in 1981.

♥ ♥ ♥

Jerry's Sweet and Sour Beans

An all time favorite, guaranteed

Serves 10 — a serving is 1-1/2 cups

Preparation: :30   Cook 1:15   Stand :00   Total 1:45

Ingredients:

1	cup chopped onions
1	clove garlic, minced
1	cup chopped celery
1/4	cup dark brown sugar
1	16 ounce can tomato sauce
1/2	cup chili sauce
1/4	cup dark molasses
1	teaspoon salt
1/4	teaspoon black pepper
2	dashes hot pepper sauce
1	pound great northern beans, or 2 - 48 ounce jars cooked beans
1	14 ounce can pineapple tidbits in juice, drained
1/2	cup sweet pickle relish

If using dried beans, cover with 2 inches of water, bring to a boil and boil 2 minutes. Remove from heat and let stand for 1 hour; then drain. Saute garlic and onions in liquid butter buds or broth. Stir in all other ingredients except pineapple, relish and beans. Simmer for 20 minutes. Add cooked beans, pineapple and relish. Stir and pour into casserole dish. Cover and bake at 350°F for 1 hour. Remove lid and bake 15 minutes more.

Options: To lower sodium, use tomato sauce with "no added salt" and eliminate the 1 teaspoon of salt.

♥ ♥ ♥

Nutrition: (per serving): 259 calories

Saturated fat . . . . 0 g
Total Fat . . . . 1 g   (3% of calories)
Protein . . . . 11 g   (17% of calories)
Carbohydrates . . . . 52 g   (80% of calories)

Cholesterol . . . . 0 mg   Sodium . . . . 626 mg
Fiber . . . . 4 g   Iron . . . . 5 mg
Vitamin A . . . . 1664 IU   Vitamin C . . . . 18 mg

Source: Gerald Nagle, 63, is a retiree who enjoys traveling. He had bypass surgery in 1988, aortic valve replacement and has diabetes.

Betty's Stuffed Peppers with Black Beans

The tangy sauce brings out the flavor of the peppers

Serves 6

Preparation: :35   Cook 1:00   Stand :00   Total 1:35

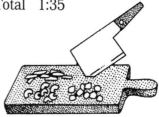

Ingredients:

6	green bell peppers
1	cup fat free textured soy protein
1	cup water
1	16 ounce can black beans, drained and pureed or 1 cup black bean flakes
1	cup rice, uncooked (do not use instant rice)
1/2	cup fat free egg substitute
1	cup onion, chopped
	pepper to taste
32	ounces tomato juice
2	tablespoons flour
1/2	cup skim milk
1/2	cup sugar

Slice the top off each pepper and clean out the inside. Save the tops. Reconstitute the soy with water so that it is softened. Drain, rinse and mash the black beans. In a large bowl, mix the soy, black beans, rice, egg substitute, chopped onion and pepper. Fill peppers and put the tops back on. Arrange in a pot and cover with the tomato juice. Simmer slowly for one hour. Occasionally shake the pot so peppers don't stick. Do not use a hot burner or peppers will burn. 15 minutes before peppers are done, mix the flour, skim milk and sugar in a small bowl. When it is smooth, add it to peppers. Continue to cook, until peppers are done and sauce is tangy and thickened.

♥ ♥ ♥

Options: use artificial sweetener instead of sugar or use less sugar. Use reduced sodium tomato juice. Include your favorite seasonings, such as garlic powder.

Nutrition: (per serving): 490 calories

Saturated fat . . . . 0 g		
Total Fat . . . . 1 g	(2% of calories)	
Protein . . . . 33 g	(27% of calories)	
Carbohydrates . . . . 88 g	(71% of calories)	

Cholesterol . . . . 0 mg	Sodium . . . . 788 mg
Fiber . . . . 8 g	Iron . . . . 8 mg
Vitamin A . . . . 1403 IU	Vitamin C . . . . 96 mg

Source: Betty Verdone is married to Carmine Verdone who is retired. Carmine has had five heart attacks, bypass surgery in 1983, and stent surgery in 1994. He also has diabetes.

> *"The Reversal Team is a family with Dr. Rogers at the head. The staff, patients and spouses are family members, all there to help and support each other."*
>
> Carmine Verdone

Best Ever Black-Eyes

Sweet and tangy – serve over rice.

Serves 8 — a serving is about 1-1/2 cups

Preparation: :20   Cook 3:00   Stand :00   Total 3:20

Ingredients:

1	pound dried black eye peas
1	cup onion, chopped
6	cups fat free broth
2	teaspoons salt
2	teaspoons paprika
1	clove garlic, minced
2	teaspoons seasoned pepper
2	teaspoons cumin
2	teaspoons onion powder
1/2	teaspoon dry mustard
1/2	teaspoon cayenne
2	green bell peppers
1	cup celery
3	cups apple juice
6	cups water, as needed
1	cup onion, chopped

Soak the dried peas in water overnight. Drain and rinse well. In a large soup pot, use one cup of the broth to saute one cup of onion with the herbs. When the onion is tender, add the rest of the broth and the black-eyes. Chop the green peppers and the celery and add them to the soup pot along with half of the apple juice. Bring to a boil and then simmer for several hours until the peas are tender. You may need to add additional water if it gets too thick during cooking. When the peas are soft and tender, add the remaining apple juice and the second cup of onions. Stir well before serving.

Options: Serve garnished with chopped green onion. Use low sodium broth and eliminate salt, if watching sodium. Serve over rice.

♥ ♥ ♥

Nutrition: (per serving): 257 calories

Saturated fat . . . . 0 g		
Total Fat . . . . 2 g	(6% of calories)	
Protein . . . . 12 g	(19% of calories)	
Carbohydrates . . . . 48 g	(75% of calories)	

Cholesterol . . . . 0 mg	Sodium . . . . 752 mg
Fiber . . . . 3 g	Iron . . . . 1 mg
Vitamin A . . . . 541 IU	Vitamin C . . . . 57 mg

Source: Diane Boehmer helped us with our initial food service and developed many delicious recipes for the program.

♥ ♥ ♥

Kathy's Grilled Cheese Sandwich

Quick and easy

Serves 1

Preparation: :10   Cook :00   Stand :00   Total :10

Ingredients:

1   envelope Butter Buds™ Mix
2   slices fat free bread
1   slice fat free mozzarella
        optional peppers
        vegetable oil cooking spray

Mix Butter Buds™ according to package instructions. Brush the liquid Butter Buds™ on the slices of bread. Place cheese in between slices. Use peppers as desired to provide more flavor.

Turn the burner on medium and spray a frying pan with vegetable oil cooking spray for one second. Cook covered for 2-1/2 to 3 minutes on each side.

Additional options include adding tomato slices, pickles, onion, salsa or other ingredients.

Nutrition: (per serving): 226 calories

Saturated fat . . . . 0 g		
Total Fat . . . . 1 g	(5% of calories)	
Protein . . . . 9 g	(16% of calories)	
Carbohydrates . . . . 45 g	(79% of calories)	
Cholesterol . . . . 2 mg	Sodium . . . . 492 mg	
Fiber . . . . 0 g	Iron . . . . 0 mg	
Vitamin A . . . . 0 IU	Vitamin C . . . . 0 mg	

Source: Kathy Williams is a homemaker who had bypass surgery in 1990.

♥ ♥ ♥

Helen's Barley Casserole

Delicious and so satisfying

Serves 6

Preparation: :15   Cook 1:30   Stand :00   Total 1:45

Ingredients:

1	cup barley	1	onion
2	16 ounce cans tomatoes	1/4	cup celery
1/4	teaspoon thyme	1/4	cup carrots
1/4	teaspoon marjoram	1/4	cup cabbage
1/4	teaspoon sweet basil	4	ounces fat free cheddar cheese
1/4	teaspoon cayenne	1/4	cup bread crumbs
1/4	teaspoon oregano, optional		
	salt and pepper to taste		

Combine the barley, seasonings, canned tomatoes with juice and the chopped vegetables. Place in a 2 quart casserole and bake for 1-1/2 hours at 350°F. Remove from oven and top with cheese and bread crumbs. Turn oven to low and heat for 15 more minutes.

Nutrition: (per serving): 219 calories

Saturated fat . . . . 0 g		
Total Fat . . . . 1 g	(5% of calories)	
Protein . . . . 12 g	(21% of calories)	
Carbohydrates . . . . 40 g	(74% of calories)	
Cholesterol . . . . 4 mg	Sodium . . . . 188 mg	
Fiber . . . . 2 g	Iron . . . . 2 mg	
Vitamin A . . . . 2284 IU	Vitamin C . . . . 44 mg	

Source: Helen Moses is a homemaker who keeps busy babysitting her grandchildren. She has coronary artery disease.

♥ ♥ ♥

Jerry's Vegetarian Chili

A Reversal Team favorite

Serves 8 — a serving is 1 cup

Preparation: :20   Cook :45   Stand :00   Total 1:05

Ingredients:

1/2	cup fat free broth	1	teaspoon cumin
1	clove garlic, minced	1	16 ounce can red kidney
1	cup onion, chopped		beans
1	green bell pepper, chopped	1	16 ounce can garbanzo
1	tablespoon chili powder, or to taste		beans
1	tablespoon cider vinegar	1	16 ounce can pinto beans
1/4	teaspoon allspice	1	16 ounce can tomatoes,
1/4	teaspoon coriander		unsalted

Put the broth in a large pot or heavy skillet over medium heat. Saute garlic, onions and green pepper in the broth until the onions become soft. Rinse and drain all beans. Add remaining ingredients and bring to a boil. Cover and reduce heat. Simmer for 45 minutes. Vary ingredients according to your preferences.

Nutrition: (per serving): 232 calories

Saturated fat . . . . 0 g		
Total Fat . . . . 2 g	(9% of calories)	
Protein . . . . 12 g	(21% of calories)	
Carbohydrates . . . . 41 g	(70% of calories)	
Cholesterol . . . . 0 mg	Sodium . . . . 585 mg	
Fiber . . . . 3 g	Iron . . . . 4 mg	
Vitamin A . . . . 963 IU	Vitamin C . . . . 38 mg	

Source: Jerry Nagle, 63, is a retiree who enjoys traveling. He had bypass surgery and aortic valve replacement in 1988. He also has diabetes.

♥♥♥

Southwestern Baked Beans

Hot and spicy

Serves 10 — a serving is 1 cup

Preparation: :10   Cook 2:00   Stand :00   Total 2:10

Ingredients:

2	vidalia onions
48	ounces canned great northern beans
1	cup catsup
15	ounces fresh salsa
2	16 ounce cans stewed tomatoes, low salt
1	tablespoon McCormick's no-salt seasoning mix

Chop the onions. Mix all ingredients in a three quart casserole and bake at 350°F for 1-1/2 to 2 hours. Great for picnics.

Nutrition: (per serving): 254 calories

Saturated fat . . . . 0 g		
Total Fat . . . . 1 g	(3% of calories)	
Protein . . . . 12 g	(19% of calories)	
Carbohydrates . . . . 49 g	(78% of calories)	
Cholesterol . . . . 0 mg	Sodium . . . . 513 mg	
Fiber . . . . 4 g	Iron . . . . 3 mg	
Vitamin A . . . . 985 IU	Vitamin C . . . . 27 mg	

Source: Sally Roulinson, 58, is a seamstress, artist and housewife. She had a heart attack in 1990, angioplasty in 1993 and bypass in 1995.

"The hardest part of deciding to start the program was becoming a vegetarian. Once I got started, with great help from the staff and the support group, it felt natural and I don't miss eating meat at all."

♥ ♥ ♥

Diane's Kidney Bean Loaf

A hearty entree especially good with tomato relish

Serves 6

Preparation: :15   Cook 1:00   Stand :10   Total 1:25

Ingredients:

1	onion
2	cups kidney beans, canned or cooked
1/2	cup dry bread crumbs
1/2	teaspoon thyme
8	ounces fat free egg substitute
1	12 ounce can tomato sauce
	vegetable oil cooking spray

Chop onion. Rinse and drain beans. Place onion, beans, thyme and bread crumbs in blender or food processor and process until smooth. Add egg substitute and mix well. If you wish to use egg white instead, use one cup of whites. Add salt, herbs and pepper as desired. Consistency of mix should resemble uncooked meatloaf. If it seems too moist, add more bread crumbs or a little uncooked oatmeal. Spray a loaf pan with vegetable oil cooking spray. Pour the bean mix into the pan and arrange mix evenly. Set the loaf pan in a pan of water and place in a pre-heated oven set for 350°F. Baste with tomato sauce frequently. Cook for 60 to 90 minutes or until the loaf is set. A knife should insert clean in center of loaf. Remove from oven and let the loaf rest for 10 minutes. Serve with tomato relish (recipe on page 126) or fat free gravy. This recipe is nice with roasted or mashed potatoes, green peas and cooked carrots seasoned with a little brown sugar. Try other beans such as black beans, lentils or red beans to vary the flavor. Crushed garlic and chick peas are a great combination in this recipe. Use your own preferences for seasoning. Try Italian blend seasonings or go with chopped green chilies and cumin for a Mexican flavor. This recipe is very versatile.

♥ ♥ ♥

Nutrition: (per serving): 154 calories

Saturated fat . . . . 0 g		
Total Fat . . . . 1 g	(6% of calories)	
Protein . . . . 8 g	(20% of calories)	
Carbohydrates . . . . 29 g	(74% of calories)	

Cholesterol . . . . 0 mg	Sodium . . . . 669 mg
Fiber . . . . 2 g	Iron . . . . 2 mg
Vitamin A . . . . 396 IU	Vitamin C . . . . 9 mg

Source: Diane Boehmer helped us establish our initial food service and developed many delicious recipes for the program.

♥ ♥ ♥

Tomato Relish

Adds flavor and zest to Kidney Bean Loaf

Serves 8

Preparation: :15   Cook :45   Stand :00   Total 1:00

Ingredients:

1	onion
1	green bell pepper
1	clove garlic
1	pinch ground cloves
3-1/2	cups canned stewed tomatoes
	brown sugar to taste
	pepper to taste

Finely chop onion, pepper and garlic. Mix all ingredients and cook to a thick consistency on very low temperature, 45 minutes or longer. Check frequently to see if additional water needs to be added. Season to taste.

Nutrition: (per serving): 47 calories

Saturated fat . . . . 0 g
Total Fat . . . . 0 g   (4% of calories)
Protein . . . . 1 g   (12% of calories)
Carbohydrates . . . . 10 g   (84% of calories)

Cholesterol . . . . 0 mg   Sodium . . . . 268 mg
Fiber . . . . 1 g   Iron . . . . 1 mg
Vitamin A . . . . 642 IU   Vitamin C . . . . 24 mg

Source: Diane Boehmer helped us establish our initial food service and developed many delicious recipes for the program.

♥ ♥ ♥

Dan's Grilled Cheese Sandwich

A grreeat lunch sandwich with lots of flavor and zip

Serves 1

Preparation: :05   Cook :05   Stand :00   Total :10

Ingredients:

2	slices fat free rye bread
2	slices fat free cheese, Swiss flavor
1	slice red onion
1	tablespoon spicy brown mustard

Use two or more slices of fat free cheese slices. Use fat free rye bread with caraway seeds.

Toast the bread. Put onion on one slice, add the cheese and top with mustard. Put the second slice of bread on the sandwich and microwave on medium high for 20 seconds until the cheese starts to melt. If you are watching sodium, eliminate mustard and use one slice of cheese.

Nutrition: (per serving): 203 calories

Saturated fat . . . . 0 g		
Total Fat . . . . 1 g	(6% of calories)	
Protein . . . . 16 g	(31% of calories)	
Carbohydrates . . . . 32 g	(63% of calories)	
Cholesterol . . . . 15 mg	Sodium . . . . 1074 mg	
Fiber . . . . 2 g	Iron . . . . 1 mg	
Vitamin A . . . . 0 IU	Vitamin C . . . . 16 mg	

Source: Dan McCafferty, a hospital development officer, had a heart attack in 1992.

"The program has taught me how to lead a health-filled life through diet, exercise and stress management."

♥ ♥ ♥

Helen's Stuffed Peppers

A fast and easy microwave recipe for busy days

Serves 4-6

Preparation: :15   Cook :15   Stand :00   Total :30

Ingredients:

1/2	cup frozen whole kernel corn	3	cups instant white rice, uncooked
1/4	cup chopped onions	1/4	teaspoon sugar
1	tablespoon water	1/8	teaspoon pepper
1/2	cup chilled tomato sauce	1	8 ounce can red kidney beans, rinsed and drained
2	tablespoons shredded fat free mozzarella cheese	6-8	large red or green peppers

In casserole dish, microwave corn and onion in water on high power for 2 minutes. Then stir in tomato sauce, uncooked rice, sugar and pepper. Cover and cook 2 to 3 minutes, stirring after the first minute. Add drained beans and stir into rice mixture. Cut peppers in half length-wise and remove seeds. Place peppers cut side down on plate; cover with plastic wrap and cook on high for 2 minutes. Spoon rice mixture into peppers, sprinkle with cheese and heat until warm.

Nutrition: (per serving): 257 calories

Saturated fat . . . . 0 g		
Total Fat . . . . 1 g	(2% of calories)	
Protein . . . . 7 g	(11% of calories)	
Carbohydrates . . . . 56 g	(87% of calories)	
Cholesterol . . . . 0 mg	Sodium . . . . 257 mg	
Fiber . . . . 1 g	Iron . . . . 3 mg	
Vitamin A . . . . 4456 IU	Vitamin C . . . . 145 mg	

Source: Helen Moses is a homemaker who keeps busy babysitting her grandchildren. Helen has coronary artery disease.

♥ ♥ ♥

Spaghetti Sauce

Simmering in a crock pot makes this a convenient sauce

Serves 8

Preparation: :10   Cook 2:00   Stand :00   Total 2:10

Ingredients:

2	cups fat free textured soy protein	1	bay leaf
46	ounces tomato juice	1-1/2	tablespoons basil
28	ounces chopped canned tomatoes, no-salt-added	1	tablespoon oregano
2	chopped onions	2	cloves garlic, minced
1	4 ounce can mushrooms, drained	2	tablespoons dried parsley
2	cups water		

Add all ingredients to a large pot. Bring to a boil, reduce heat and simmer until thick. Serve over pasta. Freezes well. Options: to further reduce sodium, use low sodium tomato juice. Garnish with fresh chopped tomatoes and chopped fresh parsley. A little fat free mozzarella sprinkled on top is also a nice touch.

Nutrition: (per serving): 191 calories

Saturated fat . . . . 0 g		
Total Fat . . . . 1 g	(3% of calories)	
Protein . . . . 19 g	(40% of calories)	
Carbohydrates . . . . 27 g	(57% of calories)	
Cholesterol . . . . 0 mg	Sodium . . . . 639 mg	
Fiber . . . . 6 g	Iron . . . . 6 mg	
Vitamin A . . . . 1695 IU	Vitamin C . . . . 51 mg	

Source: Donna Hardin, whose husband Larry is a tool and die maker, cross country biker and was a bypass surgery candidate in 1993.

♥ ♥ ♥

Cabbage Rolls

As close to "galabki" as you can get!

Serves 12

Preparation: :45   Cook 2:00   Stand :00   Total 2:45

Ingredients:

1   head of cabbage
1-1/2   cups fat free textured soy protein
1   cup warm water
2   cups cooked rice
1/4 to 1/2 cup fat free stock
3   large onions
2 to 3   garlic cloves
2   tablespoons dried dill weed
         salt and pepper to taste
2   cups tomato juice

Cut end of cabbage and core out the center of the head. Put the head of cabbage in large saucepan of boiling water. Remove the leaves from the cabbage as they come off into the pan. When they are cool, cut out part of the large "vein" about two inches from the bottom. Save the best leaves for the rolls—you will need 12-24 leaves. Set leaves aside. Any extra leaves and vein parts can be placed in a large casserole or roasting pan so that the bottom is covered. If you do not have enough, use lettuce to fill in.

Soak the soy protein in 1 cup of warm water until it is soft. Saute chopped onion and garlic in fat free stock until tender and then add cooked rice, the soy protein and dill. Use salt and pepper to taste. Fill the center of each cabbage leaf with 2-3 tablespoons rice mixture. Fold sides and roll up like a tortilla. Put all the rolls onto the bed of cabbage. Cover them with additional cabbage or lettuce leaves. Pour two cups of tomato juice over the rolls. Cover the pan and bake for 2 hours at 350°F until cabbage is tender. Serve hot with fat free sour cream on the side. Makes 24 rolls.

♥ ♥ ♥

Nutrition: (per serving): 179 calories

Saturated fat . . . . 0 g		
Total Fat . . . . 0 g	(2% of calories)	
Protein . . . . 14 g	(32% of calories)	
Carbohydrates . . . . 30 g	(66% of calories)	

Cholesterol . . . . 0 mg	Sodium . . . . 161 mg
Fiber . . . . 10 g	Iron . . . . 6 mg
Vitamin A . . . . 318 IU	Vitamin C . . . . 48 mg

Source: Helen Moses is a homemaker who keeps busy babysitting her grand-children. Helen has coronary artery disease.

"I never thought I would ever become a vege-tarian. It is real healthy for you. The doctors didn't know what my alternatives would be. I had 95% blockage in one artery and 65% in another. Diet and exercise opened up the arter-ies without surgery."

Helen Moses

♥ ♥ ♥

Sauerkraut Casserole

A quick alternative to stuffed cabbage

Serves 8

Preparation: :15   Cook 1:00   Stand :00   Total 1:15

Ingredients:

1-1/2	cups fat free textured soy protein, hydrated in 1-1/2 cups of hot water for 5 minutes	1	quart sauerkraut, drained, rinsed well and squeezed
1	onion, chopped	1/2	cup rice, uncooked
1	green bell pepper, chopped	1-1/2	cups water
1	cup chopped celery	1	teaspoon Lawry's-Hot-n-Spicey Seasoned salt
1	quart canned tomatoes, no-salt-added		

Spray large skillet with cooking spray. Saute onions, green pepper and celery until onions are transparent. Add textured soy protein and Lawry's Hot Spice. Mix well. Add tomatoes and sauerkraut to a 2-1/2 to 3 quart casserole dish. Add rice and water and mix well. Add soy protein mixture and blend well. Bake at 350°F in a covered dish, for approximately 1 hour.

Nutrition: (per serving): 175 calories

Saturated fat . . . . 0 g		
Total Fat . . . . 1 g	(6% of calories)	
Protein . . . . 15 g	(33% of calories)	
Carbohydrates . . . . 31 g	(62% of calories)	
Cholesterol . . . . 0 mg	Sodium . . . . 990 mg	
Fiber . . . . 5 g	Iron . . . . 5 mg	
Vitamin A . . . . 825 IU	Vitamin C . . . . 46 mg	

Source: Sally Roulinson, 58, is a seamstress, artist and housewife. She had a heart attack in 1990, angioplasty in 1993 and bypass in 1995.

"Becoming a vegetarian is just another challenge along life's way."

♥ ♥ ♥

Lentil Loaf

Left over Lentil Loaf makes a great sandwich

Serves 6

Preparation: :30   Cook 1:00   Stand :00   Total 1:30

Ingredients:

3/4	cup lentils	2	egg whites
1	cup shredded fat free cheddar cheese	1	teaspoon poultry seasoning, or herbs such as thyme or rosemary, seasoned pepper, garlic, black pepper to taste
1	onion, chopped		
1	cup fresh bread crumbs		

Preheat oven to 350°F. Spray a one pound loaf pan with non-stick cooking spray. Wash lentils well in cold water; drain well. Cover them with 1-1/2 to 2 cups of water in a saucepan. Cover, bring to boil, reduce heat and simmer covered for 20 minutes until soft. Mix the cheese, onion, pepper and seasonings with the cooked lentils. Add bread crumbs and egg whites. Stir well. Mix should resemble uncooked meatloaf. If it seems too moist, add additional bread crumbs. Press the mixture into the loaf pan. Cover with foil. Bake for 40-45 minutes. Turn out on platter and serve with tomato sauce or fat free gravy.

Nutrition: (per serving): 168 calories

Saturated fat . . . . 0 g		
Total Fat . . . . 1 g	(6% of calories)	
Protein . . . . 10 g	(25% of calories)	
Carbohydrates . . . . 29 g	(69% of calories)	
Cholesterol . . . . 1 mg	Sodium . . . . 146 mg	
Fiber . . . . 2 g	Iron . . . . 3 mg	
Vitamin A . . . . 15 IU	Vitamin C . . . . 4 mg	

Source: Gerry Krag is the consulting nutritionist and group facilitator for the Downriver Reversal Team.

Lasagna Roll-ups

A new twist on traditional lasagna; you'll love these roll-ups

Serves 8

Preparation: :15   Cook 1:05   Stand :00   Total 1:20

Ingredients:

Sauce:

2	cloves garlic, minced
32	ounces fat free spaghetti sauce
2	teaspoons dried Italian seasoning
1/2	teaspoon fennel seeds, optional

Filling:

8	ounces uncooked lasagna noodles
1	cup fat free cottage cheese or fat free ricotta cheese
1	10 ounce package frozen chopped spinach, thawed and squeezed dry
1/2	cup shredded carrots
2	egg whites, or 1 egg equivalent of fat free egg substitute
1/4	teaspoon salt

Topping:

1	cup fat free mozzarella cheese

Preheat oven to 350°F. Combine sauce ingredients and simmer 15 minutes. Cook noodles according to package directions, drain and rinse. Combine cottage cheese or ricotta cheese, carrots, spinach, egg whites and salt; mix well. Spread each cooked lasagna noodle with 1/4 cup filling to within 1 inch of one end. Roll firmly toward unfilled end.

Reserve 1-1/2 cups sauce. Pour remaining sauce in 8 x 12 inch pan. Arrange roll-ups seam side down in sauce. Pour reserved sauce over roll-ups. Cover and bake for 30 to 40 minutes. Sprinkle with mozzarella cheese and bake uncovered until melted.

♥ ♥ ♥

Nutrition: (per serving): 195 calories

Saturated fat	0 g	
Total Fat	1 g	(4% of calories)
Protein	12 g	(25% of calories)
Carbohydrates	35 g	(71% of calories)

Cholesterol	4 mg	Sodium	504 mg
Fiber	0 g	Iron	2 mg
Vitamin A	4831 IU	Vitamin C	10 mg

Source: Patricia Fecker is a registered nurse for the Downriver Cardiology Consultants who enjoys cooking healthy food and adapting recipes.

♥ ♥ ♥

Rice with Black Beans

A fast recipe, perfect for busy days

Serves 4

Preparation: :05   Cook :05   Stand :05   Total :15

Ingredients:

1	medium onion, chopped
1/2	cup fat free broth
1	14 ounce can stewed tomatoes
1	16 ounce can black beans
1	teaspoon oregano
1/2	teaspoon garlic powder
1-1/2	cups quick cooking brown rice, uncooked

Saute onion in broth until tender, but not browned. Add tomatoes, beans, oregano and garlic powder. Bring to boil. Stir in rice. Cover, reduce heat and simmer for 5 minutes. Remove from heat and let stand 5 minutes.

This is an ideal recipe for busy days. It can be used as a main entree or used as part of a recipe. Roll it in a fat free flour tortilla and you have a great burrito. Use it with steamed vegetables and you have a colorful and nutritious meal.

Options: add additional tomatoes and chili pepper and you have quick and easy chili. Use your imagination and create tasty variations that only take minutes.

♥ ♥ ♥

Nutrition: (per serving): 208 calories

Saturated fat . . . . 0 g		
Total Fat . . . . 1 g	(4% of calories)	
Protein . . . . 12 g	(23% of calories)	
Carbohydrates . . . . 38 g	(74% of calories)	

Cholesterol . . . . 0 mg	Sodium . . . . 307 mg
Fiber . . . . 1 g	Iron . . . . 1 mg
Vitamin A . . . . 124 IU	Vitamin C . . . . 2 mg

Source: Marie Zimolzak is a registered dietetic technician. She keeps busy with her two school age children and new baby. Her husband Frank helped us with his computer background.

"It is truly a pleasure working with people who want to change their life in such a positive way."

♥ ♥ ♥

Black Bean Vegetable Chili

A spicy, full-bodied black bean chili

Serves 8 — a serving is about 1 cup

Preparation: :45   Cook 1:05   Stand :00   Total 1:50

Ingredients:

2	cups fat free broth
2	yellow onions, peeled and cut into 1/4 inch dice
2	zucchini, cut into 1/4 inch dice
1	eggplant, cut into 1/2 inch cubes
1	red bell pepper, seeded, cored and cut into 1/4 inch dice
1	yellow bell pepper, seeded, cored and cut into 1/4 inch dice
4	cloves garlic, peeled and coarsely chopped
8	plum tomatoes, cut into 1 inch cubes
1	cup chopped Italian flat-leaf parsley
1/2	cup slivered fresh basil leaves
3	tablespoons chili powder
1-1/2	teaspoon ground cumin
1	tablespoon dried oregano
1	teaspoon freshly ground black pepper
1/2	teaspoon crushed red pepper
	salt, to taste, optional
2	cups cooked black beans
1-1/2	cups fresh corn kernels
1/2	cup chopped fresh dill
1/4	cup lemon juice
3	scallions, thinly sliced for garnish, optional

Heat 1/2 cup vegetable broth in a large casserole. Saute onions, zucchini, eggplant, peppers and garlic for 20 minutes. Add additional broth as needed to prevent sticking. Remove with slotted spoon and put in casserole dish. Add to the casserole the tomatoes, remaining broth, 1/2 cup parsley, basil and spices.

♥ ♥ ♥

Cook over low heat for 30 minutes, stirring occasionally. After 30 minutes cooking time, add black beans, corn, dill and lemon juice.

Cook an additional 15 minutes. Adjust seasonings and stir in remaining 1/2 parsley. Serve hot, garnished with some sliced scallions if desired.

Nutrition: (per serving): 180 calories

Saturated fat . . . . 0 g		
Total Fat . . . . 2 g	(8% of calories)	
Protein . . . . 8 g	(17% of calories)	
Carbohydrates . . . . 34 g	(75% of calories)	

Cholesterol . . . . 0 mg	Sodium . . . . 142 mg
Fiber . . . . 4 g	Iron . . . . 4 mg
Vitamin A . . . . 3082 IU	Vitamin C . . . . 71 mg

Source: Sheila Rogers is a retired cardiologist and is married to Dr. Joseph T. Rogers, who practices with his sons, Dr. Joseph C. and Dr. Felix J. Rogers at Downriver Cardiology Consultants in Trenton, Michigan.

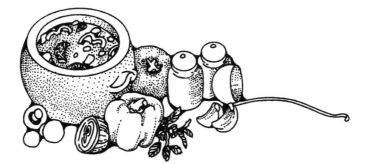

♥ ♥ ♥

Festival Couscous

A colorful combination that tastes fabulous

Serves 6 — a serving is about 2 cups

Preparation: :30   Cook :45   Stand :15   Total 1:30

Ingredients:

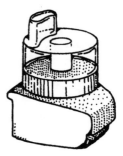

4	Japanese eggplants
1	teaspoon coarse salt to cover eggplants
1/2	cup apple juice
2	shallots
1	red onion
1	red bell pepper
1	yellow bell pepper
1	green bell pepper
6	new potatoes
1	cup chickpeas, cooked
1/4	cup raisins
2	tablespoons tomato paste
1	tablespoon coriander
1	tablespoon cumin
1	tablespoon saffron threads (optional)
1/4	cup dry white wine
2	cups dry couscous, prepared according to package
	minced parsley
	garlic pepper sauce (see next recipe)

Slice the eggplants crosswise and sprinkle with salt. Set aside. Put apple juice in a large saucepan. Add minced shallots and thinly sliced onion and saute until tender. Thinly slice the peppers, saving two slices of each for the garnish. Add the peppers to the onion and saute for five more minutes.

Pat excess moisture from the eggplants and add them to the skillet, stirring to blend. If using saffron, soften in 1 tablespoon hot water. Quarter the potatoes

♥ ♥ ♥

and add them along with the chick peas, raisins, tomato paste, coriander and saffron. Stir well and add wine. Cover and simmer gently until potatoes are cooked through, about 30 minutes. Let sit 15 minutes before serving. To serve, put the couscous on a platter, spoon the cooked vegetables over it and garnish with peppers. Sprinkle with minced parsley and serve with Garlic Pepper Sauce (recipe on following page).

If making the day before, cover and refrigerate. Gently reheat until uniformly hot. Prior to serving, prepare the couscous according to the package instructions.

Nutrition: (per serving): 390 calories

Saturated fat	0 g	
Total Fat	1 g	(2% of calories)
Protein	11 g	(12% of calories)
Carbohydrates	82 g	(84% of calories)
Alcohol	1 g	(2% of calories)

Cholesterol	0 mg	Sodium	422 mg
Fiber	2 g	Iron	3 mg
Vitamin A	1917 IU	Vitamin C	86 mg

Source: Bob Shank is a retired Episcopal priest and the executive director of the Cranbrook Peace Foundation. He has multiple risk factors for heart disease.

"The path to healing a heart is much like the peace process. It takes openess, clear communication and persistence. Neither is easy, but the rewards are well worth the effort."

Garlic Pepper Sauce

Serve with Festival Couscous

Serves 8 — a serving is 2 tablespoons

Preparation: :10   Cook :00   Stand 2:00   Total 2:10

Ingredients:

1	cup fat free yogurt, plain, whisked until smooth
1	clove garlic, minced
1	teaspoon sweet paprika
1/4	teaspoon cayenne pepper
1/4	cup fresh parsley, minced

Whisk together the yogurt, garlic, paprika and cayenne. Gently stir in minced parsley and refrigerate until ready to serve. Best if made the evening before so the spices have time to flavor the yogurt.

Nutrition: (per serving): 18 calories

Saturated fat	0 g	
Total Fat	0 g	(5% of calories)
Protein	2 g	(38% of calories)
Carbohydrates	3 g	(57% of calories)
Cholesterol	0 mg	Sodium 23 mg
Fiber	0 g	Iron 0 mg
Vitamin A	299 IU	Vitamin C 2 mg

Source: Bob Shank is a retired Episcopal priest and the executive director of the Cranbrook Peace Foundation. He has multiple risk factors for heart disease.

"The path to healing a heart is much like the peace process. It takes openess, clear communication and persistence. Neither is easy, but the rewards are well worth the effort."

♥ ♥ ♥

Stuffed Shells

Great for company

Serves 4

Preparation: :25   Cook :45   Stand :00   Total 1:10

Ingredients:

6	ounces large pasta shells		1	teaspoon paprika
10	ounces frozen chopped spinach			salt and pepper to taste
1	pound skim ricotta cheese		2	cups fat free spaghetti
3	egg whites			sauce
1	tablespoon basil		1	cup fat free mozzarella,
1	teaspoon oregano			shredded

Cook shells according to package instructions. Steam spinach and drain well. Mix spinach, ricotta, mozzarella, egg whites and seasoning. Stuff into cooked shells. Top with spaghetti sauce and mozzarella cheese. Cover with aluminum foil and bake at 375°F for 45 minutes. Can be converted to lasagna by using flat noodles and layering.

Nutrition: (per serving): 289 calories

Saturated fat . . . . 0 g		
Total Fat . . . . 1 g	(3% of calories)	
Protein . . . . 26 g	(37% of calories)	
Carbohydrates . . . . 44 g	(60% of calories)	
Cholesterol . . . . 14 mg	Sodium . . . . 160 mg	
Fiber . . . . 1 g	Iron . . . . 2 mg	
Vitamin A . . . . 6339 IU	Vitamin C . . . . 18 mg	

Source: Lou Hayward is a computer programmer who had angioplasty in 1993.

"When I started the program, I was taking 240 mg of Cardizem CD and 100 mg of Toprol XL. Now I'm taking only 50 mg of Toprol XL and hope to eventually be off that, too."

♥ ♥ ♥

Red Beans and Rice

High in protein and taste

Serves 10 — a serving is about 1 cup

Preparation: :10   Cook :40   Stand :00   Total :50

Ingredients:

3	14 ounce cans red beans or kidney beans, drained
2	medium sized onions, chopped
4	cloves minced garlic
2	medium sized green bell peppers, chopped
3	stalks celery, chopped
1	bay leaf
1	teaspoon dried thyme (use 1/2 teaspoon to start)
4	10-3/4 ounce cans fat free broth
	a few drops of hot sauce
1	pinch salt, to taste
1	pinch pepper, to taste

Rinse beans. Put all ingredients into a large saucepan. Bring to a boil. Reduce heat and simmer until thick. Remove bay leaf before serving. Serve over hot rice.

Nutrition: (per serving): 250 calories (analysis does not include rice)

Saturated fat	0 g	
Total Fat	1 g	(3% of calories)
Protein	23 g	(37% of calories)
Carbohydrates	37 g	(59% of calories)
Cholesterol	0 mg	Sodium . . . . 757 mg
Fiber	8 g	Iron . . . . 3 mg
Vitamin A	477 IU	Vitamin C . . . . 35 mg

Source: Donna Hardin, whose husband Larry is a tool and die maker, cross country biker and was a bypass surgery candidate in 1993.

♥ ♥ ♥

Broccoli Strata

Assemble the day before and then heat and serve

Serves 6

Preparation: :25   Cook :45   Stand :10   Total 1:20

Ingredients:

2	cups fresh mushrooms	1	cup fat free egg substitute
2	cups broccoli	2	cups skim milk
6	slices whole wheat bread	2	tablespoons flour
4	slices fat free cheddar cheese	1/2	teaspoon basil
4	slices fat free Swiss cheese		paprika
2	tablespoons minced onion		

Steam mushrooms and broccoli until tender-crisp—this can be done in the microwave. Toast the bread and cut in cubes. Place half the toast on the bottom of a nine inch square pan or three quart casserole. Layer the cheddar, vegetables, Swiss cheese, the rest of the toast and then the onion. In a bowl mix the egg substitute, skim milk, flour and basil. Pour over casserole. Cover and chill at least an hour or overnight. Sprinkle with paprika and bake uncovered in a 325°F oven for 45 minutes until set. Let stand 10 minutes before serving.

Nutrition: (per serving): 155 calories

Saturated fat . . . . 0 g		
Total Fat . . . . 1 g	(7% of calories)	
Protein . . . . 13 g	(34% of calories)	
Carbohydrates . . . . 23 g	(60% of calories)	
Cholesterol . . . . 6 mg	Sodium . . . . 334 mg
Fiber . . . . 1 g	Iron . . . . 1 mg
Vitamin A . . . . 720 IU	Vitamin C . . . . 29 mg

Source: Gerry Krag is the consulting nutritionist and group facilitator for the Downriver Reversal Team.

Meatless Sloppy Joe

Great for picnics

Serves 12

Preparation: :30   Cook 2:00   Stand :00   Total 2:30

Ingredients:

2	cups fat free textured soy protein
2-1/4	cups fat free broth, low sodium
1	cup chopped onions
1	cup chopped celery
4	tablespoons dry oatmeal
2 to 3	teaspoons chili powder
2 to 4	teaspoons Worcestershire sauce
1	tablespoon sugar
1	teaspoon garlic powder
1	8 ounce can tomato sauce
2	10-3/4 ounce can tomato soup, fat free

Add soy to 2 cups of broth and set aside for about 15 minutes. Saute onions and celery in 1/4 cup fat free broth or cooking sherry. Place onion, celery and soy in a crock pot. Add remaining ingredients and cook to desired thickness, about 2 hours.

Serve on fat free buns. Recipe may be cut in half to make 6 sandwiches.

Note: Pritikin makes a tomato soup with less than 1 gram of fat per serving.

Nutrition: (per serving): 228 calories

Saturated fat . . . . 0 g		
Total Fat . . . . 0 g	(1% of calories)	
Protein . . . . 12 g	(36% of calories)	
Carbohydrates . . . . 19 g	(55% of calories)	
Alcohol. . . . . 2 g	(8% of calories)	

Cholesterol . . . . 0 mg	Sodium. . . . . 479 mg
Fiber . . . . 3 g	Iron . . . . 3 mg
Vitamin A . . . . 583 IU	Vitamin C . . . . 31 mg

Source: Bill Radcliff is a retiree who does extensive volunteer work. Bill lives with his wife Diane and is retired from Detroit Edison. He had bypass surgery in 1987.

"God has given us a second chance; show Him you appreciate it."

♥ ♥ ♥

Betty's Sausage Patties

Excellent for breakfast or anytime

Serves 12

Preparation: :30   Cook :05   Stand :15   Total :50

Ingredients:

1	cup fat free textured soy protein
2	cups fat free broth, any flavor
4	cups oatmeal, quick
1	tablespoon sausage seasoning
2	teaspoons sage
2	teaspoons Italian seasoning
2	teaspoons garlic powder
2	tablespoons liquid smoke
8	ounces fat free egg substitute
1	cup onions, chopped
	vegetable oil cooking spray

Reconstitute the soy protein with 1 cup of the broth. Set aside the second cup of broth. Mix all the ingredients together and stir well. Slowly add enough of the reserved broth to moisten the mixture. Mix well. Let stand for 15 minutes. The oats will become soft. Divide the mixture in two and form six balls from each half, making 12 balls. Gently press into patties. Brown both sides on a non-stick surface sprayed lightly with vegetable oil cooking spray.

The mixture is very sticky, so keep your hands wet while forming the balls and patties. Serve as a breakfast pattie or as an entree with mashed potatoes and fat free gravy. Excellent on a hamburger bun. Make ahead and freeze in individual plastic bags and you'll always have a tasty food to eat for a meal or on the run.

Option: To lower the sodium, use less sausage seasoning.

♥ ♥ ♥

Nutrition: (per serving): 153 calories

Saturated fat . . . . 0 g	
Total Fat . . . . 1 g	(6% of calories)
Protein . . . . 22 g	(54% of calories)
Carbohydrates . . . . 17 g	(40% of calories)

Cholesterol . . . . 0 mg	Sodium . . . . 406 mg
Fiber . . . . 6 g	Iron . . . . 9 mg
Vitamin A . . . . 21 IU	Vitamin C . . . . 1 mg

Source: Betty Verdone, whose husband Carmine has had five heart attacks, bypass surgery in 1983 and stent surgery in 1994. Carmine also has diabetes.

"The only thing constant in life is change. As our lives change, sometimes for the good and sometimes for the bad, we need to be adaptable and flexible. The Reversal Team teaches this through physical therapy, relaxation and dietary change."

Carmine Verdone

♥ ♥ ♥

Spaghetti Squash Casserole

A delicious source of beta carotene

Serves 6

Preparation: :20   Cook :45   Stand :00   Total 1:05

Ingredients:

1	10 ounce package frozen chopped spinach
1	spaghetti squash, medium size
1	cup fat free ricotta cheese
1/2	cup fat free egg substitute
1/2	teaspoon dried Italian seasoning
1/4	teaspoon salt, optional
15	ounces tomato sauce
3/4	cup fat free mozzarella cheese
	vegetable oil cooking spray

Cut squash in half and remove seeds and pulp. Invert on a tray and microwave until tender, about 10-15 minutes. Let cool. Thaw spinach and drain well, pressing out excess liquid. Using a fork, remove the strands of squash from the shell. Lightly spray a 9 x 13 inch pan with non-stick cooking spray. Arrange the squash on the bottom of the pan. In a bowl, combine the spinach, ricotta cheese, egg substitute and seasonings. Mix until blended. Pour over squash. Top with tomato sauce and sprinkle with cheese. Bake in 350°F oven for 30 minutes.

Option: Use fat free cottage cheese instead of ricotta; Use no-salt-added tomato sauce.

♥ ♥ ♥

Nutrition: (per serving): 182 calories

Saturated fat . . . . 0 g		
Total Fat . . . . 2 g	(10% of calories)	
Protein . . . . 10 g	(22% of calories)	
Carbohydrates . . . . 31 g	(68% of calories)	

Cholesterol . . . . 5 mg	Sodium . . . . 539 mg
Fiber . . . . 5 g	Iron . . . . 3 mg
Vitamin A . . . . 4683 IU	Vitamin C . . . . 27 mg

Source: Gerry Krag is the consulting nutritionist and group facilitator for the Downriver Reversal Team.

♥ ♥ ♥

John's Famous Chili

This oil free recipe uses bulgur for texture

Serves 8 — a serving is one cup

Preparation: :30   Cook 2:15   Stand 1:00   Total 3:45

Ingredients:

1/4	cup fat free broth	1	40-ounce can kidney beans
2	cloves garlic, minced	1	28 ounce can tomatoes,
1	green bell pepper, diced		no-salt-added
1-1/2	cups onion, chopped	1/2	cup dry bulgur wheat
2	stalks celery, diced	1	teaspoon black pepper
1	28 ounce can great northern beans	2	tablespoons chili powder

In a large pot, saute garlic, pepper, onion and celery in the broth until vegetables are tender. Add beans, tomatoes, bulgur and seasoning. Bring to a boil over medium heat, then reduce heat and simmer for two hours. Add water to get desired thickness. Shut off heat, cover and let stand for one hour.

Nutrition: (per serving): 220 calories

Saturated fat . . . . 0 g		
Total Fat . . . . 1 g	(5% of calories)	
Protein . . . . 11 g	(21% of calories)	
Carbohydrates . . . . 41 g	(75% of calories)	
Cholesterol . . . . 0 mg	Sodium . . . . 711 mg	
Fiber . . . . 4 g	Iron . . . . 4 mg	
Vitamin A . . . . 972 IU	Vitamin C . . . . 38 mg	

Source: John DeMarsh, 74, is a retired General Motors engineer who has had coronary artery disease since 1987.

"I followed a reversal protocol on my own for several years, but since I joined the Downriver Reversal Team, I have seen my total cholesterol drop from 194 to 159 and my LDL cholesterol drop from 118 to 89."

♥ ♥ ♥

Soft Soy Tacos

Easy and enjoyable

Serves 8

Preparation: :20   Cook :05   Stand :00   Total :25

Ingredients:

1/2	cup fat free textured soy protein	2	cups chopped tomatoes
1	cup fat free broth	2	cups chopped lettuce
1	packet fat free taco seasoning mix	2	cups shredded fat free
8	10-inch flour tortillas, fat free		cheddar cheese
8	ounces fat free sour cream	1	cup salsa

Mix soy protein with broth and let stand for five minutes. In non-stick frying pan, mix protein with taco seasoning and saute. Add more water as needed to prevent sticking. Meanwhile, warm the tortillas in microwave or in a non-stick frying pan. Place some soy mix in each tortilla and top with sour cream, tomato, lettuce, cheddar cheese and salsa. Fold to eat.

Nutrition: (per serving): 243 calories

Saturated fat . . . . 0 g		
Total Fat . . . . 0 g	(1% of calories)	
Protein . . . . 14 g	(23% of calories)	
Carbohydrates . . . . 46 g	(76% of calories)	
Cholesterol . . . . 1 mg	Sodium . . . . 360 mg
Fiber . . . . 1 g	Iron . . . . 1 mg
Vitamin A . . . . 544 IU	Vitamin C . . . . 15 mg

Source: Jeanne M. Eckert, 62, is a homemaker and gardening expert who has blocked arteries.

"I believe that if I had not joined the Reversal Program a year ago, I would have had a heart attack by now. I would recommend it for anyone, even those in good health, as a preventive to heart disease"

♥ ♥ ♥

Hearty Stew

Serve with salad, brown rice, steamed vegetables and rolls

Serves 8 — a serving is about 1 cup

Preparation: :20   Cook 1:30   Stand :00   Total 1:50

Ingredients:

1-1/2 cups water
1-1/2 cups fat free textured soy chunks
2-1/2 cups low-sodium tomato juice, divided
1/4   cup low sodium soy sauce
5   potatoes, cubed
2   onions, cut in wedges
3   carrots, cut in 1/2-inch slices
1/2   teaspoon basil
1/2   teaspoon paprika
1/2   pound mushrooms, cut in half
2   zucchini, cut in 1 inch pieces
1/2   pound green beans, cut in 1 inch pieces

Mix the water and soy protein together and set aside for a few minutes. Mix the soy sauce and tomato juice together. Put half of the juice mixture in a three quart casserole and cover with potatoes, onions and carrots. Mix in the soy chunks, the basil and paprika. Cover tightly and bake at 350°F for 1-1/4 hours. Check vegetables during baking. If they seem too dry, add water. Stir the stew to make sure that everything is coated with the juice mixture. Add the mushrooms and zucchini. Add the rest of the tomato juice mixture. Cover casserole and return to oven for about 30 minutes more. If a thicker sauce is desired, add a few tablespoons of instant mashed potatoes and stir well.

Note: If watching sodium, make sure the soy chunks you purchase do not have added salt.

♥ ♥ ♥

Nutrition: (per serving): 293 calories

Saturated fat . . . . 0 g		
Total Fat . . . . 1 g	(2% of calories)	
Protein . . . . 19 g	(25% of calories)	
Carbohydrates . . . . 54 g	(73% of calories)	

Cholesterol . . . . 0 mg	Sodium . . . . 241 mg
Fiber . . . . 6 g	Iron . . . . 5 mg
Vitamin A . . . . 8436 IU	Vitamin C . . . . 48 mg

Source: Ray and Nancy Gomez; Ray Gomez, 64, is retired and has blocked arteries. Ray started running two years after his heart attack in 1980. He and Nancy have now participated in nine marathons.

"Eight years ago I was told I had triple vessel disease and needed a bypass. With diet, medication and exercise, I've been able to avoid having the bypass surgery, but I felt I needed more. I found what I needed with this program and I've been able to keep running marathons."

Ray Gomez

♥ ♥ ♥

Carol's Santa Fe Casserole

Serve with fresh corn, lettuce salad and Fruit Salad Dessert

Serves 12

Preparation: :30   Cook :45   Stand :00   Total 1:15

Ingredients:

1-3/4   cups corn meal
1/2   teaspoon baking soda
1/2   teaspoon baking powder
1/2   teaspoon cumin
1/4   teaspoon chili powder
1   cup fat free buttermilk
1   4 ounce can chopped green chilies
8   ounces fat free egg substitute
1/4   cup water
1   medium chopped onion
1/2   green or red bell pepper
        vegetable oil cooking spray
1   16 ounce can pinto or kidney beans
2   green onions, chopped
8   fluid ounces tomato juice
6   ounces shredded fat free cheese

Mix corn meal, baking soda, baking powder, cumin and chili powder together in a mixing bowl. In a small bowl, mix the buttermilk and egg substitute. Stir in the chilies and mix well. Add to corn meal and mix well. Set aside. In a non-stick skillet, saute onion and green pepper in 1/4 cup water. Cook until onion turns golden and water is evaporated. Pour off any excess liquid. Add this to corn meal mixture. Lightly spray a 9 x 13 inch pan with cooking spray. Drain and rinse beans. Put them on bottom of pan. Cover with shredded cheese, chopped green onion and tomato juice. Top with cornmeal mixture. Bake at 350°F for 30-45 minutes, or until cornbread topping is golden brown and a knife inserted in center comes out clean. Serve topped with picante or salsa.

♥ ♥ ♥

Note: If you cannot find fat free buttermilk, put a tablespoon of vinegar in a one cup measure. Add skim milk to equal one cup. Let stand for a minute, then stir well.

Option: Use two cans of beans instead of one.

Nutrition: (per serving): 252 calories

Saturated fat . . . . 0 g	
Total Fat . . . . 1 g	(2% of calories)
Protein . . . . 18 g	(29% of calories)
Carbohydrates . . . . 44 g	(69% of calories)

Cholesterol . . . . 2 mg	Sodium . . . . 410 mg
Fiber . . . . 3 g	Iron . . . . 5 mg
Vitamin A . . . . 419 IU	Vitamin C . . . . 11 mg

Source: Carol Rhora is a neurodiagnostic technician who had a heart attack in 1992. She also has hypertension.

"If not for this program, I feel that I would have had another heart attack."

Carol Rhora

♥ ♥ ♥

Imqarrun Fil-forn

Maltese for "baked macaroni"

Serves 16

Preparation: :20   Cook   1:30   Stand   :00   Total   1:50

Ingredients:

2	pounds mostaccioli	1	6 ounce can tomato paste
1	16 ounce package Gimme Lean™ beef substitute	1	tablespoon pepper
1	16 ounce package Gimme Lean™ sausage substitute	2	teaspoons sage
1	28 ounce can tomatoes, crushed and unsalted	2	8 ounce packages fat free egg substitute
1	28 ounce can tomato sauce, unsalted	1	cup fat free parmesan cheese

Cook noodles as directed on box and rinse. In a large soup pot, brown beef substitute and sausage substitute in a small amount of water. Add tomato products, pepper and sage. Cook for 30 minutes over moderate heat. Remove from heat and gently stir in the noodles, egg substitute and parmesan cheese. Pour into a 9 x 13 pan and bake at 350°F for 1 to 1-1/2 hours or until crispy on top. If you don't want it crispy, cover with aluminum foil during the last 30 minutes.

Nutrition: (per serving): 345 calories

Saturated fat . . . . 0 g		
Total Fat . . . . 1 g	(3% of calories)	
Protein . . . . 23 g	(27% of calories)	
Carbohydrates . . . . 60 g	(70% of calories)	
Cholesterol . . . . 0 mg	Sodium . . . . 445 mg	
Fiber . . . . 1 g	Iron . . . . 2 mg	
Vitamin A . . . . 905 IU	Vitamin C . . . . 25 mg	

Source: Al Spiteri, 52, is a journeyman in hydraulic repair. He had a heart attack in 1993.

♥ ♥ ♥

Baked Bean Casserole

Serve with Apple Coleslaw, steamed vegetables and Fast Fruit Trifle

Serves 16 — a serving is about 3/4 cup

Preparation: :10   Cook 1:00   Stand :00   Total 1:10

Ingredients:

2	48 ounce jars canned white beans, or any variety you prefer
1	large onion, chopped
1/2	cup fat free textured soy protein
1	cup fat free barbeque sauce
3	jalapeno peppers, chopped fine, optional
2	tablespoons brown sugar

Mix all ingredients. Put in a four quart casserole. Bake for one hour at 350°F. Serve over rice.

Nutrition: (per serving): 303 calories

Saturated fat . . . . 0 g		
Total Fat . . . . 1 g	(3% of calories)	
Protein . . . . 18 g	(23% of calories)	
Carbohydrates . . . . 55 g	(73% of calories)	
Cholesterol . . . . 0 mg	Sodium . . . . 571 mg	
Fiber . . . . 5 g	Iron . . . . 6 mg	
Vitamin A . . . . 907 IU	Vitamin C . . . . 22 mg	

Source: Betty Verdone, whose husband Carmine is a retiree with five heart attacks, bypass in 1983, and stent surgery in 1994. Carmine is also a diabetic.

"The Reversal Program has become Carmine's normal way of life with all the health benefits."

♥ ♥ ♥

Vegetarian Stew

Good old-fashioned flavor

Serves 8 — a serving is about 1 cup

Preparation: :15   Cook 1:00   Stand :05   Total 1:20

Ingredients:

1-1/2	cups fat free soy chunks	2	cups fat free broth
1-1/2	cups boiling water	4	cups sliced carrots
	vegetable oil cooking spray	4	potatoes, cubed
2	thinly sliced large onions	1	cup green beans
2	cups sliced mushrooms	1	tablespoons cornstarch
3	cloves garlic, minced	1	tablespoon cold water
1/2	cup tomato sauce		

Mix the soy chunks with boiling water. Let stand for 3-5 minutes. Spray a large pot with vegetable oil cooking spray. Saute soy chunks about 6 minutes. Add mushrooms and onion to pot and cook another 6 minutes. Add garlic and cook about 2 more minutes. Stir in the tomato sauce and the broth. Add enough water to cover the chunks. Bring to a boil. Reduce heat and simmer 10 minutes. Add carrots, potatoes and green beans. Partially cover pot and simmer for about 20 minutes or until vegetables are done. In a small bowl, mix cornstarch and water and add to stew. Increase heat and boil until sauce is thick, about 2 minutes. Season according to preferences. Try pepper, celery powder, worcestershire sauce, sage or basil.

Nutrition: (per serving): 263 calories

Saturated fat . . . . 0 g		
Total Fat . . . . 1 g	(2% of calories)	
Protein . . . . 17 g	(26% of calories)	
Carbohydrates . . . . 48 g	(72% of calories)	

Cholesterol . . . . 0 mg	Sodium . . . . 122 mg
Fiber . . . . 5 g	Iron . . . . 4 mg
Vitamin A . . . . 15710 IU	Vitamin C . . . . 30 mg

Source: Betty Verdone, whose husband Carmine is a retiree with five heart attacks, bypass in 1983, and stent surgery in 1994. Carmine is also a diabetic.

"In the beginning it takes a little 'blind faith,' but once you've followed this program for a few short months, your body will respond. When you feel good you know you are on the right road. When I entered the program in 1992, I was overweight and out of shape. Now I am lean and fit."

Carmine Verdone

Bean Burritos

Makes a filling and satisfying entree

Serves 6

Preparation: :15   Cook :10   Stand :00   Total :25

Ingredients:

1-2/3   cups cooked kidney beans or pink beans
1/2   cup fat free broth
1/2   cup tomatoes, peeled and finely chopped
1/4   cup green bell peppers, chopped
1/4   cup onions, chopped
2   tablespoons diced green chilies
1   minced garlic clove
1/4   teaspoon salt
1/2   cup fat free cheddar cheese, shredded
        bottled hot pepper sauce
6   10-inch fat free flour tortillas
        taco sauce
        fat free sour cream, optional
        tomato, cut in wedges, optional

Rinse and drain beans. Puree beans in a blender or processor and set aside. Saute in broth the chopped tomato, green pepper, onion, chilies, garlic and salt until thoroughly heated. Add mashed beans, cheese and hot pepper sauce to taste; mix well. Wrap tortillas in foil and heat at 350°F for 10 minutes. (Or, loosely wrap in plastic wrap or waxed paper and microwave at full power 30-40 seconds.) Fill each tortilla with about 1/4 cup bean mixture and roll. Serve with salsa. Top each with sour cream and garnish with tomato. Serve warm.

♥ ♥ ♥

Nutrition: (per serving): 269 calories

Saturated fat . . . . 0 g		
Total Fat . . . . 0 g	(1% of calories)	
Protein . . . . 13 g	(20% of calories)	
Carbohydrates . . . . 53 g	(79% of calories)	

Cholesterol . . . . 0 mg	Sodium . . . . 492 mg
Fiber . . . . 2 g	Iron . . . . 2 mg
Vitamin A . . . . 472 IU	Vitamin C . . . . 16 mg

Source: Al Lorenz and the Smokehouse Staff developed this recipe. Each week, Al and his staff prepare the vegetarian meals for the Reversal Team. All the meals are prepared with no added fats. They are balanced, hearty and great. The **Bean Burritos** are a favorite.

Enchilada Pie

Serve with Zesty Corn Muffins, salad and fresh corn

Serves 12

Preparation: :25   Cook :30   Stand :10   Total 1:05

Ingredients:

2-1/2	cups fat free textured soy protein
2	cups hot water
	vegetable oil cooking spray
8	fresh or thawed frozen corn tortillas, fat free
1	packet fat free taco seasoning mix
3/4	cup salsa
1/2	red or green bell pepper, chopped
1	onion, chopped
1	28 ounce can fat free refried beans
1	cup fat free sour cream
1	cup shredded fat free cheese
1	cup lettuce, shredded

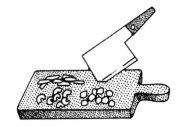

Preheat oven to 350°F. Reconstitute soy protein with hot water and let sit for 15 minutes. Spray bottom of 9 x 13 inch pan with vegetable oil cooking spray and line with tortillas. Mix pepper, onion, taco seasoning and salsa into soy protein in a frying pan and heat well. Spread refried beans on four of the tortillas and then spread 1/2 of the soy mixture. Place another layer of tortillas over the soy mixture and layer the sour cream over them. Spread the remaining soy mixture on top. Bake 25 to 30 minutes. Remove from oven and let stand for abut 10 minutes. Cut in squares and serve topped with lettuce and cheese.

Options: Add fresh chopped tomato to lettuce before serving.

♥ ♥ ♥

Nutrition: (per serving): 231 calories

Saturated fat . . . . 0 g		
Total Fat . . . . 2 g	(6% of calories)	
Protein . . . . 22 g	(38% of calories)	
Carbohydrates . . . . 32 g	(56% of calories)	

Cholesterol . . . . 2 mg	Sodium . . . . 419 mg
Fiber . . . . 6 g	Iron . . . . 5 mg
Vitamin A . . . . 236 IU	Vitamin C . . . . 12 mg

Source: Betty Verdone, whose husband Carmine is a retiree with five heart attacks, bypass in 1983, and stent surgery in 1994. Carmine is also a diabetic.

"Carmine feels so much better and his diabetes is under control with a 50% decrease in his diabetic medicine. He is much more active with less fatigue in his everyday activities."

Betty Verdone

♥ ♥ ♥

Mickie's Gingered Asparagus Fettuccine

Fresh asparagus never tasted better

Serves 4

Preparation: :15   Cook :25   Stand :00   Total :40

Ingredients:

3   large minced shallots
2   teaspoons fresh ginger root, coarsely grated
1   pound fresh asparagus
1   cup cooking wine
3/4   cup skim ricotta cheese
3/4   cup fat free yogurt
1/4   cup fat free parmesan cheese
6   ounces fettuccine, cooked
        freshly ground pepper
        salt to taste

Wash asparagus and trim by breaking off tough stem end at point where it breaks evenly. Cut into 1/2-inch pieces diagonally, starting just below the tips. In a large skillet, place the asparagus, shallots and ginger. Cover with enough wine to gently saute the asparagus until it is tender, about 10 minutes.

Blend the ricotta and yogurt together. When asparagus is done, remove from heat and stir in the yogurt mixture. Put hot pasta on plate and cover with asparagus. Top with parmesan and salt and pepper to taste.

Options: Use 2 cloves crushed garlic instead of ginger. Use fat free sour cream instead of yogurt. Use fettuccine noodles made without fat.

♥ ♥ ♥

Nutrition: (per serving): 288 calories

Saturated fat . . . . 0 g		
Total Fat . . . . 1 g	(4% of calories)	
Protein . . . . 21 g	(29% of calories)	
Carbohydrates . . . . 39 g	(54% of calories)	
Alcohol . . . . 5 g	(13% of calories)	

Cholesterol . . . . 37 mg	Sodium . . . . 174 mg
Fiber . . . . 1 g	Iron . . . . 3 mg
Vitamin A . . . . 1751 IU	Vitamin C . . . . 37 mg

Source: Mickie and Sam Sabolovich; Sam is a 46 year old retired City of Detroit police officer. He had bypass surgery in 1983 and 1993. He has had four angioplasties with two roto blade atherectomies.

"I started the program after my last surgery. Although the surgery saved my life, I was still having about 30 angina episodes each week. After six weeks into the program, my angina was almost gone. Currently I am pain free and I do just about anything I want to and life is truly great. I thank Dr. Rogers and the dedicated staff of the Downriver Reversal Team."

Mickie and Sam Sabolovich.

♥ ♥ ♥

Cabbage, White Beans and Rice

Serve with Sweet Potato Rolls and your favorite salad

Serves 6 — a serving is 2 cups

Preparation: :20   Cook :35   Stand :00   Total :55

Ingredients:

32	ounces fat free broth
1	cup onions, finely chopped
3	carrots, finely chopped
1	large celery stalk, finely chopped
1	yellow hot pepper, finely chopped (banana pepper)
1	teaspoon caraway seeds
2	cups chopped green cabbage
1	tablespoon light brown sugar
1	cup rice (white or quick-cooking brown)
1	cup water
28	ounces canned crushed tomatoes
24	ounces canned white beans, drained and rinsed
1	tablespoon cider vinegar
1/2	teaspoon ground white pepper

In large soup pot, heat 1/4-1/2 cup fat free broth and saute onion for 3 minutes. Add carrots and celery and yellow pepper; saute 3 minutes. Add caraway seeds. Cook, stirring, 1 minute. Stir in cabbage, the rest of the fat free broth and brown sugar. Simmer covered for 5 minutes. Stir in crushed tomatoes with juice, rice and water. Simmer covered for 20 minutes. Add white beans, vinegar and white pepper. Simmer uncovered for 5 minutes until heated through.

♥ ♥ ♥

Nutrition: (per serving): 445 calories

Saturated fat . . . . 0 g		
Total Fat . . . . 1 g	(3% of calories)	
Protein . . . . 34 g	(30% of calories)	
Carbohydrates . . . . 74 g	(67% of calories)	

Cholesterol . . . . 0 mg	Sodium . . . . 551 mg
Fiber . . . . 4 g	Iron . . . . 6 mg
Vitamin A . . . . 11790 IU	Vitamin C . . . . 55 mg

Source: Al Spiteri, 52, a journeyman in hydraulic repair, had a heart attack in 1993.

"I thank God I was informed about this program and I pursued it until I joined the Downriver Reversal Team. Both my weight and my cholesterol are down. I'm avoiding surgery and feeling better than I ever have. In 1995, I was shown reasons why I should stop eating sugar. I thought I felt great before, but now I'm at a whole other level of "feeling great." My weight loss had plateaued, but since giving up sugar, I have lost an additional 20 pounds to the total of 50 lost since joining the program. My cholesterol is almost down to 150 and my triglycerides are now 88. I continue to learn better ways to keep me off the operating table as I continue to participate in the program."

Al Spiteri

♥ ♥ ♥

Basic Burgers

Easy, fast, inexpensive and versatile

Serves 4

Preparation: :10   Cook :05   Stand :10   Total :25

Ingredients:

1	cup fat free textured soy protein
1/2	cup dehydrated mashed potato flakes
1/4	teaspoon garlic powder
1	tablespoon dried onion flakes
1	tablespoon fat free brown gravy mix
1	cup fat free broth

Mix the dry ingredients together in a bowl. Add the broth and stir well. Let stand for 10-15 minutes. Make four balls, the size of lemons. Press flat to form patties. Brown in a silverstone pan or grill over barbeque.

Note: burgers are easiest to form 10-15 minutes after liquid is added. These will have better flavor if burgers are cooked the day before. Take one in a baggie when you go out to eat. Order a bun with tomato, lettuce, onion, catsup and pickles. Put your Basic Burger in the bun and enjoy. A pound of soy protein makes about 16 burgers.

Options: Look for low sodium gravy mix. Hain™ brand makes a fat free, low sodium gravy mix. Vary the seasonings. Use Italian blend herbs and a little fat free parmesan and serve with marinara sauce. Or try canned chopped chilies and serve topped with salsa. Use poultry seasoning and serve with mashed potatoes, gravy, vegetables and cranberries. The addition of an egg white and a small amount of fat free bread crumbs will make the burgers easier to form.

♥ ♥ ♥

Nutrition: (per serving): 165 calories

Saturated fat . . . . 0 g		
Total Fat . . . . 0 g	(0% of calories)	
Protein . . . . 18 g	(43% of calories)	
Carbohydrates . . . . 23 g	(57% of calories)	

Cholesterol . . . . 0 mg	Sodium . . . . 37 mg
Fiber . . . . 4 g	Iron . . . . 3 mg
Vitamin A . . . . 0 IU	Vitamin C . . . . 13 mg

Source: Gerry Krag is the consulting nutritionist and group facilitator for the Downriver Reversal Team.

"Basic Burgers travel well. While driving across Pennsylvania on I-80, where exits are few and far between, I went through a Burger King and ordered a Veggie Whopper with no mayonnaise. I used a "Basic Burger" out of the cooler and had a filling and satisfying meat-less sandwich. Basic Burgers are excellent for lunch boxes, picnics and eating at home."

Gerry Krag

♥ ♥ ♥

Chop Suey

Serve with Oriental Salad and Maple Glazed Winter Vegetables

Serves 8 — a serving is 1 cup

Preparation: :20   Cook :20   Stand :05   Total :45

Ingredients:

1-1/3 cup water
1-2/3 cups fat free textured soy protein
1   cup fat free broth, no added salt
1 to 3 cloves garlic, minced
8   ounces mushrooms, sliced
2   cups celery, diagonally sliced
1   10 ounce package peas, frozen
2   cups bean sprouts, fresh
1   cup fat free broth, no salt added
2   tablespoons cornstarch
1   tablespoon low sodium soy sauce, or to taste
1/2   cup cold water
1   tablespoon molasses
1   teaspoon ground ginger, or to taste
       seasoned pepper to taste
1/4   cup sliced scallions

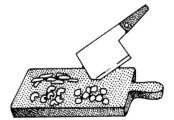

Mix the water and soy protein together. Let stand for 3 to 5 minutes, stirring occasionally. In a large skillet, saute the garlic, mushrooms and celery in one cup of the broth until the mushrooms are tender. Add the peas, sprouts, soy protein and the second cup of broth. Cover and cook over medium heat for about 5-10 minutes until the celery is tender crisp. In a small container, blend the cornstarch, cold water, molasses, seasonings and soy sauce. Add to the chop suey and cook over medium heat, stirring constantly until the sauce thickens. Add additional water to thin the sauce, if needed. Serve over rice garnished with the chopped scallions. Best if prepared the day before, but hold peas and sprouts until reheating to preserve crunch.

♥ ♥ ♥

Options: to enhance the flavor of the sauce, add 1 tablespoon cooking sherry. Use some chopped onion with the mushrooms, if desired. To control the sodium, use reduced sodium soy sauce and do not use canned vegetables, garlic salt or bouillon.

Nutrition: (per serving): 158 calories (Analysis does not include rice)

Saturated fat . . . . 0 g		
Total Fat . . . . 0 g	(2% of calories)	
Protein . . . . 17 g	(44% of calories)	
Carbohydrates . . . . 21 g	(54% of calories)	

Cholesterol . . . . 0 mg	Sodium . . . . 96 mg
Fiber . . . . 5 g	Iron . . . . 4 mg
Vitamin A . . . . 285 IU	Vitamin C . . . . 21 mg

Source: Gerry Krag is the consulting nutritionist and group facilitator for the Downriver Reversal Team.

"The longer you follow the program, the easier it gets. I have observed this again and again with Reversal Team members. I have also experienced this myself. Eating an occasional higher fat food releases a cascade of reactions that makes one crave more higher fat foods. However, by consistently sticking with low-fat vegetarian foods, your body will experience fewer cravings and healthy foods will satisfy."

Gerry Krag

Sasaki

Serve with Oriental Spinach Salad

Serves 6 — a serving is about one cup

Preparation: :15   Cook :10   Stand :05   Total :30

Ingredients:

1-1/2	cups fat free textured soy protein	2	cups fresh mung bean sprouts
1-1/2	cups water		
1/4	cup fat free broth	1/2	cup low sodium soy sauce
4	cups shredded cabbage	1	tablespoon sugar
1/2	cup green onions	6	cups cooked rice
1-1/2	cups finely chopped celery		

Mix water and soy protein together, let stand for five minutes. Meanwhile, saute cabbage in broth until cabbage is hot. Add the soy protein and the rest of the ingredients. Stirring constantly, cook until heated through, about five minutes. Serve over hot rice.

Nutrition: (per serving): 419 calories (analysis includes rice)

Saturated fat . . . . 0 g		
Total Fat . . . . 1 g	(1% of calories)	
Protein . . . . 24 g	(23% of calories)	
Carbohydrates . . . . 79 g	(76% of calories)	
Cholesterol . . . . 0 mg	Sodium . . . . 593 mg	
Fiber . . . . 5 g	Iron . . . . 7 mg	
Vitamin A . . . . 138 IU	Vitamin C . . . . 30 mg	

Source: Sally Roulinson, 58, is a seamstress and artist. She had a heart attack in 1990, angioplasty in 1993 and bypass in 1995.

". . . I don't miss eating meat at all."

♥ ♥ ♥

Barbeque Sandwiches

Serve with Vegetable Soup, Raspberry Fruit Salad and carrot slices

Serves 4

Preparation: :15　　Cook :30　　Stand :00　　Total :45

Ingredients:

1-1/2	cups fat free textured soy protein	2	tablespoons sugar
1	cup water	1/2	teaspoon cloves
1	large onion, chopped	2	tablespoons mustard
1	green or yellow bell pepper, chopped	1	tablespoon vinegar
1/4	cup fat free broth	1	cup low sodium catsup

Mix the water and soy protein together and let stand for five minutes. Saute the onion and pepper in broth until transparent. Add soy protein and remainder of ingredients. Cover and simmer on low heat for 30 minutes. Stir occasionally. To keep a gravy-like consistency, you may need to add water. Serve on toasted buns.

Nutrition: (per serving): 258 calories

Saturated fat . . . . 0 g		
Total Fat . . . . 1 g	(2% of calories)	
Protein . . . . 25 g	(40% of calories)	
Carbohydrates . . . . 38 g	(59% of calories)	
Cholesterol . . . . 0 mg	Sodium . . . . 497 mg
Fiber . . . . 7 g	Iron . . . . 5 mg
Vitamin A . . . . 118 IU	Vitamin C . . . . 22 mg

Source: Sally Roulinson, 58, is a seamstress and artist. She had a heart attack in 1990, angioplasty in 1993 and bypass in 1995.

"For me, stress management is one of the most important parts of the program because stress is hard to deal with on your own."

Wild Mushroom and Red Pepper Baked Pasta

A great dish for lots of company

Serves 8-12 — a serving is about 2 cups

Preparation: :45   Cook 1:00   Stand :00   Total 1:45

Ingredients:

1	pound macaroni, uncooked
2	diced medium red onions or 1 red and 1 white
1	red bell pepper, diced in 1/2 inch pieces
1	pound mushrooms
10	green onions, sliced
4	fluid ounces red wine
1/2	cup chopped parsley, fresh
1	teaspoon ground sage
12	slices whole wheat bread, cubed
2	cups fat free broth
1/2	teaspoon salt
1/2	teaspoon fresh ground black pepper, or more if preferred
	vegetable oil cooking spray
1/4	cup fat free parmesan cheese

Preheat oven to 350°F. For variety, use colored vegetable macaroni. Follow package instructions and cook macaroni, but remove from heat when pasta is al dente, tender yet still firm to the bite. Drain, but do not rinse. Transfer to a large cookie sheet to cool to room temperature. Dice the onion and pepper. Quarter the mushrooms. For variety, select chanterelles, portabellas, shitake and field mushrooms. Cook the mushrooms in wine with the onions and pepper. Cook until tender and slightly browned, about 6 minutes. Remove from heat and add the green onions, parsley and sage. Transfer to a very large bowl and add the pasta and the cubed bread, mixing well. Stir in the broth and salt and pepper.

♥ ♥ ♥

Transfer to a very large oven proof casserole sprayed lightly with vegetable oil cooking spray. Cover tightly and bake until very hot, about 30-45 minutes. Remove from oven and top with fat free parmesan cheese. This makes 8 very large servings. Overheating will dry out the casserole

Options: include one teaspoon of cinnamon and increase the pepper.

Nutrition: (per serving): 385 calories

Saturated fat	0 g	
Total Fat	2 g	(6% of calories)
Protein	16 g	(16% of calories)
Carbohydrates	73 g	(75% of calories)
Alcohol	1 g	(3% of calories)

Cholesterol	1 mg	Sodium	424 mg
Fiber	3 g	Iron	4 mg
Vitamin A	533 IU	Vitamin C	23 mg

Source: Bob Shank is a retired Episcopal priest who is now the executive director of the Cranbrook Peace Foundation. He has multiple risk factors for coronary artery disease.

"The path to healing a heart is much like the peace process. It takes openess, clear communication and persistence. Neither is easy, but the rewards are well worth the effort."

♥ ♥ ♥

Sandwich Spread

Brown baggers delight

Serves 5

Preparation: :15   Cook :00   Stand :00   Total :15

Ingredients:

4	ounces fat free soy based sandwich slices
4	hard boiled egg whites
1	tablespoon sweet pickle relish
1/4	cup fat free mayonnaise
10	slices fat free whole wheat bread

Finely mince or grind the sandwich slices and egg whites. Stir in the relish and mayonnaise. Spread on five slices of bread. Add sliced tomato, onion, lettuce as desired. Top with remainder of bread.

Note: if you are watching sodium, use low sodium bread. Many breads have 120-200 mg. sodium per slice. Also, look for sandwich slices that are lower in sodium.

Nutrition: (per serving): 216 calories

Saturated fat . . . . 0 g		
Total Fat . . . . 0 g	(0% of calories)	
Protein . . . . 15 g	(28% of calories)	
Carbohydrates . . . . 39 g	(72% of calories)	
Cholesterol . . . . 0 mg	Sodium . . . . 713 mg	
Fiber . . . . 4 g	Iron . . . . 0 mg	
Vitamin A . . . . 3 IU	Vitamin C . . . . 0 mg	

Source: Sally Roulinson, 58, is a seamstress and artist. She had a heart attack in 1990, angioplasty in 1993 and bypass in 1995.

♥ ♥ ♥

Southwest Spaghetti

Great with salad, Zesty Corn Muffins and sliced tomatoes

Serves 6

Preparation: :15   Cook :45   Stand :00   Total 1:00

Ingredients:

1/2	pound pasta, cooked	16	ounces canned tomatoes
1/4	cup fat free broth	2	cups frozen corn, cooked
1	chopped onion	1/2	teaspoon Worcestershire sauce
1	green bell pepper, chopped		pinch cayenne pepper
1	clove garlic, minced	2	cups grated fat free cheddar
1	cup fat free textured soy pro-tein		cheese
			fat free bread crumbs
1	cup water		

Cook pasta according to package directions. Saute onion, pepper and garlic in broth until transparent. Add soy protein and water and stir well. Stir in tomatoes, corn, seasonings and 1 cup of the cheese. Heat gently until the cheese starts to melt. Spray a 3 quart casserole with vegetable oil cooking spray. Put cooked pasta in bottom. Add the soy mixture. Top with remaining cup of cheese and sprinkle some bread crumbs on top. Bake until heated through in a 350°F oven, about 20 minutes. Do not bake too long or cheese will be tough.

Nutrition: (per serving): 336 calories

Saturated fat . . . . 0 g		
Total Fat . . . . 2 g	(4% of calories)	
Protein . . . . 30 g	(36% of calories)	
Carbohydrates . . . . 51 g	(60% of calories)	
Cholesterol . . . . 28 mg	Sodium . . . . 404 mg	
Fiber . . . . 4 g	Iron . . . . 4 mg	
Vitamin A . . . . 790 IU	Vitamin C . . . . 31 mg	

Source: Sally Roulinson, 58, is a seamstress and artist. She had a heart attack in 1990, angioplasty in 1993 and bypass in 1995.

♥ ♥ ♥

Spaghetti Sauce Calderone

A nice thick sauce with lots of flavor

Serves 6 — a serving is about 3/4 cup

Preparation: :15   Cook 2:00   Stand :00   Total 2:15

Ingredients:

28	ounces canned tomatoes
12	ounces tomato paste
1	large diced onion
3	cloves garlic, minced or whole
1	stalk celery, diced
1	bay leaf
1	teaspoon parsley, dried, or 2 tsp. fresh
1/2	teaspoon oregano
1/4	teaspoon cayenne pepper
	salt and pepper to taste
1/2	cup fat free textured soy protein, optional
	water to hydrate soy

Combine tomatoes and paste in a blender and blend until well mixed. In a large saucepan, combine all ingredients except the soy and water. Bring to a boil and then cover and simmer until sauce is thick, about two hours. Stir occasionally. If sauce sticks to bottom, reduce heat even more. If using the soy protein, mix it with enough water, about 1/3 cup, so that it is well moistened and has the texture of ground meat. Add to sauce after about one hour of simmering. As the sauce continues to simmer, check to make sure it isn't getting too thick. If it begins to stick to bottom, add a little water. Remove bay leaf before serving. This recipe can be easily doubled. Freezes well. Makes 6 cups.

♥ ♥ ♥

Nutrition: (per serving): 168 calories

Saturated fat . . . . 0 g		
Total Fat . . . . 1 g	(6% of calories)	
Protein . . . . 10 g	(25% of calories)	
Carbohydrates . . . . 29 g	(69% of calories)	

Cholesterol . . . . 0 mg	Sodium . . . . 386 mg
Fiber . . . . 4 g	Iron . . . . 4 mg
Vitamin A . . . . 2477 IU	Vitamin C . . . . 57 mg

Source: Frances and Fred Calderone; Fred, 69, is a retired diesel mechanic, heavy equipment. He had a heart attack in 1993 and angioplasty in 1993 and 1994. Fred's hobbies are gardening and toy trains.

"Before joining this program, I had a heart attack. One artery was 90% blocked and so I had an angioplasty. Then I attended cardiac rehabilitation, but never followed up. One year later, another artery was 90% blocked, plus the first artery was starting to block again. I had a second angioplasty. So I decided to join the reversal program and now my cholesterol is down from 243 to 129. My weight has gone from 210 to 175. Plus the other numbers are where they should be. So you see, the program does work. I would highly recommend it. Also, I would like to say that I feel great. I have more energy than before — best in three years. The staff that runs the program are great — very supportive. Plus the members are the most supportive people that you can find. I am very proud to be a member of this program."

Fred Calderone

♥ ♥ ♥

Sharon's Lasagna

Serve with salad, Italian bread and zucchini

Serves 8

Preparation: :15   Cook 1:00   Stand :00   Total 1:15

Ingredients:

2	16 ounce packages fat free ricotta cheese
1	cup fat free parmesan cheese
3	egg whites
3	tablespoons fresh parsley, chopped
16	ounces fat free mozzarella cheese, shredded
1	8 ounce box of lasagna noodles, uncooked
25	ounces fat free spaghetti sauce (sodium reduced) (save jar after emptying sauce)
1	cup water

Mix ricotta cheese, 3/4 cup parmesan cheese, egg whites, mozzarella and parsley, set aside. Spread 1/2 cup of sauce on bottom of 9 x 13 inch baking pan. Place 3 uncooked lasagna noodles on top of sauce. Spread half of the ricotta mixture on the noodles. Spread 1/3 of the remaining spaghetti sauce on top of cheese. Repeat layers until ingredients are used. Sprinkle remaining 1/4 cup parmesan cheese on top. Make sure all noodles are covered. Take 1 cup water and swish out spaghetti sauce from jar. Pour into each corner of pan. Cover tightly with foil and bake for 45-50 minutes in a 350°F oven. Remove foil and bake until browned, about 15 minutes longer.

Options: Use basil, oregano and pepper to add flavor to ricotta.

♥ ♥ ♥

Nutrition: (per serving): 289 calories

Saturated fat . . . . 0 g		
Total Fat . . . . 1 g	(4% of calories)	
Protein . . . . 43 g	(58% of calories)	
Carbohydrates . . . . 29 g	(38% of calories)	

Cholesterol . . . . 0 mg	Sodium . . . . 795 mg
Fiber . . . . 1 g	Iron . . . . 2 mg
Vitamin A . . . . 542 IU	Vitamin C . . . . 13 mg

Source: Sharon Bommarrito is the daughter of Helen Moses; Helen has been a Reversal Team member since 1992.

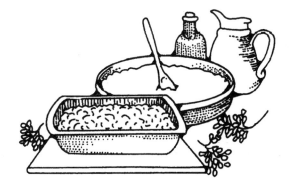

Jeanne's "Chicken" & Dumplings

A tasty replacement for an old favorite

Serves 6

Preparation: :10   Cook :45   Stand :00   Total :55

Ingredients:

46	ounces fat free broth
2	cloves garlic, minced
1	onion, quartered
1	stalk celery, chopped into 2 inch pieces
2	potatoes, peeled and halved
4	carrots, peeled and halved
1	bay leaf
1	tablespoon poultry seasoning pepper, to taste
1/2	lemon

Dumplings:

1	cup self-rising flour
1	tablespoon finely chopped onions, optional
1/2	cup skim milk
1-1/2	teaspoons vinegar
1	egg white

Place all soup ingredients, except lemon, into a large dutch oven. Squeeze lemon over ingredients; add fresh lemon rind to taste. Cover and bring to a boil. Reduce heat and simmer for 20-25 minutes.

Dumplings: Mix vinegar and milk and let stand. Beat egg white until almost stiff. Add milk mixture to flour. Add onion and mix well. Add egg white and mix again. Drop by spoonfuls into simmering soup and simmer 10 more minutes covered and 10 minutes uncovered..

Options: Drop Oven Biscuits: Preheat oven to 325°F. Use dumpling recipe and drop by tablespoons on non-stick cookie pan. Bake 15-20 minutes until toothpick comes out clean. Serve with soups or stews. These are good with hot fat free gravy mixed with peas, onions and soy protein for a quick meal. Another option is to mix a little fat free cheese into the biscuits and serve them with chili.

♥ ♥ ♥

Nutrition: (per serving): 154 calories

Saturated fat . . . . 0 g	
Total Fat . . . . 1 g	(3% of calories)
Protein . . . . 6 g	(16% of calories)
Carbohydrates . . . . 31 g	(81% of calories)

Cholesterol . . . . 0 mg	Sodium . . . . 175 mg
Fiber . . . . 2 g	Iron . . . . 2 mg
Vitamin A . . . . 13,766 IU	Vitamin C . . . . 30 mg

Source: Jeanne M. Eckert, 62, is a homemaker and gardening expert. In addition to having coronary artery disease, she has blockages in the arteries of her legs. Jean's mother was a preparing chef who taught her to cook.

"I believe if I had not joined the Reversal Program a year ago, I would have had a heart attack by now. I would recommend it for anyone, even those in good health, as a preventative to heart disease."

Jeanne M. Eckert

Easy Pot Pie

Serve with bran muffins, classic molded salad and steamed broccoli

Serves 6

Preparation: :30   Cook :30   Stand :00   Total 1:00

Ingredients:

1	tablespoon dried onion flakes
2/3	cup skim milk
1-1/2	cups sliced carrots
1	cup potatoes, cubed
1`	chopped medium onion
1	stalk celery, chopped
1	teaspoon minced garlic
1/3	cup fat free textured soy protein
1	cup frozen peas
2-3	cups fat free broth
1	cup self rising flour

Preheat oven to 375°F. Place dry onion flakes in milk and set aside. Place carrots and potato in a small amount (1/4 cup) water and cook in microwave on high for about four minutes, stir and return to microwave for three more minutes. (These can also be simmered on stove top until tender). Add celery, onion and garlic and microwave again on high for two minutes. Put cooked vegetables in 9 x 13 inch baking pan. Stir in soy protein, the peas and broth. Add seasonings as desired (try such seasonings as pepper, seasoned pepper, poultry seasoning, rosemary or thyme). Mix flour, onion flakes and milk together until blended. Dough should be a spreadable consistency. If it is too stiff, add a little skim milk. Spread the dough mixture on top of vegetables to form a crust and bake 20-30 minutes until top is golden brown.

♥ ♥ ♥

Nutrition: (per serving): 212 calories

Saturated fat . . . . 0 g		
Total Fat . . . . 1 g	(3% of calories)	
Protein . . . . 11 g	(21% of calories)	
Carbohydrates . . . . 40 g	(76% of calories)	

Cholesterol . . . . 0 mg	Sodium . . . . 410 mg
Fiber . . . . 3 g	Iron . . . . 3 mg
Vitamin A . . . . 8168 IU	Vitamin C . . . . 24 mg

Source: Jeanne M. Eckert, 62, is a homemaker and gardening expert. In addition to having coronary artery disease, she has blockages in the arteries of her legs. Jean's mother was a preparing chef who taught her to cook.

> *"I believe if I had not joined the Reversal Program a year ago, I would have had a heart attack by now. I would recommend it for anyone, even those in good health, as a preventative to heart disease."*
>
> Jeanne M. Eckert

♥ ♥ ♥

Pasta and Bean Stew

With salad, a side vegetable and a good bread: a quick, tasty dinner

Serves 4 — a serving is 1-1/2 cups

Preparation: :15   Cook :15   Stand :00   Total :30

Ingredients:

1	cup canned tomatoes	16	ounces canned kidney beans, drained
3/4	cup uncooked shell macaroni		
1/4	cup onions, chopped	1	14 ounce can fat free broth
1/4	cup green bell peppers, chopped		
1	teaspoon Italian seasoning	8	ounces canned garbanzo beans, drained
1	teaspoon Worcestershire sauce		
1	clove finely chopped garlic		

Combine all ingredients in a 2 quart saucepan. Heat to a boil, stirring occasionally. Cover and simmer for about 15 minutes, stirring occasionally, until pasta is tender.

Nutrition: (per serving): 264 calories

Saturated fat . . . . 0 g		
Total Fat . . . . 2 g	(5% of calories)	
Protein . . . . 13 g	(20% of calories)	
Carbohydrates . . . . 50 g	(75% of calories)	
Cholesterol . . . . 0 mg	Sodium . . . . 659 mg	
Fiber . . . . 3 g	Iron . . . . 3 mg	
Vitamin A . . . . 440 IU	Vitamin C . . . . 19 mg	

Source: Charles Hodge is a journeyman millwright and volunteer fire fighter, who has coronary artery disease.

"Thank God for this life saving program."

♥ ♥ ♥

Bean Stuffed Spuds

A quick and tasty side dish

Serves 4

Preparation: :20   Cook :00   Stand :00   Total :20

Ingredients:

4	medium baking potatoes
1	8 ounce can red kidney beans
1/2	cup salsa
1	cup fat free cottage cheese
1/2	cup shredded fat free cheddar cheese

Scrub potatoes and prick with fork. Microwave on high for 14 to 17 minutes, rearranging potatoes after 7 minutes. Drain and rinse beans. In a small microwave bowl, stir together beans and salsa. Cover with plastic wrap and cook on high 2 to 4 minutes, stirring after 1-1/2 minutes. Roll potatoes to loosen skin, press potatoes to separate and open them. Spoon cottage cheese into potatoes, then pour salsa mixture over potatoes. Sprinkle with shredded cheese and microwave on high, uncovered, for one minute or until cheese melts.

Nutrition: (per serving): 329 calories

Saturated fat . . . . 0 g		
Total Fat . . . . 0 g	(1% of calories)	
Protein . . . . 20 g	(24% of calories)	
Carbohydrates . . . . 61 g	(75% of calories)	

Cholesterol . . . . 7 mg	Sodium . . . . 602 mg
Fiber . . . . 2 g	Iron . . . . 3 mg
Vitamin A . . . . 181 IU	Vitamin C . . . . 33 mg

Source: Helen Moses is a homemaker who keeps busy babysitting her grand-children. Helen has coronary artery disease.

♥ ♥ ♥

Elbow Macaroni Skillet Dinner

A zesty and colorful meal

Serves 8

Preparation: :20   Cook :40   Stand :00   Total 1:00

Ingredients:

1	onion, chopped	1	16 ounce can kidney beans, rinsed and drained
1	green bell pepper, chopped		
2	cloves garlic, minced	1	10 ounce package frozen corn, thawed
1	tablespoon chili powder		
1/2	teaspoon salt	8	ounces macaroni, elbow type, cooked and drained
1/2	teaspoon ground cumin		
1/2	cup fat free broth	1/2	cup shredded fat-free cheddar cheese
1	28 ounce can tomatoes, undrained		

In a large skillet, heat broth over medium-high heat. Add onion, green pepper, garlic, chili powder, salt and cumin; saute 4 minutes or until vegetables are tender. Stir in tomatoes, breaking them up with the spoon. Add kidney beans and corn; bring to a boil. Cover, reduce heat and simmer, stirring occasionally, for 15 minutes. If sauce gets too thick, add a little water. Toss with macaroni, sprinkle with cheese and serve.

Nutrition: (per serving): 373 calories

Saturated fat . . . . 0 g		
Total Fat . . . . 1 g	(3% of calories)	
Protein . . . . 20 g	(22% of calories)	
Carbohydrates . . . . 70 g	(75% of calories)	
Cholesterol . . . . 0 mg	Sodium . . . . 552 mg	
Fiber . . . . 6 g	Iron . . . . 7 mg	
Vitamin A . . . . 1030 IU	Vitamin C . . . . 42 mg	

Source: Fred Calderone, 69, retired diesel mechanic, had a heart attack in 1993.

♥ ♥ ♥

Green Goddess Pasta Sauce

Easy and colorful

Serves 4

Preparation: :20   Cook :00   Stand :00   Total :20

Ingredients:

4   cups fresh spinach
8   ounces spinach pasta
10-1/2 ounces 1% fat tofu or fat free tofu
          to taste: paprika, black pepper, salt
1   teaspoon oregano
1   teaspoon basil
1/4   cup finely chopped onions
1/4   cup fat free parmesan cheese, optional
          chopped tomato, as desired

Steam spinach until wilted. Cook pasta as directed on package. Puree tofu cake with spinach, adding seasonings and chopped onion as desired. Drain pasta. Serve pasta with the pureed sauce. Garnish with parmesan and chopped tomato.

Nutrition: (per serving): 235 calories

Saturated fat . . . . 0 g		
Total Fat . . . . 2 g	(9% of calories)	
Protein . . . . 15 g	(26% of calories)	
Carbohydrates . . . . 38 g	(64% of calories)	
Cholesterol . . . . 41 mg	Sodium . . . . 212 mg	
Fiber . . . . 1 g	Iron . . . . 4 mg	
Vitamin A . . . . 3816 IU	Vitamin C . . . . 16 mg	

Source: Babsi Riegler is a yoga instructor for the Reversal Team. She also has a degree in psychology.

♥ ♥ ♥

Chickpea and Rice Casserole

Serve over rice for an easy, easy meal

Serves 6

Preparation: :10   Cook :25   Stand :00   Total :35

Ingredients:

3/4	cup fat free textured soy protein	8	ounces mushrooms, sliced
1	chopped onion	1	cup frozen peas
3	chopped carrots	1	cup frozen corn
25	ounces fat free spaghetti sauce		black pepper to taste
16	ounces canned chickpeas, rinsed and drained	1	teaspoon Italian seasoning

Simmer the soy protein, onion, carrots and sauce for 25 to 30 minutes. Add remaining ingredients, as desired. Vary the vegetables according to your preference. Continue to simmer until vegetables are tender and sauce is uniformly heated. Add water as needed to prevent sticking. Serve over rice. To reduce salt, look for fat free spaghetti sauce that is lower in sodium.

Nutrition: (per serving): 237 calories

Saturated fat . . . . 0 g		
Total Fat . . . . 1 g	(4% of calories)	
Protein . . . . 15 g	(24% of calories)	
Carbohydrates . . . . 41 g	(72% of calories)	
Cholesterol . . . . 0 mg	Sodium . . . . 270 mg	
Fiber . . . . 5 g	Iron . . . . 4 mg	
Vitamin A . . . . 10435 IU	Vitamin C . . . . 17 mg	

Source: Ronald Konopka, 52, is an autostylist who had angioplasty in 1988 and 1990 and bypass surgery in 1994.

Side Dishes

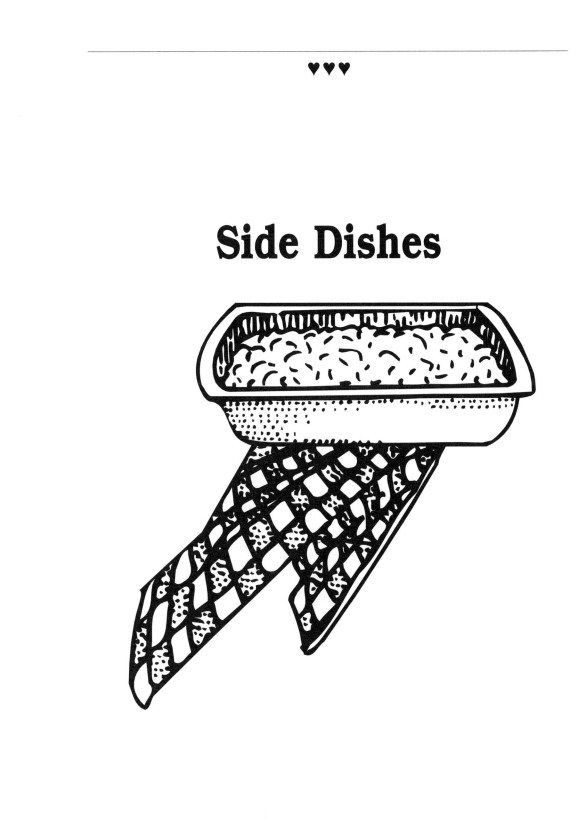

Side Dishes

Jerry's Frency Fries 195

Vegetarian Portabella 196

Sally's Potatoes 197

Ethel's Sweet Potatoes 198

Maple Glazed Winter Vegetables 199

Celery, Peppers and Pasta 200

Pasta and Broccoli with
    Tomatoes 201

Vegetable Pie 202

Potatoes, Peppers and
    Asparagus 203

Hominy Skillet Side Dish 204

Mashed Parrots 205

Vegetable Rice Casserole 206

Moussaka 208

Gravy 210

Mashed Potatoes 211

Barley Pilaf 212

Reversal Moors and Christians .213

Bev's Pasta Kraut Surprise 214

Golden Harvest Casserole 215

Zesty Twice Baked Potatoes . . .216

Baked Green Tomatoes
    with Zucchini 217

Broccoli Marinara 218

Pat's Potatoes 220

Zucchini Bake 221

Eggplant with Spinach
    Spiral Pasta 222

♥ ♥ ♥

Jerry's French Fries

If you have been craving French fries, try these

Serves 4

Preparation: :15   Cook :35   Stand :00   Total :50

Ingredients:

2	large baking potatoes
1	large sweet potato
1	egg white
1	tablespoon pungent seasoning, such as seasoned pepper, cayenne or chili powder

Cut the potatoes and sweet potato into thin fries. In a large bowl, lightly beat the egg white with a fork until foamy. Stir in the seasoning. Add the potatoes and toss to coat well. Using a non-stick cookie sheet or one sprayed with a non-stick cooking spray, spread the potatoes in a single layer. Bake at 450°F for 30-35 minutes, or until the potatoes are crisp and browned.

Nutrition: (per serving): 235 calories

Saturated fat . . . . 0 g		
Total Fat . . . . 1 g	(2% of calories)	
Protein . . . . 6 g	(10% of calories)	
Carbohydrates . . . . 52 g	(88% of calories)	
Cholesterol . . . . 0 mg	Sodium . . . . 48 mg
Fiber . . . . 2 g	Iron . . . . 2 mg
Vitamin A . . . . 10555 IU	Vitamin C . . . . 36 mg

Source: Gerald Nagle, 63, is a retiree who enjoys traveling. In 1988, he had bypass surgery and aortic valve replacement. He also has diabetes.

♥ ♥ ♥

Vegetarian Portabella

An elegant meal, appetizer or side dish

Serves 4

Preparation: :15   Cook :30   Stand :00   Total :45

Ingredients:

5	Portabella mushrooms	1/2	cup fat free broth
1	green bell pepper	1/2	cup red wine vinegar
1	yellow bell pepper		fat free red wine
1	red bell pepper		vinegar dressing, to
1	onion		taste

Preheat oven to 325°F. De-stem portabella mushrooms and gently score top of mushrooms. Spray cookie sheet with non-stick cooking spray, place mushrooms on pan and bake until brown (approximately 10-15 minutes). After cooking, refrigerate until cool. Cut peppers and onions into strips. Saute onions and peppers in broth and cook until tender. Add mushrooms and red wine vinegar; saute a few minutes longer. After cooking, apply red wine vinegar dressing to taste. Good hot or cold. Use mushrooms themselves in a bun or burrito. Or, serve as a side dish or on rice or angel hair pasta.

Nutrition: (per serving): 66 calories

Saturated fat . . . . 0 g		
Total Fat . . . . 0 g	(3% of calories)	
Protein . . . . 2 g	(12% of calories)	
Carbohydrates . . . . 9 g	(57% of calories)	
Alcohol . . . . 3 g	(38% of calories)	

Cholesterol . . . . 0 mg	Sodium . . . . 10 mg
Fiber . . . . 1 g	Iron . . . . 0 mg
Vitamin A . . . . 2226 IU	Vitamin C . . . . 90 mg

Source: Josh Hodge is the son of Charles Hodge. Charles Hodge has coronary artery disease and has been a Reversal Team member since early 1995.

♥ ♥ ♥

Sally's Potatoes

Your family will love this easy, tasty casserole

Serves 10

Preparation: :05   Cook :30   Stand :00   Total :35

Ingredients:

1	cauliflower	40	ounces frozen shredded
1	green or red bell pepper		hash brown potatoes
2	vidalia onions	1	12 ounce can corn
1/2	cup fat free broth		

Use frozen shredded potatoes with no added fat, such as "Simply Potatoes™;" you will need 2 packages, each weighing 1 pound, 4 ounces.

Steam the head of cauliflower and let it cool. Chop the pepper and onions. Using a non-stick fry pan, cook the onion and pepper in a small amount of fat free broth. When the onion is tender, add the potatoes using additional liquid to prevent sticking. As the potatoes begin to brown, add the drained corn. Chop the steamed cauliflower. Once the potatoes are browned, add the cauliflower to the casserole and cook until uniformly heated. Serve with salad and fat free corn chips. Delicious with bean dishes.

Nutrition: (per serving): 160 calories

Saturated fat . . . . 0 g		
Total Fat . . . . 1 g	(6% of calories)	
Protein . . . . 4 g	(11% of calories)	
Carbohydrates . . . . 33 g	(83% of calories)	
Cholesterol . . . . 0 mg	Sodium . . . . 116 mg	
Fiber . . . . 1 g	Iron . . . . 2 mg	
Vitamin A . . . . 91 IU	Vitamin C . . . . 37 mg	

Source: Sally Roulinson, 58, is a seamstress and artist. She had a heart attack in 1990, angioplasty in 1993 and bypass in 1995.

♥ ♥ ♥

Ethel's Sweet Potatoes

Great for holiday meals

Serves 6

Preparation: :20   Cook 1:00   Stand :00   Total 1:20

Ingredients:

3-1/2   pounds sweet potatoes
1/2   cup orange marmalade or apricot preserves
1/4   cup brown sugar, to taste
1/2   cup orange juice
3   egg whites
           vegetable oil cooking spray

Peel and slice potatoes. Steam or boil until tender, about 30 minutes. Drain and mash. Add marmalade, sugar and juice. Beat egg whites to form stiff peaks. Stir gently into potatoes. Coat a 6 cup casserole with non-stick cooking spray. Add mixture and bake at 350°F until puffy and set, about 40 minutes.

Nutrition: (per serving): 396 calories

Saturated fat . . . . 0 g		
Total Fat . . . . 1 g	(2% of calories)	
Protein . . . . 6 g	(6% of calories)	
Carbohydrates . . . . 90 g	(91% of calories)	
Cholesterol . . . . 0 mg	Sodium . . . . 67 mg	
Fiber . . . . 2 g	Iron . . . . 2 mg	
Vitamin A . . . . 53105 IU	Vitamin C . . . . 68 mg	

Source: Ethel Kennedy is a dental assistant with elevated cholesterol and hypertension

"The diet and the program have controlled the elevation of my cholesterol and hypertension and brought me to a positive attitude with more ambition to exercise."

♥ ♥ ♥

Maple Glazed Winter Vegetables

This unique combination will please your palate

Serves 10

Preparation: :30   Cook :10   Stand :00   Total :40

Ingredients:

1	pound carrots, peeled and cut in 3 x 1/4 inch strips	2	tablespoons maple syrup
1	pound parsnips, peeled and cut in 3 x 1/4 inch strips	1-1/4	teaspoons salt, optional
1	pound rutabagas, peeled and cut in 3 x 1/4 inch strips	1/4	teaspoon cinnamon ground pepper, to taste
2	tablespoons lemon juice	1	packet Butter Buds™ Mix, if desired

Steam vegetables until tender-crisp, about 8 minutes. Combine remaining ingredients in large bowl. Add vegetables and toss gently. Adjust seasonings and serve hot. If not sweet enough, add 1/4 cup melted brown sugar or additional maple syrup.

Vegetables can be prepared ahead and chilled in a covered container for up to two days. Reheat gently, then add remaining ingredients as described above.

Nutrition: (per serving): 91 calories

Saturated fat . . . . 0 g		
Total Fat . . . . 0 g	(3% of calories)	
Protein . . . . 2 g	(7% of calories)	
Carbohydrates . . . . 20 g	(90% of calories)	
Cholesterol . . . . 0 mg	Sodium . . . . 30 mg	
Fiber . . . . 2 g	Iron . . . . 1 mg	
Vitamin A . . . . 12760 IU	Vitamin C . . . . 25 mg	

Source: Judith Caplan Phillips is the general manager of an ad specialty supplier who had a bypass in 1992 and has diabetes.

♥ ♥ ♥

Celery, Peppers and Pasta

Simple, easy and good

Serves 8

Preparation: :20   Cook :15   Stand :00   Total :35

Ingredients:

3	cups celery, chopped
1	cup diced green bell peppers
1/4	cup fat free broth
29	ounce can stewed tomatoes
1/4	teaspoon black pepper
3	cups pasta, cooked, or 1-1/2 cups uncooked pasta

If using uncooked pasta, cook according to package directions. Saute celery and green pepper in broth until slightly tender and crisp, about 5 minutes. Add more fat free broth if needed to prevent burning. Add tomatoes (broken up), and black pepper. Simmer uncovered until mixture thickens, about 5 minutes. Stir in cooked pasta. Cook until well heated. Serve hot.

Nutrition: (per serving): 122 calories

Saturated fat . . . . 0 g		
Total Fat . . . . 1 g	(4% of calories)	
Protein . . . . 4 g	(14% of calories)	
Carbohydrates . . . . 25 g	(82% of calories)	
Cholesterol . . . . 0 mg	Sodium . . . . 302 mg
Fiber . . . . 1 g	Iron . . . . 2 mg
Vitamin A . . . . 710 IU	Vitamin C . . . . 28 mg

Source: Ruby Dedenbach is a homemaker who had bypasses in 1988 and 1992, stent surgery in 1995.

♥ ♥ ♥

Pasta and Broccoli with Tomatoes

A colorful and tasty side dish

Serves 4

Preparation: :15   Cook :30   Stand :00   Total :45

Ingredients:

1	cup macaroni, uncooked	1/4	teaspoon garlic powder
2	tomatoes, medium sized	1	cup frozen broccoli, cuts
1	small onion, chopped		or florets
1	teaspoon parsley	1/4	cup shredded fat free
1/2	cup fat free broth		cheddar cheese
1	teaspoon dried Italian seasoning, crushed		

Cook pasta in 4 cups of water and then drain. While pasta is cooking, chop tomatoes and seed if desired. Saute onions in broth until tender. Add tomatoes, parsley, Italian seasoning and garlic. Heat mixture until hot, then add broccoli. Cover and cook over medium heat for 4 minutes. Add a small amount of water if needed to prevent burning. Stir in pasta and cook for 3 more minutes or until broccoli is tender-crisp. Transfer to a serving dish and sprinkle with cheese.

Nutrition: (per serving): 148 calories

Saturated fat . . . . 0 g		
Total Fat . . . . 1 g	(4% of calories)	
Protein . . . . 10 g	(26% of calories)	
Carbohydrates . . . . . . 26 g	(70% of calories)	
Cholesterol . . . . 2 mg	Sodium . . . . 156 mg	
Fiber . . . . 2 g	Iron . . . . 2 mg	
Vitamin A . . . . 904 IU	Vitamin C . . . . 39 mg	

Source: Helen Moses is a homemaker who keeps busy babysitting her grandchildren. Helen has coronary artery disease.

♥ ♥ ♥

Vegetable Pie

A tasty way to serve vegetables

Serves 6

Preparation: :20   Cook :30   Stand :00   Total :50

Ingredients:

2	cups potatoes, grated and drained
2	egg whites
1	teaspoon cajun spice or seasoning of choice
1	medium onion
2	medium size zucchini
8	ounces mushrooms

Preheat oven to 425°F. After grating and draining potatoes, add spices to slightly beaten egg whites. Then add egg mixture to potatoes; mix well. Spray 9 inch pie pan with non-stick cooking spray. Place potatoes into pie pan, pressing firmly as a pie "dough." Place in oven and bake for 10-15 minutes or until lightly browned. Meanwhile, slice onion, mushrooms and zucchini thinly. Remove pie pan from oven and layer vegetables in pie pan. Sprinkle with salt and pepper if desired and return to oven for 15 minutes or until done. Cut and serve.

Nutrition: (per serving): 82 calories

Saturated fat . . . . 0 g		
Total Fat . . . . 0 g	(2% of calories)	
Protein . . . . 3 g	(17% of calories)	
Carbohydrates . . . . 17 g	(81% of calories)	
Cholesterol . . . . 0 mg	Sodium . . . . 27 mg	
Fiber . . . . 1 g	Iron . . . . 1 mg	
Vitamin A . . . . 186 IU	Vitamin C . . . . 14 mg	

Source: Jeanne M. Eckert, 62, is a homemaker and gardening expert who has blocked arteries.

♥ ♥ ♥

Potatoes, Peppers and Asparagus

Try this taste-tempting combination

Serves 4

Preparation: :20   Cook :20   Stand :00   Total :40

Ingredients:

	vegetable oil cooking spray
2	red potatoes, halved and sliced thin
1	onion, peeled and sliced in 1/4 inch slices
1	clove garlic, minced
1/2	small red bell pepper, sliced
1/2	small yellow bell pepper, sliced
	freshly ground black pepper
1/2	pound asparagus, steamed tender-crisp

Spray a large skillet with vegetable oil cooking spray. Heat to medium high, then lay potato slices on bottom of pan. Place onion slices and garlic on top of potatoes; cover, reduce heat and cook for about 5 minutes. Turn potatoes and onions; add peppers, cover and cook for 5 more minutes or until potatoes are done. Add black pepper to taste. Stir well, then add cooked asparagus and heat through gently.

Nutrition: (per serving): 155 calories

Saturated fat . . . . 0 g		
Total Fat . . . . 1 g	(3% of calories)	
Protein . . . . 5 g	(13% of calories)	
Carbohydrates . . . . 32 g	(83% of calories)	
Cholesterol . . . . 0 mg	Sodium . . . . 15 mg	
Fiber . . . . 2 g	Iron . . . . 2 mg	
Vitamin A . . . . 1013 IU	Vitamin C . . . . 58 mg	

Source: Gail Gibson is the wife of Jim Gibson who had bypass surgery in 1991.

♥ ♥ ♥

Hominy Skillet Side Dish

Tasty Tex-Mex

Serves 4

Preparation: :20   Cook :30   Stand :05   Total :55

Ingredients:

1/4	cup fat free broth	1/2 to 3/4 package taco	
1/2	cup coarsely chopped onions		seasoning mix
1/2	cup coarsely chopped green	1/2	teaspoon bottled hot
	bell peppers		pepper sauce
1	14 ounce can hominy, drained	1/2	cup water
1	16 ounce can tomatoes,	1	cup shredded fat free
	chopped		cheddar cheese

In a 10 inch skillet, saute onion, green pepper and hominy in broth. Cook, stirring often until vegetables are wilted. Stir in tomatoes, taco mix, hot pepper sauce and water. Simmer, stirring occasionally, until slightly thickened (about 25 minutes). Top with shredded cheese. Let stand 5 minutes. Serve with fat free tortilla chips.

Nutrition: (per serving): 71 calories

Saturated fat . . . . 0 g		
Total Fat . . . . 1 g	(10% of calories)	
Protein . . . . 3 g	(11% of calories)	
Carbohydrates . . . . 24 g	(79% of calories)	
Cholesterol . . . . 0 mg	Sodium . . . . 686 mg
Fiber . . . . 1 g	Iron . . . . 1 mg
Vitamin A . . . . 833 IU	Vitamin C . . . . 30 mg

Source: Ruby Dedenbach is a homemaker who had bypass surgery in 1988 and 1992 and stent surgery in 1995.

♥♥♥

Mashed Parrots

A wonderful combination of potatoes and carrots

Serves 6

Preparation: :20   Cook :40   Stand :00   Total 1:00

Ingredients:

3   large potatoes, boiled, drained and peeled
3   carrots, steamed
        hot water, as needed
        salt to taste or any other spices you like

Puree potatoes and carrots until mashed potato consistency is reached, using hot water as needed. Serve with veggie burgers or use as you would mashed potatoes.

Nutrition: (per serving): 188 calories

Saturated fat . . . . 0 g		
Total Fat . . . . 0 g	(1% of calories)	
Protein . . . . 4 g	(9% of calories)	
Carbohydrates . . . . 42 g	(90% of calories)	

Cholesterol . . . . 0 mg	Sodium . . . . 90 mg
Fiber . . . . 2 g	Iron . . . . 2 mg
Vitamin A . . . . 10141 IU	Vitamin C . . . . 28 mg

Source: Babsi Riegler is a yoga instructor for the Reversal Team. She also has a degree in psychology.

♥ ♥ ♥

Vegetable Rice Casserole

Good flavor and it's easy to prepare

Serves 10

Preparation: :25   Cook :45   Stand :00   Total 1:10

Ingredients:

1/2   cup fat free broth
2   green bell peppers, cut into strips
1   cup chopped onions
2   cups chopped cauliflower
2   cups chopped broccoli
2   cloves chopped garlic
1/2   teaspoon dried thyme
1   teaspoon bouillon granules, fat free
3   cups hot water
1-1/2   cups uncooked brown rice
1   tablespoon low sodium soy sauce

In large skillet, add broth, green pepper, 1/2 cup chopped onions, cauliflower, broccoli and garlic. Cook over high heat for 5 minutes until tender-crisp. Water may be added if needed to prevent burning. Stir in thyme. Remove from heat; set aside. Dissolve bouillon granules in hot water in 2 quart casserole dish; stir in rice, remaining 1/2 cup onion and soy sauce. Cover and bake at 350°F for 20 minutes. Remove casserole from oven and stir in sauteed vegetable mixture. Cover and bake an additional 10-20 minutes or until all liquid is absorbed and rice is tender. If casserole dries out, add a little water. Add soy sauce to taste when serving.

♥ ♥ ♥

Nutrition: (per serving): 128 calories

Saturated fat . . . . 0 g	
Total Fat . . . . 1 g	(7% of calories)
Protein . . . . 4 g	(11% of calories)
Carbohydrates . . . . 26 g	(82% of calories)

Cholesterol . . . . 0 mg	Sodium . . . . 150 mg
Fiber . . . . 1 g	Iron . . . . 1 mg
Vitamin A . . . . 371 IU	Vitamin C . . . . 45 mg

Source: William Kenneth Smith who had a heart attack and bypass surgery in 1989.

Moussaka

A fat free version of the traditional Greek dish

Serves 8

Preparation: :45   Cook :35   Stand :00   Total 1:20

Ingredients:

1	cup onion, chopped
1/4	cup fat free broth
3	cloves garlic
1	28 ounce can tomatoes (no salt added)
1/2	cup apple juice
1	teaspoon oregano
1	teaspoon basil
1/8	teaspoon pepper
2	eggplants, medium size
1	16 ounce can evaporated skim milk
2	tablespoons flour
1/4	cup fat free egg substitute
1/4	teaspoon nutmeg
1/4	teaspoon paprika
1/4	teaspoon cinnamon

Mince the garlic and saute with onion in broth until tender. Add tomatoes, apple juice, oregano, pepper and basil. Stir well, cooking until bubbly. Reduce heat and simmer gently for 10-15 minutes. Wash eggplant and remove stem caps. Slice into rounds about 1/2 inch thick. Place eggplant slices on cookie sheets and broil on both sides until golden brown. The moisture of the eggplant prevents it from sticking to the pan. When both sides are brown, turn the oven on bake and set for 350°F. Continue to bake the eggplant until tender, about five minutes. Set aside. In a medium saucepan, mix the flour, canned milk, egg substitute and remaining seasonings. Cook on medium heat until sauce is bubbly, stirring constantly. When sauce thickens, cook for one more minute. Remove from heat and set aside. Cover the bottom of a 9 x 13 inch pan with

1/3 of the tomato sauce. Add 1/2 of the eggplant slices and cover with 1/3 of the tomato sauce. Add remaining eggplant and tomato sauce. Cover the top with the cream sauce. Bake in a 350°F oven for 35 minutes.

Options: Before the last 10 minutes of baking, sprinkle fat free cheese on the top. For a "meatier" moussaka, hydrate one cup of fat free textured soy protein in one cup of fat free broth. Stir into the tomato sauce after it has simmered. One cup of fat free sour cream added to the cooked and cooled cream sauce adds flavor to this dish.

Nutrition: (per serving): 101 calories

Saturated fat	0 g	
Total Fat	1 g	(5% of calories)
Protein	6 g	(24% of calories)
Carbohydrates	17 g	(70% of calories)

Cholesterol	2 mg	Sodium	76 mg
Fiber	1 g	Iron	1 mg
Vitamin A	917 IU	Vitamin C	34 mg

Source: Gerry Krag is the consulting nutritionist and group facilitator for the Downriver Reversal Team.

♥ ♥ ♥

Gravy

Nice over lentil loaf or on mashed potatoes

Serves 4 — a serving is about 1/2 cup

Preparation: :05   Cook :20   Stand :00   Total :25

Ingredients:

2	cups fat free chicken broth or fat free vegetable broth	1/4	teaspoon garlic powder pepper and salt, to taste
2-1/2	tablespoons flour or corn starch		rosemary, poultry seasonings or other herbs to taste

Select fat free broth or prepare your own by refrigerating broth and removing all fat from surface. This must be done very carefully. If fat does not harden, it will be hard to judge if your broth is fat free. If broth appears oily, do not use it. Use a fat free vegetable broth instead.

Mix flour and herbs into cool or room temperature broth. Put in a saucepan and stir until well blended. Stir constantly, over medium heat, until gravy begins to bubble. Reduce heat and continue to stir until the gravy thickens. If gravy gets too thick, thin with a little water. Serve over potatoes or use as a base for vegetarian stew.

Nutrition: (per serving): 32 calories

Saturated fat . . . . 0 g		
Total Fat . . . . 0 g	(6% of calories)	
Protein . . . . 3 g	(37% of calories)	
Carbohydrates . . . . 5 g	(57% of calories)	
Cholesterol . . . . 0 mg	Sodium . . . . 180 mg	
Fiber . . . . 0 g	Iron . . . . 0 mg	
Vitamin A . . . . 8 IU	Vitamin C . . . . 0 mg	

Source: Gerry Krag is the consulting nutritionist and group facilitator for the Downriver Reversal Team.

♥ ♥ ♥

Mashed Potatoes

Enjoy mashed potatoes without guilt

Serves 1

Preparation: :10   Cook :30   Stand :00   Total :40

Ingredients:

1	large potato, peeled, sliced and boiled until tender
1	teaspoon Molly McButter butter flavored sprinkles
	skim milk, as needed
	salt and pepper to taste
	favorite herbs to taste
1	tablespoon fat free sour cream

Drain potato and add the Molly McButter™. Mash well, adding milk as needed. Mix in the sour cream and continue mixing until light and fluffy. Season as desired. Serve at once. For eight servings, use 8 potatoes, 8 teaspoons Molly McButter™ and 8 tablespoons fat free sour cream.

Variation: serve with fat free gravy or stir in some fresh chopped chives. Mash potatoes with the skins on to increase fiber.

Nutrition: (per serving): 200 calories

Saturated fat . . . . 0 g		
Total Fat . . . . 0 g	(1% of calories)	
Protein . . . . 4 g	(8% of calories)	
Carbohydrates . . . . 46 g	(91% of calories)	
Cholesterol . . . . 0 mg	Sodium . . . . 130 mg	
Fiber . . . . 1 g	Iron . . . . 2 mg	
Vitamin A . . . . 5 IU	Vitamin C . . . . 24 mg	

Source: Gerry Krag is the consulting nutritionist and group facilitator for the Downriver Reversal Team.

♥ ♥ ♥

Barley Pilaf

A delicious side dish that goes well with almost anything

Serves 4

Preparation: :35   Cook :00   Stand :05   Total :40

Ingredients:

4	tablespoons white wine	1	tablespoon thyme, fresh, or
1	cup barley, quick cooking		2 teaspoons, dried
1	clove garlic, minced		black pepper, to taste
2-1/2	cups fat free broth	1/4	cup chives or chopped
1/2	cup orzo		green onion

In a frying pan, heat wine. Add barley and saute until golden (about 3-5 minutes). Add garlic and saute for 1 minute more. Pour in broth and bring to boil. Add orzo and thyme. Stir and cover. Reduce heat to low and simmer for 10 minutes. Remove from heat and let set for 5 minutes to absorb remaining liquid. Stir in chives or green onions. Season with pepper before serving.

Nutrition: (per serving): 244 calories

Saturated fat . . . . 0 g		
Total Fat . . . . 1 g	(3% of calories)	
Protein . . . . 7 g	(11% of calories)	
Carbohydrates . . . . 50 g	(82% of calories)	
Alcohol . . . . 1 g	(4% of calories)	
Cholesterol . . . . 0 mg	Sodium . . . . 8 mg	
Fiber . . . . 1 g	Iron . . . . 3 mg	
Vitamin A . . . . 243 IU	Vitamin C . . . . 3 mg	

Source: Judith Caplan Phillips is the general manager of an ad specialty supplier who had a bypass in 1992 and is a diabetic.

"This is not a one day sale. We have all made a long term commitment and most of us have been coming to the Downriver Reversal Team for two or more years. This program has been the glue that holds us together."

♥ ♥ ♥

Reversal Moors and Christians

A tasty combination of beans and rice

Serves 8

Preparation: :15   Cook :30   Stand :00   Total :45

Ingredients:

2-1/2	cups water	2	cups cooked black beans
1	onion, diced	1	cup fat free broth
2	cloves garlic, crushed	1	cup long grain rice
1/2	cup seeded, de-ribbed and		salt and pepper, to taste
	chopped green bell peppers		
2	tomatoes, peeled, seeded and chopped		

In a large pot, heat 1/2 cup water over medium heat. Add the onion, garlic and green pepper and saute until tender. Add the tomatoes, black beans and broth. Let simmer stirring frequently, until heated through. Add the rice and the remaining water, cover and cook over low heat, stirring occasionally, until rice is tender, about 20 minutes. Add salt and pepper to taste and enjoy.

Nutrition: (per serving): 143 calories

Saturated fat . . . . 0 g		
Total Fat . . . . 0 g	(3% of calories)	
Protein . . . . 5 g	(14% of calories)	
Carbohydrates . . . . 30 g	(83% of calories)	
Cholesterol . . . . 0 mg	Sodium . . . . 201 mg	
Fiber . . . . 1 g	Iron . . . . 2 mg	
Vitamin A . . . . 234 IU	Vitamin C . . . . 15 mg	

Source: Al Spiteri, 52, is a journeyman in hydraulic repair. He had a heart attack in 1993.

"Staying out of the hospital and off the operating room table for two years now."

♥ ♥ ♥

Bev's Pasta Kraut Surprise

This is one of Bev's favorites, so be sure to try it

Serves 4

Preparation: :05   Cook :20   Stand :00   Total :25

Ingredients:

1/2   cup chopped onions
1   cup fat free broth
4   cups cooked pasta
1   16 ounce can sauerkraut, rinsed and drained
        pepper to taste

In a large frying pan, simmer the broth with the onion until onion becomes translucent. Add the kraut and simmer until it starts to turn golden, almost brown. Add the cooked pasta and pepper and toss well. When the pasta is heated uniformly, serve and enjoy.

Options: use wine or apple juice instead of broth. Season with your favorite herbs.

Nutrition: (per serving): 108 calories

Saturated fat . . . . .0 g		
Total Fat . . . . .1 g	(6% of calories)	
Protein. . . . . .4 g	(16% of calories)	
Carbohydrates . . . . . . .21 g	(78% of calories)	
Cholesterol . . . . .19 mg	Sodium. . . . . .754 mg	
Fiber . . . . .1 g	Iron . . . . .2 mg	
Vitamin A . . . . .79 IU	Vitamin C . . . . .18 mg	

Source: Beverly A. Grobbin is our data manager, a group facilitator and also works in our exercise facility. She enjoys cooking and traveling.

♥ ♥ ♥

Golden Harvest Casserole

A sumptuous side dish

Serves 6

Preparation: :25   Cook :55   Stand :30   Total 1:50

Ingredients:

3	cups eggplant, peeled and diced	1	cup whole kernel corn
1	cup zucchini, sliced	1	tablespoon chopped
2	teaspoons salt		parsley
1/2	cup chopped onions	1/2	teaspoon basil
	vegetable oil cooking spray	1/2	teaspoon oregano
1/2	cup uncooked rice	1/4	teaspoon pepper
3	cups tomatoes, peeled and cubed	1/2	cup grated fat free
1/2	cup diced green bell peppers		parmesan cheese

Place eggplant and zucchini in colander; sprinkle with 1 teaspoon of salt. Let stand 30 minutes. Preheat oven to 350°F. Spray 3 quart casserole with non-stick cooking spray. Saute onion in small amount of water. Put sauteed onion in casserole dish along with the rest of the ingredients, reserving 1/4 cup of parmesan cheese for topping. Cover and bake for 55-65 minutes, or until veggies and rice are tender. Sprinkle with reserved cheese and serve.

Nutrition: (per serving): 139 calories

Saturated fat . . . . 0 g		
Total Fat . . . . 1 g	(6% of calories)	
Protein . . . . 4 g	(11% of calories)	
Carbohydrates . . . . 29 g	(84% of calories)	
Cholesterol . . . . 0 mg	Sodium . . . . 800 mg	
Fiber . . . . 2 g	Iron . . . . 2 mg	
Vitamin A . . . . 859 IU	Vitamin C . . . . 37 mg	

Source: Pat Nevin-Normandin is a yoga instructor and group facilitator for the Reversal Team. She and her husband love to travel.

♥ ♥ ♥

Zesty Twice-Baked Potatoes

A tasty potato dish that's high in protein

Serves 2

Preparation: 1:30   Cook :00   Stand :00   Total 1:30

Ingredients:

2	large potatoes	1	dash pepper
1	cup fat free cottage cheese	2	tablespoons fat free
1	teaspoon horseradish		cheddar cheese, shredded
2	tablespoons sliced green onions		

Pierce potatoes with fork. Preheat oven to 350°F. Place potatoes on center rack and bake 45-60 minutes until tender; cool. Cut baked potatoes in half lengthwise. Scoop out centers, leaving 1/2 inch shell. Mash potato with cottage cheese and horseradish. Stir in green onion slices and a dash of pepper. Add a few drops of skim milk if mixture seems very dry. Spoon into shells. Bake at 350°F for 20 minutes and then remove from oven and sprinkle tops with cheese. Return to oven and bake for about 10 minutes.

Nutrition: (per serving): 348 calories

Saturated fat . . . . 0 g		
Total Fat . . . . 0 g	(14% of calories)	
Protein . . . . 8 g	(12% of calories)	
Carbohydrates . . . . 78 g	(74% of calories)	
Cholesterol . . . . 0 mg	Sodium . . . . 34 mg	
Fiber . . . . 3 g	Iron . . . . 4 mg	
Vitamin A . . . . 25 IU	Vitamin C . . . . 50 mg	

Source: Marie Zimolzak is a registered dietetic technician. She keeps busy with her two school age children and new baby. Her husband Frank helped us with his computer background.

"It is truly a pleasure working with people who want to change their life in such a positive way."

♥ ♥ ♥

Baked Green Tomatoes with Zucchini

A delicious way to use end of season tomatoes

Serves 4

Preparation: :20   Cook 1:00   Stand :00   Total 1:20

Ingredients:

2	zucchini squash, or more	1	cup grated fat free cheddar
1	onion, sliced		cheese
1	green or red bell pepper, sliced		pepper to taste
4	green tomatoes		seasonings of your choice,
1	tablespoon brown sugar		such as basil
6	fat free soda crackers, crushed		

Cut the zucchini in 1/2 inch slices and layer them in a pan so they are about 2 to 3 inches deep. Layer onion and pepper on top of zucchini and top with slices of the green tomatoes. Sprinkle the brown sugar over the tomatoes and cover with cracker crumbs. Cover with foil and bake at 350°F for one hour. Sprinkle cheese over top and bake for a little while longer to melt the cheese. Do not bake too long or cheese will get tough.

Nutrition: (per serving): 124 calories

Saturated fat . . . . 0 g		
Total Fat . . . . 0 g	(3% of calories)	
Protein . . . . 12 g	(39% of calories)	
Carbohydrates . . . . 18 g	(58% of calories)	
Cholesterol . . . . 0 mg	Sodium . . . . 223 mg	
Fiber . . . . 1 g	Iron . . . . 1 mg	
Vitamin A . . . . 1162 IU	Vitamin C . . . . 55 mg	

Source: Ruby Dedenbach is a homemaker who had bypasses in 1989 and 1992, and stent surgery in 1995.

Broccoli Marinara

Sweet tomato sauce with tender broccoli florets

Serves 4

Preparation: :20   Cook :20   Stand :00   Total :40

Ingredients:

4	cups broccoli florets (1 medium size head)
1/4	cup fat free broth
2	cloves minced garlic
1	28 ounce can low sodium chopped tomatoes
2	tablespoons golden raisins, chopped
1/8	teaspoon cayenne pepper
1-1/2	tablespoons water chestnuts, chopped
6	ounces pasta
2	tablespoons minced parsley

Steam broccoli until tender, about 3-5 minutes. Remove from heat and rinse in cold water and set aside. Place broth and garlic in large saucepan and simmer until garlic turns golden and liquid has evaporated. Add tomatoes, raisins, cayenne pepper and simmer uncovered for 15 minutes. Add the water chestnuts and simmer for 5 more minutes. Cook pasta according to package, omitting the salt. Drain and place in a large heated bowl. Put the broccoli in the warm sauce, tossing to heat through. Pour over pasta and sprinkle with parsley.

Options: Use cauliflower instead of broccoli. Use organically-grown ingredients whenever possible.

Note: The leftover broccoli stems can be peeled and sliced for tasty appetizers.

♥ ♥ ♥

Nutrition: (per serving): 241 calories

Saturated fat . . . . 0 g		
Total Fat . . . . 2 g	(6% of calories)	
Protein . . . . 10 g	(16% of calories)	
Carbohydrates . . . . 47 g	(78% of calories)	

Cholesterol . . . . 31 mg	Sodium . . . . 71 mg
Fiber . . . . 3 g	Iron . . . . 4 mg
Vitamin A . . . . 3345 IU	Vitamin C . . . . 109 mg

Source: Dr. Sheila Rogers is a retired cardiologist and is married to Dr. Joseph T. Rogers who continues to practice with his sons, Dr. Joseph C. Rogers and Dr. Felix J. Rogers at Downriver Cardiology Consultants in Trenton, Michigan.

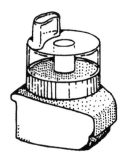

♥ ♥ ♥

Pat's Potatoes

Very easy to prepare

Serves 4

Preparation: :25   Cook :40   Stand :00   Total 1:05

Ingredients:

4	large potatoes, 6 inch bakers
2	onions, thinly sliced
28	ounces canned tomatoes, chopped
1	8 ounce can tomato sauce

Put half of the potatos on the bottom of a three quart casserole. Layer the sliced onions on top. Top with the rest of the potatoes. Pour the tomatoes with juice and sauce over all. Bake at 350°F oven for one hour.

Nutrition: (per serving): 303 calories

Saturated fat . . . . 0 g		
Total Fat . . . . 1 g	(2% of calories)	
Protein . . . . 8 g	(10% of calories)	
Carbohydrates . . . . 66 g	(87% of calories)	

Cholesterol . . . . 0 mg	Sodium . . . . 343 mg
Fiber . . . . 3 g	Iron . . . . 4 mg
Vitamin A . . . . 1199 IU	Vitamin C . . . . 67 mg

Source: Pat McKenna, 61, is a homemaker with diabetes who had bypass surgery in 1991. She also had a kidney bypass in 1991.

"I feel this program is adding years to my life. My heart surgery saved my life, but even after the surgery, I didn't feel good. The diet is keeping me alive and I feel good."

♥ ♥ ♥

Zucchini Bake

Nice oven baked flavor

Serves 4

Preparation: :15   Cook :30   Stand :00   Total :45

Ingredients:

	vegetable oil cooking spray	1/3	cup corn meal
1 to 2	zucchini, sliced	1/3	cup flour
1	egg white		seasoned salt, to taste
1	tablespoon skim milk		other seasonings, as desired

Spray cookie sheet with vegetable oil cooking spray. Beat egg white with milk in a shallow bowl. In a separate bowl, mix the flour, corn meal and seasonings. Dip the zucchini slices in the liquid and then coat with dry mixture. Put on cookie sheet and bake at 400°F for 30 minutes, turning once during baking. Bake until golden and tender. Use your imagination for seasonings. Onion powder is nice; Italian blend seasons also work well.

Nutrition: (per serving): 93 calories

Saturated fat . . . . 0 g	
Total Fat . . . . 1 g	(6% of calories)
Protein . . . . 4 g	(15% of calories)
Carbohydrates . . . . 18 g	(79% of calories)

Cholesterol . . . . 0 mg	Sodium . . . . 193 mg
Fiber . . . . 0 g	Iron . . . . 0 mg
Vitamin A . . . . 183 IU	Vitamin C . . . . 3 mg

Source: Joyce Gill is a homemaker. Her husband Jim has coronary artery disease.

♥ ♥ ♥

Eggplant with Spinach Spiral Pasta

A great meal for company or your family

Serves 4

Preparation: :40   Cook :30   Stand :05   Total 1:15

Ingredients:

1/4	cup fat free broth
1	eggplant, cubed
1	onion, chopped
2	cloves garlic, minced
1	green bell pepper, chopped
15	ounces canned tomatoes, chopped
4	ounces spinach or whole wheat pasta spirals
1	cup skim milk
1	tablespoon cornstarch
1/2	teaspoon oregano
1	teaspoon basil
1	pinch nutmeg
	pinch seasoned pepper
2	tablespoons fat free parmesan cheese
1/4	cup shredded fat free cheese

In a saucepan, combine the broth with the eggplant, onion, garlic, peppers and tomatoes. Cover and simmer for 15 minutes. Cook pasta according to package directions, but remove from heat while pasta is still firm. Drain and set aside. Combine milk, cornstarch, oregano, basil, nutmeg and seasoned pepper. At medium high heat, bring to a boil, stirring constantly. Once sauce is thickened, remove from heat and let stand 5 minutes. Stir in the parmesan and fat free shredded cheese. Place noodles in a 2 or 3 quart casserole or other baking dish. Top with eggplant mix. Spoon the sauce over vegetables. Bake in a moderate 350°F oven until heated through, about 20-30 minutes. If desired, place under broiler for a few minutes until top is lightly browned.

♥ ♥ ♥

Nutrition: (per serving): 224 calories

Saturated fat . . . . 0 g		
Total Fat . . . . 1 g	(4% of calories)	
Protein . . . . 12 g	(21% of calories)	
Carbohydrates . . . . 42 g	(74% of calories)	

Cholesterol . . . . 2 mg	Sodium . . . . 390 mg
Fiber . . . . 2 g	Iron . . . . 2 mg
Vitamin A . . . . 1165 IU	Vitamin C . . . . 54 mg

Source: Connie Wedel has diabetes and multiple risk factors for heart disease. She enjoys spending winters in Florida.

"After 12 months, my carotid doppler test showed that my carotid arteries had opened up dramatically."

Connie Wedel

♥♥♥

Desserts

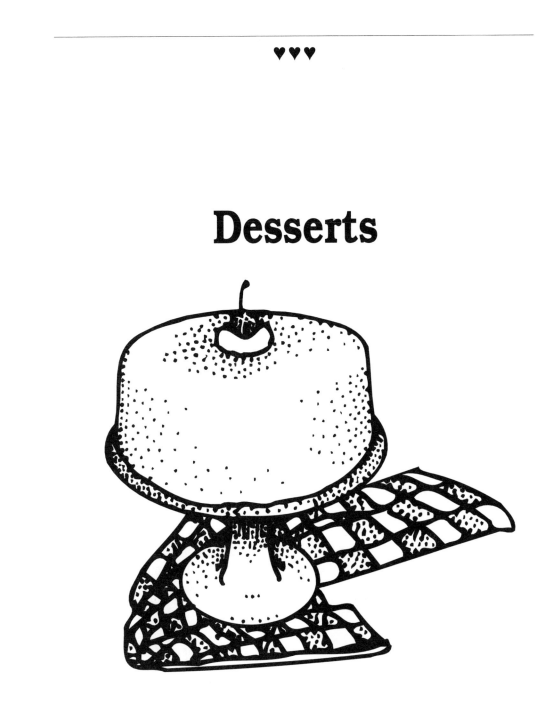

Desserts

Fruit Salad Dessert 227

Applesauce Cake 228

Prune Cake 230

Rich Date Cake 232

Dave's Delectable Dessert 234

Easy Ice Box Pie 235

Rosemary's Apple Cake 236

Bread Pudding 238

Fake Shake 239

Estella's Chocolate Orange
    Cheesecake 240

Carrot Cupcakes 242

Chocolate Cake 244

Light Fruitcake 246

Seven Minute Frosting 248

Cream Cheese Sauce 249

Bob's Steamed Carrot Cake . . .250

Nutty Apple Cake 252

Angel Food Fruit Pudding 254

Whipped Topping 256

Carol's Orange Yogurt Cake . . .258

Jerry's Cinnamon Biscotti 260

Fruit Ravioli 262

Fast Fruit Trifle 263

French Apple Dessert 264

Peaches 'n Cream 266

Pumpkin Pie 268

Pavlova 270

Rice Pudding 272

Raspberry Freeze 273

Easy Frozen Dessert 274

Spice Cookies 275

Old-Fashioned
    Oatmeal Cookies 276

Moe's Pumpkin Cake 277

Pat's Cinnamon Rolls 278

Rennet Pudding 280

Strawberry-Rhubarb Squares . .281

Lazy Cherry Cobbler 282

Pie Crust 283

Marilyn's Oatmeal Cookies 284

♥ ♥ ♥

Fruit Salad Dessert

Light and tangy

Serves 8

Preparation: :10   Cook :15   Stand :45   Total 1:10

Ingredients:

2	3 ounce packages Tapioca pudding mix
4	cups orange juice
20	ounces canned pineapple chunks in juice; do not drain
2	10 ounce cans mandarin orange sections, drained
3	bananas, sliced
1	pound frozen raspberries, or any combination of fruit you like thawed and drained

Cook pudding as directed, using orange juice in place of milk. Let cool. Add the pineapple, mandarin oranges and bananas. Fold in the raspberries, stirring only enough to mix. Chill well before serving.

Nutrition: (per serving): 271 calories

Saturated fat . . . . 0 g			
Total Fat . . . . 1 g	(3% of calories)		
Protein . . . . 2 g	(3% of calories)		
Carbohydrates . . . . 64 g	(94% of calories)		
Cholesterol . . . . 0 mg	Sodium . . . . 32 mg		
Fiber . . . . 2 g	Iron . . . . 1 mg		
Vitamin A . . . . 845 IU	Vitamin C . . . . 83 mg		

Source: Carol Rhora is a neurodiagnostic technician who had a heart attack in 1992 and has hypertension.

"If not for this program, I feel that I would have had another heart attack."

♥ ♥ ♥

Applesauce Cake

Please everyone with this special dessert

Serves 10

Preparation: :30   Cook :45   Stand :00   Total 1:15

Ingredients:

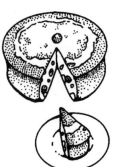

1-3/4   cups sifted flour
1   teaspoon baking soda
1-1/2   teaspoons cinnamon
1/4   teaspoon cloves
5   ounces prunes, stewed and pureed
1   cup sugar
1/4   cup fat free egg substitute
1   cup unsweetened applesauce
1   cup raisins
1/2   teaspoon salt
1   teaspoon nutmeg
3/4   teaspoon allspice

Sift flour, baking soda, salt and spices together three times. Cream sugar with prunes until thoroughly mixed. Add egg substitute and mix thoroughly. Add sifted dry ingredients and applesauce alternately in small amount, beating well after each addition. Stir in raisins. Pour into loaf pans sprayed with non-stick cooking spray. Bake at 350°F for 45 to 60 minutes or until toothpick inserted in center of cake comes out clean. Turn cake immediately out on wire rack to cool.

Note: two 2-1/2 ounce jars of baby food prunes may be substituted for 5 ounces of pureed stewed prunes. Do not use baby food prunes containing tapioca.

♥ ♥ ♥

Nutrition: (per serving): 262 calories

Saturated fat . . . . 0 g		
Total Fat . . . . 0 g	(2% of calories)	
Protein . . . . 3 g	(5% of calories)	
Carbohydrates . . . . 61 g	(93% of calories)	

Cholesterol . . . . 0 mg	Sodium . . . . 204 mg
Fiber . . . . 1 g	Iron . . . . 1 mg
Vitamin A . . . . 293 IU	Vitamin C . . . . 2 mg

Source: Patrick Beaudrie, 59, is a retiree who had a heart attack and bypass surgery in 1989.

"With a dedicated staff and the help of the support group, you can't go wrong. I've lost 28 pounds and my cholesterol numbers are right where they should be. My latest thallium stress test shows significant improvement. I plan on being around for a long time! A big part of the program's success is the support group and of course Dr. Rogers. Without him, there would be no program."

Patrick Beaudrie

♥ ♥ ♥

Prune Cake

This is a luscious dessert

Serves 16

Preparation: :20   Cook :50   Stand :00   Total 1:10

Ingredients:

Cake:

2	cups flour
1	teaspoon baking soda
1	teaspoon cinnamon
1/4	teaspoon cloves
1/4	teaspoon allspice
1/2	teaspoon nutmeg
1/4	teaspoon salt
5	egg whites
1-1/2	cup sugar
1	cup applesauce
1/2	cup fat free buttermilk (see note)
1	cup pitted prunes, stewed and mashed

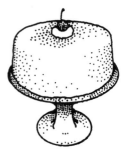

Icing:

2	cups confectioners' sugar
1-1/2	teaspoons lemon juice
1/4	teaspoon almond extract
	water, as needed (approximately 2 tablespoons)

Sift together first 7 ingredients; set aside. In a large mixing bowl, beat together egg whites and sugar until thoroughly combined. Add applesauce; mix well. Add flour mixture alternating with buttermilk, mixing well between additions. Add prunes; mix well. Heat oven to 350°F. Spray bundt-style pan with non-stick cooking spray, and pour batter into pan. Bake 45 to 50 minutes or until toothpick inserted into middle of cake comes out clean. Turn cake onto a wire rack and cool completely.

♥ ♥ ♥

Icing:

Combine sugar, lemon juice, almond extract and enough water to make the consistency of a thick glaze. Drizzle over cake.

Note: To make 1/2 cup fat free buttermilk, add 1-1/2 teaspoons lemon juice or vinegar to 1/2 cup skim milk. Let stand 5 minutes.

Nutrition: (per serving): 236 calories

Saturated fat . . . . 0 g		
Total Fat . . . . 0 g	(1% of calories)	
Protein . . . . 3 g	(5% of calories)	
Carbohydrates . . . . 55 g	(94% of calories)	
Cholesterol . . . . 0 mg	Sodium . . . . 107 mg
Fiber . . . . 0 g	Iron . . . . 1 mg
Vitamin A . . . . 203 IU	Vitamin C . . . . 1 mg

Source: Paul Bodrie is a Catholic lay pastoral assistant and university instructor who had heart attacks in 1989 and 1992 and angioplasty in 1989.

"I was in bad shape, taking about 9 nitrobids each day for frequent, painful angina. Within four weeks of joining the Reversal Team, my angina was almost gone and I have not had to take any nitrobid since that time. I have lost 60 pounds and feel great. I am physically, mentally and spiritually better off than I have been in years. Before I started the program, my doctor said I needed bypass surgery. Now, I am no longer a candidate for surgery and he is recommending the program to his patients."

Paul Bodrie

♥ ♥ ♥

Rich Date Cake

Sweet and moist and full of beta carotene

Serves 15

Preparation: :20 Cook :35 Stand :00 Total :55

Ingredients:

5	ounces pitted dates
3	cups flour
1	cup sugar
2	teaspoons cinnamon
2	teaspoons baking soda
1	teaspoon baking powder
1 ·	teaspoon salt
1/2	teaspoon ginger
1	cup plain fat free yogurt
8	ounces fat free egg substitute
3/4	cup packed light brown sugar
4	ounces pureed stewed prunes
1	teaspoon vanilla
2	cups lightly packed shredded carrots

Preheat oven to 350°F. Spray a 9 x 13 inch glass baking dish with non-stick spray. Combine dates and 1/3 cup water in small saucepan. heat over medium heat, stirring and mashing dates with a spoon until all water evaporates and dates are very soft and smooth. In large bowl, mix flour, sugar, cinnamon, baking powder, baking soda, salt and ginger. In medium bowl, with wire whisk or fork, beat yogurt, egg substitute, brown sugar, prunes and vanilla until smooth. Stir in shredded carrots and pureed dates until blended. Stir carrot mixture into flour mixture just until flour is moistened. Pour batter into baking dish. Bake 30-35 minutes until toothpick inserted in center of cake comes out clean. Cool cake in pan on wire rack. Sprinkle with confections' sugar if you like.

♥ ♥ ♥

Note: 1 jar of baby food prunes may be substituted for the 4 ounces pureed stewed prunes. Do not use baby prunes containing tapioca.

Nutrition: (per serving): 230 calories

Saturated fat . . . . 0 g		
Total Fat . . . . 0 g	(1% of calories)	
Protein . . . . 4 g	(8% of calories)	
Carbohydrates . . . . 52 g	(91% of calories)	

Cholesterol . . . . 0 mg	Sodium . . . . 318 mg
Fiber . . . . 1 g	Iron . . . . 1 mg
Vitamin A . . . . 4297 IU	Vitamin C . . . . 2 mg

Source: Paul Bodrie is a Catholic lay pastoral assistant and university instructor who had heart attacks in 1989 and 1992 and angioplasty in 1989.

"I heard about the program through my cousin's wife. I wasn't sure I could commit to not eating meat, fish and chicken. But after only six weeks, I was full of energy and down from 9 to 2 nitro tablets a day. I wouldn't be able to teach full time if it wasn't for this program"

Paul Bodrie

Dave's Delectable Dessert

For special occasions

Serves 8

Preparation: :20   Cook :00   Stand :10   Total :30

Ingredients:

6	cups fat free ice cream	4	fluid ounces of creme de menthe
1-1/2	cups crushed fat free cookies or graham crackers		peppermint extract, as needed

Soften the ice cream by letting it stand for 10-15 minutes. Chocolate fat free cookies work best, but others will do. Mix cookies in a blender or food processor until well crushed. If cookies are dry, add a few tablespoons of skim milk. Press the cookies into a 9 inch pie pan to form a thin crust. Set aside. In a large bowl, mix the ice cream with the creme de menthe until well blended. Taste test the mixture. If needed, add peppermint extract. Spread into the crust and cover with plastic wrap. Freeze. Remove pie 10-15 minutes before serving so that it will be easier to cut. Garnish each piece with a little creme de menthe and a mint leaf.

Option: Use fat free, sugar free frozen ice cream or yogurt.

Nutrition: (per serving): 134 calories

Saturated fat . . . . 0 g		
Total Fat . . . . 1 g	(1% of calories)	
Protein. . . . . 2 g	(7% of calories)	
Carbohydrates . . . . 22 g	(66% of calories)	
Alcohol. . . . . 5 g	(26% of calories)	
Cholesterol. . . . . 0 mg	Sodium. . . . . 54 mg	
Fiber . . . . 1 g	Iron . . . . 1 mg	
Vitamin A. . . . . 29 IU	Vitamin C. . . . . 0 mg	

Source: Dave Durbin, program director, exercise physiologist and group facilitator, has a degree in exercise physiology and is a marathon runner.

♥ ♥ ♥

Easy Ice Box Pie

A Reversal Team favorite

Serves 12

Preparation: :15   Cook :00   Stand :30   Total :45

Ingredients:

1-1/2	cups crushed fat free cookies or fat free graham crackers
3	ripe bananas, sliced
4	1 ounce packages of fat free, sugar free instant pudding, vanilla flavor
6	cups skim milk, for the pudding

Cover the bottom of a 9 x 13 inch pan with a thin layer of the crushed graham crackers or cookies, using about 1 cup. Set the remainder aside for the topping. Slice bananas and layer over the crushed graham crackers. Make the pudding according to package directions, but use 1-1/2 cups of skim milk for each box instead of 2 cups. Pour pudding over the banana slices and sprinkle reserved crumbs on top. Refrigerate until well chilled.

Nutrition: (per serving): 100 calories

Saturated fat . . . . 0 g		
Total Fat . . . . 0 g	(3% of calories)	
Protein . . . . 4 g	(18% of calories)	
Carbohydrates . . . . 20 g	(79% of calories)	
Cholesterol . . . . 2 mg	Sodium . . . . 453 mg	
Fiber . . . . 0 g	Iron . . . . 0 mg	
Vitamin A . . . . 272 IU	Vitamin C . . . . 4 mg	

Source: Ida Verdone, married to Jim Verdone, who has coronary artery disease.

♥ ♥ ♥

Rosemary's Apple Cake

A delightful dessert

Serves 12

Preparation: :35   Cook 1:02   Stand :00   Total 1:37

Ingredients:

6   cups apples, peeled and sliced
1-1/2 cups sugar
4   ounces fat free egg substitute
2   cups flour
2   teaspoons baking soda
1   dash salt
1   teaspoon cinnamon
1   cup raisins
Sauce:
1/2   cup brown sugar
1/2   cup sugar
2   tablespoons flour
1   cup water
1   teaspoon vanilla

Preheat oven to 350°F. In large mixing bowl, pour sugar over sliced apples. Mix and let stand until sugar gets syrupy. Add the rest of the ingredients and mix together. Spray a 9 x 13 inch pan with non-stick spray and pour batter into pan. Bake cake for 50 to 55 minutes.

Sauce:

Mix sugars with flour in a saucepan. Add water gradually. Cook until clear or about 7 minutes. Remove from heat and add vanilla. Pour over hot cake.

Option: Bake with less sugar or use sugar substitute such as "Sugar Twin™."

♥ ♥ ♥

Nutrition: (per serving): 344 calories

Saturated fat	0 g	
Total Fat	1 g	(2% of calories)
Protein	4 g	(4% of calories)
Carbohydrates	81 g	(94% of calories)

Cholesterol	0 mg	Sodium	186 mg
Fiber	1 g	Iron	1 mg
Vitamin A	64 IU	Vitamin C	6 mg

Source: Paul Bodrie is a Catholic lay pastoral assistant and university instructor. He is married to Rosemary, who developed this recipe. Paul had heart attacks in 1989 and 1992 and had angioplasty in 1989.

"I heard about the program through my cousin's wife and I came to try it out. I wasn't sure I could commit to not eating meat, fish and chicken. But, after only six weeks, I was full of energy and down from nine to only one or two nitro tablets a day. I wouldn't be able to teach full time if it wasn't for this program."

Paul Bodrie

Bread Pudding

The traditional favorite is now low-fat

Serves 9

Preparation: :10   Cook 1:00   Stand :00   Total 1:10

Ingredients:

3/4   cup fat free egg substitute
1-1/2   cups sugar (see options)
3   cups bread cubes
1   20 ounce can crushed pineapple in juice,
        drained

Combine all ingredients and stir well. Pour into lightly sprayed 10 x 8 x 2 inch baking dish. Bake at 325°F for 40-45 minutes, until a knife inserted in center comes out clean.

Options: Reduce sugar to one cup or even less. Or use sugar substitute that can be cooked, such as "Sugar Twin™." Use fat free bread. 100% whole wheat bread increases the fiber level. Raisins can be added if desired. Use 1/2 cup. Simmer them in a little water until they are soft and plump. Drain and add to ingredients.

Nutrition: (per serving): 269 calories

Saturated fat . . . . 0 g		
Total Fat . . . . 1 g	(4% of calories)	
Protein . . . . 3 g	(5% of calories)	
Carbohydrates . . . . 62 g	(92% of calories)	
Cholesterol . . . . 1 mg	Sodium . . . . 194 mg	
Fiber . . . . 0 g	Iron . . . . 1 mg	
Vitamin A . . . . 24 IU	Vitamin C . . . . 6 mg	

Source: Paul Bodrie is a Catholic lay pastoral assistant and university instructor. He had heart attacks in 1989 and 1992 and had angioplasty in 1989.

♥ ♥ ♥

Fake Shake

Craving a milk shake? Try a fake shake!

Serves 2

Preparation: :05   Cook :00   Stand :00   Total :05

Ingredients:

1-1/2   bananas, peeled and frozen
1   cup skim milk
1/2   teaspoon cinnamon, optional
1   tablespoon carob, optional
1   tablespoon instant coffee (decaf), optional

Break frozen bananas into 1-2 inch pieces. Place in blender, cover with milk and add one of the optional flavorings, if desired. Blend for 2 minutes or until creamy.

Nutrition: (per serving): 130 calories

Saturated fat . . . . 0 g		
Total Fat . . . . 1 g	(4% of calories)	
Protein . . . . 5 g	(16% of calories)	
Carbohydrates . . . . 26 g	(80% of calories)	
Cholesterol . . . . 2 mg	Sodium . . . . 64 mg
Fiber . . . . 0 g	Iron . . . . 0 mg
Vitamin A . . . . 317 IU	Vitamin C . . . . 9 mg

Source: Babsi Riegler is a yoga instructor for the Reversal Team. She also has a degree in psychology.

♥ ♥ ♥

Estella's Chocolate Orange Cheesecake

A rich and creamy dessert

Serves 15

Preparation: :20   Cook 1:00   Stand 3:10   Total 4:30

Ingredients:

	vegetable oil cooking spray
1/3	cup graham cracker crumbs (look for fat free crackers) approximately 6 crackers, crumbled
	skim milk in a spray bottle
4	8 ounce packages fat free cream cheese
1-1/3	cups sugar, or equivalent sugar substitute (exception: Equal™)
16	ounces fat free egg substitute
2	tablespoons orange juice
1	teaspoon orange peel, grated
1/4	cup unsweetened cocoa powder
2	tablespoons sugar

Heat oven to 325°F. Lightly spray a 9 x 13 inch pan with vegetable oil cooking spray. Sprinkle graham cracker crumbs over bottom and sides of pan. Lightly spray crumbs with skim milk. In a large bowl, beat cream cheese at medium speed until smooth and creamy. Gradually add sugar, beating until smooth. Continue beating at low speed and add egg substitute, 1/2 cup at a time, beating until just blended. Add orange juice and orange peel. Beat 2 minutes at medium speed, scraping bowl occasionally.

In a small bowl, reserve 1-1/2 cups of the batter. Pour remaining batter into crumb lined pan. Mix the reserved batter and cocoa and sugar until well blended. Drop spoonfuls of chocolate batter in pan. Swirl chocolate batter into batter in pan. Swirl chocolate through light batter to create a marble effect. Bake at 325°F for one hour or until set. Cool for 10 minutes. Refrigerate several hours or overnight. Store in refrigerator.

♥ ♥ ♥

Nutrition: (per serving): 137 calories

Saturated fat	0 g	
Total Fat	0 g	(3% of calories)
Protein	7 g	(20% of calories)
Carbohydrates	26 g	(77% of calories)

Cholesterol	0 mg	Sodium	285 mg
Fiber	0 g	Iron	1 mg
Vitamin A	33 IU	Vitamin C	1 mg

Source: Estella Johnson helped with our food service during the first years of our program. She developed many bread and dessert recipes that have become Team favorites.

Carrot Cupcakes

These flavorful cupcakes are a good source of beta carotene

Serves 18

Preparation: :10   Cook :20   Stand :15   Total :45

Ingredients:

4	cups shredded carrots, lightly packed
1-1/2	cups sugar
1	8 ounce can crushed pineapple in juice, drained
1	cup pureed prunes
4	large egg whites
2	teaspoons vanilla
2	cups flour
2	teaspoons baking soda
2	teaspoons cinnamon
1/2	teaspoon salt
3/4	cup golden raisins, optional

Preheat oven to 375°F. Coat 18, 2-3/4 inch muffin tin cups with non-stick cooking spray; set aside. In large bowl, combine carrots, sugar, pineapple, pureed prunes, egg whites and vanilla. Stir to blend thoroughly. Add remaining ingredients except raisins; mix completely. Stir in raisins, if using. Spoon batter into prepared muffin tins, dividing equally. Bake about 20 minutes until pick inserted into centers comes out clean. Cool in pan 15 minutes. Turn onto rack to cool completely. Store in airtight container up to 1 week.

♥ ♥ ♥

Nutrition: (per serving): 165 calories

Saturated fat . . . . 0 g
Total Fat . . . . 0 g   (1% of calories)
Protein . . . . 3 g   (7% of calories)
Carbohydrates . . . . 38 g   (92% of calories)

Cholesterol . . . . 0 mg   Sodium . . . . 179 mg
Fiber . . . . 1 g   Iron . . . . 1 mg
Vitamin A . . . . 7060 IU   Vitamin C . . . . 4 mg

Source: Connie Wedel has diabetes and multiple risk factors for heart disease. She enjoys spending winters in Florida.

"After 12 months, my carotid doppler test showed that my carotid arteries had opened up dramatically."

Connie Wedel

♥ ♥ ♥

Chocolate Cake

A chocolate lovers' dream

Serves 12

Preparation: :15   Cook :35   Stand :40   Total 1:30

Ingredients:

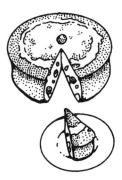

2	cups flour
3/4	cup unsweetened cocoa powder
2	cups sugar
2	teaspoons baking soda
1	teaspoon baking powder
1/4	teaspoon salt
10	ounces pureed prunes
2	teaspoons vanilla
4	egg whites, beaten
1	cup skim milk
1	cup boiling water

Sift together flour, cocoa, sugar, baking soda, baking powder and salt into mixing bowl. Stir until blended. Add prunes, vanilla, egg whites and milk; stir just until blended. Add boiling water and stir until blended. Pour batter into a 9 x 13 inch pan sprayed with non-stick cooking spray. Bake at 350°F for 35 to 45 minutes, or until wooden toothpick inserted into center of cake comes out clean. Let cake cool 10 minutes in pan, then invert onto wire rack to finish cooling. Frost with Seven Minute Frosting, if desired.

Note: 4 (2-1/2 oz.) jars of baby food pureed prunes may be substituted for the 10 ounces of pureed prunes. Do not use baby food prunes containing tapioca. If making your own pureed prunes, blend 1-1/2 cups firmly packed prunes, 8 tablespoons water and 1-1/2 teaspoons vanilla in a food processor or blender until smooth.

♥ ♥ ♥

Nutrition: (per serving): 304 calories

Saturated fat . . . . 0 g
Total Fat . . . . 1 g   (3% of calories)
Protein . . . . 6 g   (7% of calories)
Carbohydrates . . . . 68 g   (89% of calories)

Cholesterol . . . . 0 mg   Sodium . . . . 284 mg
Fiber . . . . 1 g   Iron . . . . 1 mg
Vitamin A . . . . 512 IU   Vitamin C . . . . 1 mg

Source: Sandy Williams is a registered dietitian who worked at Downriver Cardiology Consultants. She shared this recipe and it was adapted for the Reversal Program.

♥ ♥ ♥

Light Fruitcake

Great for the holidays

Serves 16

Preparation: :45   Cook :45   Stand 1:00   Total 2:30

Ingredients:

1/4	cup brandy
1	6 ounce can frozen orange juice concentrate, thawed and undiluted
1	cup cranberries, chopped
1	8 ounce package pitted dates, chopped
1	tablespoon grated orange rind
1	teaspoon vanilla
4	ounces fat free egg substitute
8	ounces canned pineapple tidbits in juice, drained
2	cups flour
1-1/4	teaspoons baking soda
1/4	teaspoon salt
1/2	teaspoon cinnamon
1/4	teaspoon nutmeg
1/4	teaspoon allspice
	non-stick cooking spray
1/2	cup brandy

Combine first three ingredients; cover and let stand for one hour. Combine dates and the next four ingredients; add to cranberry mixture. Combine flour and the next five ingredients; add to fruit mixture and stir well. Spoon batter into a six cup bundt pan sprayed with non-stick spray. Bake at 325°F for 40 to 45 minutes or until wooden toothpick inserted in center of cake comes out clean. Cool cake in pan for 20 minutes; remove from pan and let cool on wire rack.

♥ ♥ ♥

Bring 1/2 cup brandy to boil; let cool. Moisten several layers of cheesecloth in brandy and wrap around fruitcake. Cover cake with plastic wrap and then aluminum foil. Store cake in refrigerator at least 1 week before serving.

Nutrition: (per serving): 161 calories

Saturated fat . . . . 0 g		
Total Fat . . . . 0 g	(2% of calories)	
Protein . . . . 3 g	(7% of calories)	
Carbohydrates . . . . 30 g	(74% of calories)	
Alcohol . . . . 4 g	(17% of calories)	

Cholesterol . . . . 0 mg	Sodium . . . . 112 mg
Fiber . . . . 1 g	Iron . . . . 1 mg
Vitamin A . . . . 54 IU	Vitamin C . . . . 17 mg

Source: Paul Bodrie is a Catholic lay pastoral assistant and university instructor. He had heart attacks in 1989 and 1992 and had angioplasty in 1989.

"I was in bad shape, taking about 9 nitrobids each day for frequent, painful angina. Within four weeks of joining the Reversal Team, my angina was almost gone and I have not had to take any nitrobid since that time. I have lost 60 pounds and feel great. I am physically, mentally, and spiritually better off than I have been in years. Before I started the program, my doctor said I needed bypass surgery. Now, I am no longer a candidate for surgery and he is recommending the program to his patients."

Paul Bodrie

♥ ♥ ♥

Seven-Minute Frosting

A great topping for chocolate cake

Serves 12

Preparation: :03　　Cook :07　　Stand :00　　Total :10

Ingredients:

3	egg whites
1-1/2	cups brown sugar
1	teaspoon cream of tartar
1/4	cup warm water
1	teaspoon vanilla

Combine egg whites, brown sugar, cream of tartar and warm water in top of double boiler. Beat with mixer until frosting forms stiff peaks, 5-7 minutes. Remove from heat. Beat in vanilla.

Nutrition: (per serving): 62 calories

Saturated fat	0 g	
Total Fat	0 g	(0% of calories)
Protein	1 g	(6% of calories)
Carbohydrates	15 g	(94% of calories)

Cholesterol	0 mg	Sodium	38 mg
Fiber	0 g	Iron	1 mg
Vitamin A	0 IU	Vitamin C	0 mg

Source: Diane Boehmer helped us establish our initial food service and developed many delicious recipes for the program.

♥ ♥ ♥

Cream Cheese Sauce

Wonderful on carrot cake and other desserts

Serves 4

Preparation: :10   Cook :00   Stand :00   Total :10

Ingredients:

3/4	cup fat free cream cheese
1/4	cup fat free mayonnaise
1/4	teaspoon lemon juice
1	tablespoon sugar

Place all ingredients in a bowl and whisk until fluffy. Serve as a dollop on the side or on top of carrot cake, steamed vegetables or fruit.

Nutrition: (per serving): 57 calories

Saturated fat	0 g	
Total Fat	0 g	(0% of calories)
Protein	6 g	(1% of calories)
Carbohydrates	8 g	(99% of calories)

Cholesterol	0 mg	Sodium	303 mg
Fiber	0 g	Iron	0 mg
Vitamin A	0 IU	Vitamin C	1 mg

Source: Bob Shank is a retired Episcopal priest who is now the executive director of the Cranbrook Peace Foundation. He has multiple risk factors for coronary artery disease.

"The path to healing a heart is much like the peace process. It takes openess, clear communication and persistence. Neither is easy, but the rewards are well worth the effort."

Bob's Steamed Carrot Cake

A gourmet's delight

Serves 6

Preparation: :45   Cook 3:00   Stand :00   Total 3:45

Ingredients:

	vegetable oil cooking spray
1/2	cup brown sugar
1/4	cup whole wheat pastry flour
1/4	cup unbleached flour
1	teaspoon baking powder
1/2	teaspoon baking soda
1	tablespoon vanilla nut butter extract
1/2	cup raisins
1	carrot, large, peeled and grated
1	potato, medium, peeled and grated
1	dash each: ginger, mace, nutmeg
2	dashes cinnamon

Spray a one-quart mold lightly with vegetable oil cooking spray. Simmer enough water in a pot or pan large enough to hold the mold. In a large bowl, mix the sugar, flours, baking powder and baking soda. Add the extract, raisins, carrot, potato, ginger, cinnamon, mace and nutmeg. Mix thoroughly, using your hands. Spoon mixture into the prepared mold and cover and seal tightly with aluminum foil (if the mold has a lid, use it). Place the mold into the pan of water so that the water comes no more than halfway up the side of the mold and steam, covered for three hours.

Remove mold and let cool for 10 minutes. Uncover and invert onto a plate. Serve warm or at room temperature with a dollop of Cream Cheese Sauce (see recipe on page 249).

♥ ♥ ♥

Nutrition: (per serving): 163 calories

Saturated fat . . . . 0 g		
Total Fat . . . . 0 g	(2% of calories)	
Protein . . . . 3 g	(6% of calories)	
Carbohydrates . . . . 37 g	(91% of calories)	

Cholesterol . . . . 0 mg	Sodium . . . . 139 mg
Fiber . . . . 1 g	Iron . . . . 1 mg
Vitamin A . . . . 3382 IU	Vitamin C . . . . 6 mg

Source: Bob Shank is a retired Episcopal priest who is now the executive director of the Cranbrook Peace Foundation. He has multiple risk factors for coronary artery disease.

"The path to healing a heart is much like the peace process. It takes openess, clear communication and persistence. Neither is easy, but the rewards are well worth the effort."

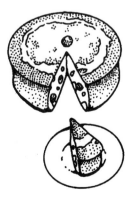

♥ ♥ ♥

Nutty Apple Cake

The water chestnuts add a fat free crunch to this dessert

Serves 8

Preparation: :25   Cook :35   Stand :00   Total 1:00

Ingredients:

4   cups Granny Smith apples, unpeeled and diced
1   cup sugar
1/2   cup flour
2   teaspoons baking powder
2   egg whites
1   tablespoon strained prunes or applesauce
1   teaspoon vanilla
1/2   cup raisins
2   tablespoons water chestnuts, chopped or fat free granola or wheat
        germ
2   cups vanilla fat free frozen yogurt
        vegetable oil cooking spray

Preheat oven to 400°F. Spray a bundt pan with vegetable oil cooking spray and then flour the pan, shaking out excess. Combine apples and sugar in a bowl and set aside.

In a small bowl, mix the egg whites, applesauce and vanilla. Combine the flour with the baking powder and sift. Then add to apple mixture along with egg mixture. Stir, do not beat, until thoroughly mixed. Fold in raisins and water chestnuts (or granola or wheat germ). Pour into prepared pan.

Bake for 30 to 40 minutes, pricking apples with toothpick to see if done. Remove from oven and cool on wire rack. Can be served hot or cold. Top each serving with 1/4 cup frozen yogurt.

♥ ♥ ♥

Nutrition: (per serving): 269 calories

Saturated fat	0 g	
Total Fat	1 g	(2% of calories)
Protein	5 g	(7% of calories)
Carbohydrates	61 g	(91% of calories)

Cholesterol	0 mg	Sodium	152 mg
Fiber	1 g	Iron	0 mg
Vitamin A	55 IU	Vitamin C	4 mg

Source: Judith Caplan Phillips is the general manager of an ad specialty supplier who had a bypass in 1992 and is a diabetic.

"This program touches lives. We've all taken pieces of our hearts and given them to one another. We've taken this program home and involved our families and friends. We are planting seeds of change."

Judith Caplan Phillips

Angel Food Fruit Pudding

A colorful and creamy treat

Serves 6

Preparation: :45   Cook :00   Stand 1:00   Total 1:45

Ingredients:

1/2	angel food cake
1	6 ounce package instant vanilla fat free pudding
2-3/4	cups skim milk (for pudding)
1	pint fresh strawberries, washed and sliced
1	8 ounce can pineapple chunks, drained
8	ounces canned apricots, drained and sliced
8	ounces canned sliced peaches, drained
1	batch fat free whipped topping

Cup up cake into bite size pieces. Make pudding according to package directions using skim milk. Mix with cake and set aside. Set a small amount of the strawberries aside for the top. Mix remaining strawberries with the other fruits and set aside. Prepare the fat free whipped topping following the recipe on next page. In a large bowl, place 1/2 of the pudding mixture. Layer 1/2 fruit mixture on top of the pudding mixture. Top with 1/2 of the whipped topping. Repeat layers and garnish with the strawberries that have been set aside. Best if chilled well before serving. To make this "aesthetically pleasing to the eye" use a large glass bowl, positioning strawberries on the outside. The red is a beautiful contrast when finished.

Option: Use sugar free pudding.

♥ ♥ ♥

Nutrition: (per serving): 155 calories

Saturated fat . . . . 0 g		
Total Fat . . . . 1 g	(3% of calories)	
Protein . . . . 5 g	(12% of calories)	
Carbohydrates . . . . 33 g	(85% of calories)	

Cholesterol . . . . 2 mg	Sodium . . . . 93 mg
Fiber . . . . 1 g	Iron . . . . 1 mg
Vitamin A . . . . 864 IU	Vitamin C . . . . 35 mg

Source: Pat Nevin-Normandin is a yoga instructor and group facilitator for the Reversal Team. She and her husband love to travel.

♥ ♥ ♥

Whipped Topping

For lovers of whipped cream

Serves 4

Preparation: :10   Cook :10   Stand :30   Total :50

Ingredients:

1/2	cup water	1	cup skim milk, divided
2	teaspoons cornstarch		
1	packet gelatin	3	tablespoons fat free sour cream
1	teaspoon fat free and sugar free instant vanilla pudding mix (dry mix)—or—	2	teaspoons sugar, or sugar substitute
1	teaspoon vanilla		

Put water in a small sauce pan. Add cornstarch and stir until blended. Heat over moderate burner, stirring constantly, until bubbly. After about one minute, when the starch is completely dissolved and thickened, remove from heat.

In a small bowl, sprinkle the gelatin over half of the skim milk and let stand for a minute. Mix well to blend gelatin into the milk. Add to the hot starch and stir well, mixing until smooth. If gelatin doesn't dissolve, put the pan back on the burner to provide enough heat to dissolve gelatin, but do not overheat, or gelatin will clot. The mixture should be smooth and gelatinous. Set aside to cool. In a medium sized bowl, mix the dry pudding mix, the sour cream, the sweetener and the remaining skim milk. Mix well, until blended. Add the cooled gelatin/starch and mix or blend very well. If there are any lumps in the mixture, blend well until smooth. Refrigerate until well chilled and gelatin sets. Beat or blend until frothy before serving. Add sugar or vanilla as desired. Whipped Topping will set when refrigerated. Blending it will soften the topping. If used on refrigerated desserts and parfaits, it will be slightly firm.

Note: 1/2 cup of "Kool-whip Lite" has 4 fat grams. *This recipe has none.* Most commercial "fat free" whipped toppings contain fat. Because a serving is 2 tablespoons, the amount of fat is less than 1/2 fat gram and can legally be "fat free." Who can eat just 2 tablespoons? The type of fat in "fat free" whipped toppings is usually highly saturated. If this recipe seems too laborious, mix a little dry instant vanilla pudding mix into some fat free sour cream for a quick topping.

Nutrition: (per serving): 71 calories

Saturated fat . . . . 0 g		
Total Fat . . . . 0 g	(2% of calories)	
Protein . . . . 4 g	(35% of calories)	
Carbohydrates . . . . 6 g	(63% of calories)	
Cholesterol . . . . 0 mg	Sodium . . . . 44 mg	
Fiber . . . . 1 g	Iron . . . . 1 mg	
Vitamin A . . . . 129 IU	Vitamin C . . . . 0 mg	

Source: Gerry Krag is the consulting nutritionist and group facilitator for the Downriver Reversal Team.

♥ ♥ ♥

Carol's Orange Yogurt Cake

A mellow, golden cake with tart orange topping

Serves 10

Preparation: :10   Cook :45   Stand :45   Total 1:40

Ingredients:

Cake:

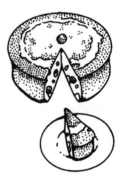

3	cups uncooked Farina
1/2	cup unbleached white flour
2	teaspoons baking powder
1	teaspoon baking soda
1-1/2	cups honey
2	cups plain fat free yogurt
4	tablespoons frozen orange juice concentrate
1	tablespoon fresh orange zest

Syrup:

6	ounces frozen orange juice concentrate
6	ounces water
3	tablespoons cornstarch

Preheat oven to 350°F. Sift together farina, flour, baking powder and soda. Stir yogurt, orange juice concentrate, orange zest and honey into dry ingredients. Pour batter into 9 x 13 inch baking pan that has been sprayed lightly with vegetable oil cooking spray. Bake until top is golden brown (approximately 45 minutes.)

To make syrup, stir cornstarch into water. Blend with orange juice concentrate. Heat over medium heat, stirring constantly, until thickened. Pour syrup over cake and poke every few inches with a toothpick to help absorb syrup. Serve when cake is cooled and syrup is absorbed.

♥ ♥ ♥

Nutrition: (per serving): 119 calories

Saturated fat . . . . 0 g
Total Fat . . . . 0 g   (1% of calories)
Protein . . . . 1 g   (2% of calories)
Carbohydrates . . . . 29 g   (97% of calories)

Cholesterol . . . . 0 mg   Sodium . . . . 78 mg
Fiber . . . . 0 g   Iron . . . . 0 mg
Vitamin A . . . . 35 IU   Vitamin C . . . . 17 mg

Source: Carol Rhora is a neurodiagnostic technician who had a heart attack in 1992 and has hypertension.

"If not for this program, I feel that I would have had another heart attack."

Carol Rhora

Jerry's Cinnamon Biscotti

A crunchy biscuit-like cookie

Serves 36

Preparation: :45   Cook 1:00   Stand :00   Total 1:45

Ingredients:

3	egg whites
6	tablespoons honey
2	cups flour
2/3	cup brown sugar, packed
3/4	teaspoon baking powder
1/4	teaspoon baking soda
	dash salt
2/3	cup yellow raisins, well chopped
1-1/2	teaspoons ground cinnamon

Preheat oven to 325°F. Lightly spray a cookie sheet with vegetable oil cooking spray and dust lightly with flour. Set aside. In a small bowl, mix egg whites and honey until blended and set aside. In a larger bowl, mix all the dry ingredients. Make a depression in the center of the flour mixture and pour in the egg white mixture and the raisins. Mix until the dough is blended and smooth. Set dough on a lightly floured surface and divide in two. Roll each portion into a 12 inch cylinder. Put on baking sheet at least six inches apart. Bake at 325°F until golden, about 35 to 40 minutes. Remove from oven and reduce the oven to 300°F. Move the logs onto a cutting board and let cool slightly. Using a sharp bread knife, cut logs into 1/2 inch slices. Arrange on baking sheet so cookies are standing upright. Bake until crisp, about 15 minutes.

Option: Use 1-1/2 teaspoon ground anise instead of cinnamon.

♥ ♥ ♥

Nutrition: (per serving): 56 calories

Saturated fat	0 g	
Total Fat	0 g	(2% of calories)
Protein	1 g	(8% of calories)
Carbohydrates	13 g	(90% of calories)

Cholesterol	0 mg	Sodium	30 mg
Fiber	0 g	Iron	0 mg
Vitamin A	0 IU	Vitamin C	0 mg

Source: Jerry Nagle, 63, is a retiree who enjoys traveling. In 1988, he had bypass surgery and aortic valve replacement. He also has diabetes.

♥ ♥ ♥

Fruit Ravioli

A Reversal Team favorite

Serves 16

Preparation: :40   Cook 2:00   Stand :00   Total 2:40

Ingredients:

1	12 ounce package blackberries, frozen
1	12 ounce package strawberries, frozen
1	12 ounce package raspberries, frozen
1	package phyllo dough
	vegetable oil cooking spray; 16 one-second sprays

Remove half the fruit from each bag and place in a deep pan. Cover fruit with water and simmer until thick, about 1 or 2 hours. Meanwhile, open the dough and place a damp towel over the sheets. Layer 4 sheets with a very light spray between each one. Cut these into quarters. Place a blackberry, a strawberry and a raspberry in the center of each quarter. Fold the dough over and seal the edges by folding over twice. Continue the process until all the dough is used. Bake at 350 for 15-20 minutes until golden. Serve with fruit sauce.

Option: Any fruit will work in this recipe. The sauce can be a different fruit that blends or complements the baked fruit.

Nutrition: (per serving): 41 calories

Saturated fat . . . . 0 g		
Total Fat . . . . 1 g	(22% of calories)	
Protein. . . . . 0 g	(5% of calories)	
Carbohydrates . . . . 7 g	(73% of calories)	
Cholesterol. . . . . 0 mg	Sodium. . . . . 5 mg
Fiber . . . . 2 g	Iron . . . . 0 mg
Vitamin A. . . . . 68 IU	Vitamin C. . . . . 22 mg

Source: Diane Boehmer helped us establish our initial food service and developed many delicious recipes for the program.

♥ ♥ ♥

Fast Fruit Trifle

Need a dessert right now? Here is your recipe!

Serves 8

Preparation: :15   Cook :10   Stand :20   Total :35

Ingredients:

1/4	angel food cake	1	cup skim milk
4	fluid ounces sherry or fruit flavored syrup	1	package fat free and sugar free instant vanilla pudding
2	cups fruit, cut into bite size pieces	1	cup fat free sour cream

Use a deep glass bowl. Cut the cake into one inch slices and layer the bottom. Pour the sherry or syrup over the cake. Fruit can be fresh, frozen or canned. Fresh strawberries are great, but thawed, frozen strawberries or raspberries work well, too. Mixed fruits are nice in almost any combination. If you are using fruit that has a lot of juice, make sure it is drained.

Layer the fruit over the cake. In a medium sized mixing bowl, stir the milk and pudding mix together until well blended. Add the sour cream and mix very well. Spread over the fruit. Chill before serving. This can be made the day before.

Nutrition: (per serving): 79 calories

Saturated fat . . . . 0 g		
Total Fat . . . . 0 g	(3% of calories)	
Protein . . . . 3 g	(18% of calories)	
Carbohydrates . . . . 12 g	(60% of calories)	
Alcohol. . . . . 2 g	(19% of calories)	
Cholesterol . . . . 1 mg	Sodium. . . . . 40 mg	
Fiber . . . . 1 g	Iron . . . . 0 mg	
Vitamin A . . . . 70 IU	Vitamin C . . . . 2 mg	

Source: Gerry Krag is the consulting nutritionist and group facilitator for the Downriver Reversal Team.

♥ ♥ ♥

French Apple Dessert

Lovely, light and luscious . . .

Serves 12

Preparation: :25 Cook :30 Stand :00 Total :55

Ingredients:

5	apples, peeled and sliced
2	cups flour
	vegetable oil cooking spray
1/2	cup sugar
1/2	teaspoon baking soda
1/2	teaspoon cream of tartar
1	cup sour skim milk
2	egg whites

Topping:

1/4	cup sugar
1/2	teaspoon cinnamon
1/4	teaspoon nutmeg

Spray two 9 inch pie pans with vegetable oil cooking spray. Divide apples evenly between the pans and set aside. If you do not have sour skim milk, place 1 tablespoon vinegar in a one cup measuring cup and add enough skim milk to fill the cup. Let sit for 5 minutes.

In a mixing bowl, combine flour, sugar, baking soda, cream of tartar, sour milk and egg whites. Mix well. Divide the batter and pour over apples. Bake at 350°F for 25-30 minutes. Invert onto serving plates, so apples are on top.

Combine all topping ingredients and sprinkle over top. Serve warm.

♥ ♥ ♥

Nutrition: (per serving): 189 calories

Saturated fat . . . . 0 g
Total Fat . . . . 1 g   (3% of calories)
Protein . . . . 4 g   (8% of calories)
Carbohydrates . . . . 42 g   (89% of calories)

Cholesterol . . . . 0 mg   Sodium . . . . 64 mg
Fiber . . . . 1 g   Iron . . . . 0 mg
Vitamin A . . . . 86 IU   Vitamin C . . . . 5 mg

Source: Jerry Nagle, 63, is a retiree who enjoys traveling. In 1988 he had bypass surgery and aortic valve replacement. He also has diabetes.

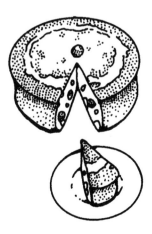

♥ ♥ ♥

Peaches 'n Cream

A refreshing, light pie . . .

Serves 8

Preparation: :25   Cook :40   Stand 2:00 Total 3:05

Ingredients:

1-1/2 cups crushed fat free cookies or graham crackers
2   tablespoons skim milk
3-1/2 cups peaches
1/3   cup flour
1/3   cup sugar
1/4   teaspoon nutmeg
1   cup evaporated skim milk

Set oven to 250°. Use either canned, fresh or frozen sliced peaches. If using canned, make sure they are well drained. If using frozen, make sure they are defrosted and drained. Mix the crushed cookies and 2 tablespoons of skim milk together. Press into a ten inch pie pan to form a thin crust. In a small bowl, mix the flour, sugar and nutmeg. Put the peaches in a large bowl and add the dry ingredients, tossing lightly so that peaches get coated. Pour the peach mix into the crust and arrange evenly. Pour the canned evaporated skim milk over all. Bake at 350° for 35-45 minutes until set. Chill at least two hours before serving.

Options: use artificial sweetener, such as Sweet and Low or Sweet One, instead of sugar. Serve with a raspberry sauce garnish. make with apples instead of peaches, baking until the apples are tender and liquid is set. use 1/4 cup fat free sour cream with the evaporated skim milk; mix well before pouring over fruit.

This recipe can be used with the pie crust recipe on page 283.

♥ ♥ ♥

Nutrition: (per serving): 114 calories

Saturated fat . . . . 0 g		
Total Fat . . . . 0 g	(2% of calories)	
Protein . . . . 4 g	(13% of calories)	
Carbohydrates . . . . 24 g	(86% of calories)	

Cholesterol . . . . 1 mg	Sodium . . . . 40 mg
Fiber . . . . 0 g	Iron . . . . 0 mg
Vitamin A . . . . 531 IU	Vitamin C . . . . 5 mg

Source: Gerry Krag is the consulting nutritionist and group facilitator for the Downriver Reversal Team.

♥♥♥

Pumpkin Pie

Enjoy this on Thanksgiving or anytime

Serves 8

Preparation: :30   Cook :45   Stand 1:00   Total 2:15

Ingredients:

2	cups canned pumpkin or use fresh cooked pumpkin
1	cup evaporated skim milk
1/2	cup fat free egg substitute
3/4	cup packed brown sugar
1	teaspoon cinnamon
1/2	teaspoon ginger or nutmeg
1/4	teaspoon ground cloves, optional
1/2	teaspoon salt, optional
1	cup crushed fat free cookies
	skim milk
	vegetable oil cooking spray

Preheat oven to 425°F. In medium size bowl, mix pumpkin, evaporated milk, egg substitute, sugar and spices until well blended. Set aside. In a small bowl, mix enough skim milk into the cookies to moisten them, about 2 tablespoons. In a 10-inch pie pan sprayed with non-stick cooking spray, press the damp cookies to form a thin crust. Pour in the filling. If your pan is smaller than 10 inches, there will be extra batter. It can be baked separately in a small dish and used as a pudding. Trim the crust at the point where the filling meets the crust. Exposed crust may become tough. Bake for 15 minutes in a 425°F oven, then reduce heat to 350°F and bake for 30-40 minutes. Cool and refrigerate. Can be made the day before.

Options: top with fat free yogurt, sweetened with a little sugar or artificial sweetener. Also nice with frozen fat free yogurt or ice cream. This recipe can be used with the pie crust recipe on page 283.

♥ ♥ ♥

Nutrition: (per serving): 96 calories

Saturated fat .... 0 g		
Total Fat .... 0 g	(4% of calories)	
Protein .... 3 g	(13% of calories)	
Carbohydrates ...... 20 g	(83% of calories)	

Cholesterol .... 1 mg	Sodium .... 44 mg
Fiber .... 1 g	Iron .... 2 mg
Vitamin A .... 13636 IU	Vitamin C .... 3 mg

Source: Gerry Krag is the consulting nutritionist and group facilitator for the Downriver Reversal Team.

♥ ♥ ♥

Pavlova

A light and beautiful dessert

Serves 8

Preparation: :25   Cook 1:00   Stand 1:00   Total 2:25

Ingredients:

3/4   cup sugar
1   tablespoon cornstarch
1   pinch salt
3   egg whites, at room temperature
1   teaspoon lemon juice

Preheat oven to 300°F. Mix dry ingredients together and set aside. In a large mixing bowl, beat the egg whites until very stiff. The egg whites should remain in the bowl, even when upside down. Very gradually, spoonful by spoonful, add the dry ingredients, beating well as each is added. Add the lemon juice and continue to beat. Line a pie pan with foil and add the egg white mixture. Fill pan evenly, but build a lip around the edge. Reduce the oven temperature to 225°F and put the Pavlova in for one hour. After one hour shut off the oven but let the Pavlova rest in the warm oven for one hour.

To serve, remove from pan and carefully pull off the foil. Place on serving plate. Fill with softened fat free frozen yogurt and top with fruit. Kiwis, strawberries and raspberries are especially nice.

This recipe may not work on humid, hot days. It does not work with sugar substitutes.

♥ ♥ ♥

Nutrition: (per serving): 84 calories

Saturated fat . . . . 0 g		
Total Fat . . . . 0 g	(0% of calories)	
Protein . . . . 1 g	(6% of calories)	
Carbohydrates . . . . 20 g	(94% of calories)	

Cholesterol . . . . 0 mg	Sodium . . . . 69 mg
Fiber . . . . 0 g	Iron . . . . 1 mg
Vitamin A . . . . 0 IU	Vitamin C . . . . 0 mg

Source: Pavlova was developed by a chef in Australia to honor the dancer. This version was given to us by two friends from Ireland.

♥ ♥ ♥

Rice Pudding

Old fashioned flavor

Serves 6

Preparation: :15   Cook 1:20   Stand :00   Total 1:35

Ingredients:

1-1/3	cups quick cooking rice, white or brown	5	cups skim milk
1/2	cup sugar	2	teaspoons vanilla
1/4	teaspoon salt	1	packet Butter Buds™ Mix
1/2	teaspoon nutmeg	1/2	cup fat free egg substitute
1/2	teaspoon cinnamon	4	tablespoons skim milk

In a large saucepan, mix the first 8 ingredients. Cook over medium heat until mix comes to a gentle boil. Simmer 20 minutes, stirring occasionally. Put a little of the hot mixture into a small bowl and add the egg substitute and milk, stirring well. Now add this egg mixture to the saucepan. Cook over low heat for 1 hour, stirring occasionally. Raisins can be added.

Nutrition: (per serving): 152 calories

Saturated fat .... 0 g		
Total Fat .... 1 g	(3% of calories)	
Protein.............. 7 g	(19% of calories)	
Carbohydrates .... 30 g	(78% of calories)	
Cholesterol........... 4 mg	Sodium........... 208 mg	
Fiber .... 0 g	Iron .... 0 mg	
Vitamin A.......... 437 IU	Vitamin C........... 2 mg	

Source: Lauretta MacDonald is married to Alec, who had a heart attack in 1978, bypasses in 1982 and 1991, and abdominal aneurysm repaired in 1995.

♥ ♥ ♥

Raspberry Freeze

Serve with fresh fruit and whipped topping

Serves 8

Preparation: :10   Cook :00   Stand :20   Total :30

Ingredients:

1   tablespoon vinegar
1   cup skim milk
1   cup fat free sour cream
1/3   cup sugar, or equivalent artificial sweetener
2   cups frozen raspberries, one 12 ounce bag,
         thawed

Pour the vinegar in a measuring cup. Add enough milk to equal one cup. Stir in the sour cream and sugar until well mixed. Add the berries and mix well. Pour into a 10 inch pie pan and freeze. Remove from freezer and let stand for 10-15 minutes. Cut into pie shaped wedges. Garnish with fat free whipped topping and fresh fruit. Options: make a crust of fat free crushed cookies pressed into the pie pan. Pour the mixture over the crust.

Nutrition: (per serving): 112 calories

Saturated fat	0 g	
Total Fat	0 g	(1% of calories)
Protein	1 g	(5% of calories)
Carbohydrates	26 g	(93% of calories)

Cholesterol	1 mg	Sodium	16 mg
Fiber	1 g	Iron	0 mg
Vitamin A	100 IU	Vitamin C	11 mg

Source: Gerry Krag is the consulting nutritionist and group facilitator for the Downriver Reversal Team.

♥ ♥ ♥

Easy Frozen Dessert

A great substitute for ice cream

Serves 2

Preparation: :10   Cook :00   Stand :00   Total :10

Ingredients:

1   cup frozen strawberries, or other frozen fruit
         sweetener, equivalent to 2 teaspoons
1   tablespoon lemon juice
2   cups fat free yogurt, plain

In a food processor or blender, chop frozen fruit until coarse. Add sweetener and lemon juice. With machine on low, blend in the yogurt, processing until thoroughly mixed and semi-frozen. Serve at once or store in freezer while you are eating your meal. If left too long in freezer, it will freeze ice hard.

Nutrition: (per serving): 160 calories

Saturated fat . . . . 0 g		
Total Fat . . . . 0 g	(3% of calories)	
Protein . . . . 13 g	(34% of calories)	
Carbohydrates . . . . 25 g	(64% of calories)	
Cholesterol . . . . 4 mg	Sodium . . . . 175 mg	
Fiber . . . . 1 g	Iron . . . . 1 mg	
Vitamin A . . . . 51 IU	Vitamin C . . . . 36 mg	

Source: The Rev. Edie Gause is married to Ken Miller, a diabetic who had heart attacks in 1987 and 1988. He had bypass surgery in 1988.

"Cooking fat free has opened a whole new world of grains and flavors as well as a new world of heart health."

♥ ♥ ♥

Spice Cookies

Kids love these

Serves 30

Preparation: :20   Cook :09   Stand :00   Total :29

Ingredients:

	vegetable oil cooking spray	1	teaspoon cinnamon
1-1/2	cups flour	1/4	teaspoon nutmeg
1/2	cup sugar	1/2	cup Karo light or dark corn
1/2	teaspoon baking soda		syrup
1/2	teaspoon salt	3	egg whites

Spray cookie sheet with cooking spray. In a large bowl, combine flour, sugar, baking soda, salt, cinnamon and nutmeg. Stir in corn syrup and egg whites until well blended. Dough will be thick and slightly sticky. Drop by rounded teaspoonfuls onto sprayed cookie sheet. Bake at 350°F for 7-9 minutes until set. Cookies will be soft when pressed. Do not over bake. Cool on wire rack.

Nutrition: (per serving): 54 calories

Saturated fat . . . . 0 g		
Total Fat . . . . 0 g	(2% of calories)	
Protein . . . . 1 g	(7% of calories)	
Carbohydrates . . . . 12 g	(91% of calories)	

Cholesterol . . . . 0 mg	Sodium . . . . 62 mg
Fiber . . . . 0 g	Iron . . . . 0 mg
Vitamin A . . . . 0 IU	Vitamin C . . . . 0 mg

Source: Marilyn Waltz is a receptionist in a law office who enjoys golf. She had bypass surgery and a heart attack in 1984.

♥ ♥ ♥

Old-Fashioned Oatmeal Cookies

A great treat anytime of the day

Serves 24

Preparation: :30   Cook :10   Stand :10   Total :50

Ingredients:

1	cup raisins	1/2	teaspoon baking powder
1	cup water	1	teaspoon baking soda
3/4	cup applesauce	1	teaspoon cinnamon
1-1/2	cups sugar	1/2	teaspoon ground cloves
1/2	cup fat free egg substitute	1	teaspoon salt
1	teaspoon vanilla	2-1/2	cups rolled oats
2-1/2	cups flour		

Simmer raisins and water in saucepan over low heat until raisins are plump, 20-30 minutes. Drain raisin liquid into measuring cup. Add enough water to make 1/2 cup. Preheat oven to 400°F. Mix applesauce, sugar, egg substitute and vanilla. Stir in raisin liquid. In a large bowl, stir together flour, baking powder, baking soda, salt and spices. Blend in applesauce mixture. Add rolled oats and raisins. Drop rounded teaspoonfuls of dough about 2" apart on ungreased baking sheet. Bake 8 to 10 minutes or until lightly browned. Makes 6 to 7 dozen.

Nutrition: (per serving): 140 calories

Saturated fat . . . . 0 g		
Total Fat . . . . 0 g	(3% of calories)	
Protein . . . . 2 g	(6% of calories)	
Carbohydrates . . . . 32 g	(91% of calories)	
Cholesterol . . . . 0 mg	Sodium . . . . 141 mg	
Fiber . . . . 0 g	Iron . . . . 1 mg	
Vitamin A . . . . 6 IU	Vitamin C . . . . 0 mg	

Source: Patrick Beaudrie, 59, is a retiree who had bypass surgery in 1989.

♥ ♥ ♥

Moe's Pumpkin Cake

Great with Cream Cheese Sauce

Serves 20

Preparation: :20   Cook :45   Stand :00   Total 1:05

Ingredients:

8	fluid ounces fat free egg substitute	1/2	teaspoon salt, optional
1/2	cup applesauce	2	teaspoons cinnamon
3/4	cups sugar	1/2	teaspoon ginger
15	ounces canned solid-pack pumpkin	1/2	teaspoon cloves
2	cups all-purpose flour	1/2	teaspoon nutmeg
2	teaspoons baking soda	3/4	cup raisins
2	teaspoons baking powder		

Prepare 13 x 9 inch pan with vegetable oil cooking spray. Preheat oven to 350°F. In a mixing bowl, beat together egg substitute, applesauce, sugar and pumpkin. In a separate bowl, sift together flour, baking soda, baking powder, salt, cinnamon, ginger, cloves and nutmeg. Slowly beat the flour mixture into the pumpkin mixture. Add raisins. Pour batter into pan and bake for 40-45 minutes. Remove from oven and allow cake to cool before cutting.

Nutrition: (per serving): 107 calories

Saturated fat . . . . 0 g		
Total Fat . . . . 0 g	(2% of calories)	
Protein . . . . 3 g	(10% of calories)	
Carbohydrates . . . . 24 g	(88% of calories)	
Cholesterol . . . . 0 mg	Sodium . . . . 179 mg	
Fiber . . . . 1 g	Iron . . . . 1 mg	
Vitamin A . . . . 4692 IU	Vitamin C . . . . 1 mg	

Source: Maureen Paulin is a dietetic intern who volunteers in our program. She is also an All-American NAIA volleyball player.

♥ ♥ ♥

Pat's Cinnamon Rolls

A traditional favorite is now fat free.

Serves 15

Preparation: :40   Cook :30   Stand 1:10   Total 2:20

Ingredients:

5 to 5-1/2 cups flour
2   packets rapid rise yeast
1/2   cup water
1-1/2   tablespoons ground cinnamon
1-1/2   cups sugar
1   teaspoon salt
1/2   cup skim milk
1/2   cup fat free egg substitute
1   8 ounce package raisins
1/2   cup applesauce

In large bowl, combine 2 cups of the flour, 1/2 cup of the sugar, undissolved yeast and salt. Heat water and milk until very warm (120-130°F). Stir into dry ingredients. Stir in egg substitute, applesauce and enough remaining flour to make soft dough. Knead on lightly floured surface until smooth and elastic, about 4-6 minutes. Cover and let rest on floured surface for 10 minutes.

Roll dough to 20 x 10 inch rectangle. Brush applesauce on dough. Evenly sprinkle with remaining sugar, cinnamon and raisins. Beginning at long end, roll up tightly, as for a jelly roll. Pinch seam to seal. With a sharp knife, cut roll into 15 pieces. Place cut sides up in a 13 x 9 inch pan sprayed with vegetable oil cooking spray. Cover. Let rise in warm, draft free place until doubled in size, about 30 to 60 minutes.

Bake at 375°F for 30 minutes or until done. Remove from pan and cool on wire rack. Brush with Powdered Sugar Glaze, if desired:

♥ ♥ ♥

Powdered Sugar Glaze:

In small bowl, combine one cup sifted powdered sugar and 1 - 3 tablespoons skim milk. Stir until smooth.

Option: Sugar can be decreased to 1/3 cup to reduce each roll by 60 calories.

Nutrition: (per serving): 286 calories

Saturated fat . . . . 0 g		
Total Fat . . . . 1 g	(2% of calories)	
Protein . . . . 5 g	(8% of calories)	
Carbohydrates . . . . 65 g	(91% of calories)	

Cholesterol . . . . 0 mg	Sodium . . . . 164 mg
Fiber . . . . 0 g	Iron . . . . 1 mg
Vitamin A . . . . 20 IU	Vitamin C . . . . 1 mg

Source: Patrick Beaudrie, 59, is a retiree who had a heart attack and bypass surgery in 1989.

"With a dedicated staff and the help of the support group, you can't go wrong. I've lost 28 pounds and my cholesterol numbers are right where they should be. My latest thallium stress test shows significant improvement. I plan on being around for a long time! A big part of the program's success is the support group and of course Dr. Rogers. Without him, there would be no program."

Patrick Beaudrie

♥ ♥ ♥

Rennet Pudding

An easily digested dessert

Serves 4

Preparation: :10   Cook :00   Stand :35   Total :45

Ingredients:

1	rennet tablet
1	tablespoon water
2	cups skim milk
4	tablespoons sugar or 10 drops artificial sweetener
1	teaspoon vanilla extract

Set out four 6 ounce custard cups. In one cup place the water and the rennet tablet which will dissolve in about 5 minutes. Heat the milk until warm, not hot, either in the microwave or on the stove. Put the sugar, flavoring and dissolved rennet into the milk. Mix briefly and pour into the custard cups. Let set for 10 minutes. Chill well before serving.

Nutrition: (per serving): 92 calories

Saturated fat . . . . 0 g		
Total Fat . . . . 0 g	(2% of calories)	
Protein. . . . . 4 g	(18% of calories)	
Carbohydrates . . . . 18 g	(80% of calories)	
Cholesterol. . . . . 2 mg	Sodium. . . . . 63 mg	
Fiber . . . . 0 g	Iron . . . . 0 mg	
Vitamin A . . . . 249 IU	Vitamin C . . . . 1 mg	

Source: Esther Kirschner is married to Stan Kirschner, who has had stent surgery and bypass surgery in 1995.

♥ ♥ ♥

Strawberry-Rhubarb Squares

A great finish to any meal

Serves 9

Preparation: :20   Cook 1:00   Stand :00   Total 1:20

Ingredients:

2	cups rhubarb, 1/2" thick, sliced
2	cups strawberries, halved
3	tablespoons cornstarch
1	cup dark brown sugar, firmly packed
1-1/2	cups quick cooking rolled oats

1/2	cup whole wheat flour
1	teaspoon cinnamon
4	ounces plum baby food

Preheat oven to 350°F. Mix first three ingredients and 1/2 cup of brown sugar together and set aside. Then mix the other 1/2 cup of brown sugar with the oats, flour and cinnamon. Add oat mixture to strawberry-rhubarb mixture. Fold in baby food and stir until well blended. Spray 8 x 8 inch pan with non-stick cooking spray. Pour batter into pan and bake for approximately 1 hour. Serve warm with fat free frozen yogurt or cool and cut into bars.

Options: 4 cups of other fruit can be used instead of rhubarb and strawberries. Other flavors of baby food can be used.

Nutrition: (per serving): 163 calories

Saturated fat	0 g	
Total Fat	1 g	(6% of calories)
Protein	3 g	(8% of calories)
Carbohydrates	35 g	(85% of calories)

Cholesterol	0 mg	Sodium	6 mg
Fiber	1 g	Iron	2 mg
Vitamin A	56 IU	Vitamin C	20 mg

Source: Pat Nevin-Normandin is a yoga teacher and group facilitator for the Reversal Team. She and her husband love to travel.

♥ ♥ ♥

Lazy Cherry Cobbler

Sure to be a family favorite

Serves 12

Preparation: :10   Cook :30   Stand :00   Total :40

Ingredients:

2	20 ounce cans cherry pie filling		1-1/2	cups self rising flour
1/2	20 ounce can water		1	cup skim milk
1/2	teaspoon almond extract		1	cup sugar

Preheat oven to 375°. Combine cherries, water and almond extract. Mix well. Place in ungreased 9 x 13 inch baking pan. In a mixing bowl, combine dry ingredients and mix well. Add milk and stir until well mixed. Pour evenly over cherries. Then run a knife through the mixture as if marbelizing. Bake 25 to 40 minutes until golden brown.

Options: use sugar reduced pie filling. Use other fruits such as blueberries. To make an 8 x 8 inch pan, use one can of fruit and 1/4 cup water, one cup self-rising flour, 2/3 cup milk and 2/3 cup sugar.

Nutrition: (per serving): 242 calories

Saturated fat . . . . 0 g		
Total Fat . . . . 0 g	(2% of calories)	
Protein . . . . 3 g	(4% of calories)	
Carbohydrates . . . . 57 g	(94% of calories)	
Cholesterol . . . . 0 mg	Sodium . . . . 188 mg	
Fiber . . . . 0 g	Iron . . . . 1 mg	
Vitamin A . . . . 118 IU	Vitamin C . . . . 0 mg	

Source: Jeanne M. Eckert is a homemaker and gardening expert. In addition to having coronary artery blockages, she has blockages in the arteries of her legs. Jean's mother was a preparing chef who taught her to cook.

♥ ♥ ♥

Pie Crust

A fat free crust for fruit or cream pies

Serves 8

Preparation: :30   Cook :35   Stand :00   Total 1:05

Ingredients:

1	packet Butter Buds™ Mix	1/4	cup sugar
1-1/2	cups rice flour	1/2	cup skim milk
1/2	cup self rising flour		vegetable oil cooking spray

Stir dry ingredients into a bowl until well mixed. Add milk and mix with a fork until the dry ingredients are damp throughout. Knead the dough to form a ball. If it is too sticky, sprinkle on more self rising flour. Cut dough into two pieces and press into two balls. Roll out on a clean dish towel or pastry cloth, using self rising flour to prevent the dough from sticking. Prepare a nine or ten inch pie pan by spraying lightly with vegetable oil cooking spray. Spray the top edge of the pan to prevent crust edges from sticking. Place the first half in the pie pan. Trim edges as needed. Use second ball for top crust. Press the two crusts together using the tines of a fork dipped in flour. Use your favorite pie recipes with this crust. Works best with precooked or canned fillings.

Nutrition: (per serving): 169 calories

Saturated fat . . . . 0 g		
Total Fat . . . . 1 g	(4% of calories)	
Protein . . . . 3 g	(7% of calories)	
Carbohydrates . . . . 38 g	(89% of calories)	
Cholesterol . . . . 0 mg	Sodium . . . . 92 mg
Fiber . . . . 0 g	Iron . . . . 0 mg
Vitamin A . . . . 31 IU	Vitamin C . . . . 0 mg

Source: Gerry Krag is the consulting nutritionist and group facilitator for the Downriver Reversal Team.

♥ ♥ ♥

Marilyn's Oatmeal Cookies

Old fashioned flavor without the fat

Serves 48

Preparation: :25   Cook :10   Stand :15   Total :40

Ingredients:

1	cup brown sugar	2	cups oatmeal
1	cup whole wheat pastry flour	1	cup raisins
1	cup all-purpose flour	1/2	cup fat free egg substitute
1	teaspoon soda	3/4	cup applesauce
1	teaspoon cinnamon	1/2	cup skim milk
1	teaspoon nutmeg	1	teaspoon vanilla

Sift sugar, flour, soda and spices into a mixing bowl. Add oats and raisins. In a small container, mix egg substitute, applesauce, milk and vanilla. Add to dry ingredients. Beat well. Drop by teaspoon on non-stick baking sheet. Bake at 350°F for about 15 minutes.

Nutrition: (per serving): 57 calories

Saturated fat . . . . 0 g		
Total Fat . . . . 0 g	(6% of calories)	
Protein . . . . 1 g	(10% of calories)	
Carbohydrates . . . . 12 g	(85% of calories)	
Cholesterol . . . . 0 mg	Sodium . . . . 3 mg	
Fiber . . . . 0 g	Iron . . . . 0 mg	
Vitamin A . . . . 9 IU	Vitamin C . . . . 0 mg	

Source: Marilyn Waltz is a receptionist in a law office who enjoys golf. She had a bypass and heart attack in 1984.

♥ ♥ ♥

Index

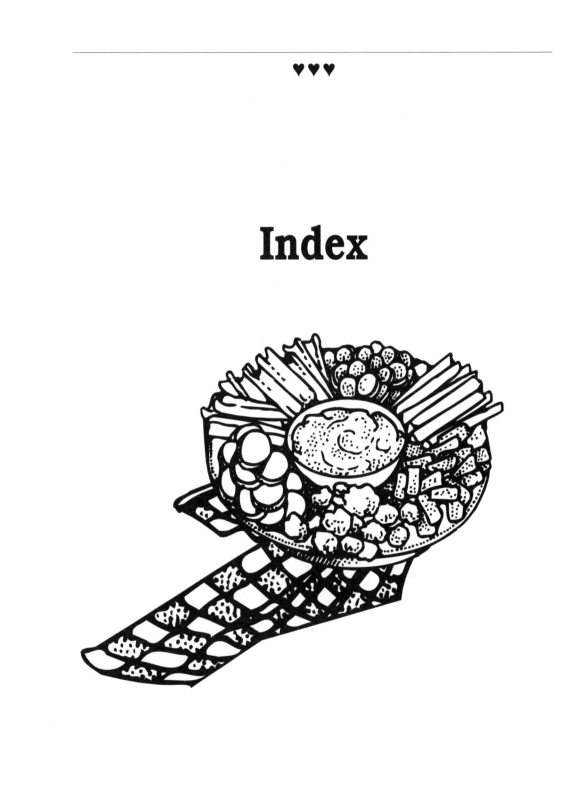

A

Al's Carrot Muffins 94
Angel Food Fruit Pudding 254

Appetizers
Bob's Special Vegetable Pate .26
Curried Yogurt Dip
  with Broccoli 24
Deviled Eggs 29
Garbanzo Ghanoush 32
Mexican Bean Dip 23
Pickled Plum Mayonnaise . . .25
Salsa Grande 33
Spinach Dip 22
Taco Chips 21
Tofu Cucumber Dip 28
Triple Deck Mexican
  Tortillas 30
Apple Coleslaw 44
Apple Muffins 93

Apples
Apple Coleslaw 44
Apple Muffins 93
Applesauce Cake 228
French Apple Dessert 264
Nutty Apple Cake 252
Applesauce Cake 228

Asparagus
Mickie's Gingered
  Asparagus 166

B

Babsi's Famous Rice Salad 40
Babsi's Navy Bean Soup 74
Baked Bean Casserole 159
Baked Green Tomatoes
  with Zucchini 217

Banana
Easy Ice Box Pie 235

Barbeque
Easy Barbeque Sandwiches 175
Barbeque Sandwiches 175
Barley Pilaf 212
Basic Burgers 170
Black Bean
  Vegetable Chili 138

Beans
Babsi's Navy Bean Soup 76
Baked Bean Casserole 159
Bean Burritos 162
Bean Stuffed Spuds 189
Best Ever Black-Eyes 118
Betty's Stuffed Green
  Peppers 116
Black Bean Vegetable Chili .138
Cabbage White Beans
  and Rice 168
Carol's Santa Fe Casserole .156
Chickpea and Rice Casserole192
Deviled Eggs 29
Diane's Kidney Bean Loaf . .124
Donna's Vegetarian Chili . .107
Enchilada Pie 164
Jerry's Sweet and
  Sour Beans 115
Jerry's Vegetarian Chili . . .122
John's Famous Chili 152
Key West Ten Can Soup 71
Lentil Loaf 133
Mexican Bean Dip 23
Mildred's Minestrone 66
Mixed Bean Salad 39
Mock Tuna Salad 41
Pasta and Bean Stew 188
Raspberry Fruit Salad 50
Red Beans and Rice 144
Reversal Moors and
  Christians 213
Rice with Baked Beans 136
Rice with Black Beans 136
Southwest Baked Beans . . .123
Taco Salad 48
Triple Deck Mexican
  Tortillas 30

Beer
Cabbage and Beer Soup 68

Beets
Beet Soup 72
Beet Soup a la Doris 77

Berries
Angel Food Fruit Pudding . .254
Blueberry Spice Vinegar . . .52
Fast Fruit Trifle 263
Fruit Ravioli 262

Fruit Salad Dessert 227
Raspberry Freeze 273
Strawberry Rhubarb
  Squares 281
Best Ever Black-Eyes 118
Betty's Sausage Patties 148
Bev's Pasta Kraut Surprise . . .214
Blueberry Spice Vinegar 52
Bob's Special Vegetable Plate . . .26
Bob's Steamed Carrot Cake . . .250

Bran
Bran Muffins 91
Fran's Bran Muffins 100
Bran Muffins 91
Bread Pudding 238

Breads
Al's Carrot Muffins 94
Apple Muffins 93
Basic White Bread 88
Bran Muffins 91
Edie's Granola 97
Estella's Dark Pumpernickel
  Batter Bread 98
Estella's Fat Free
  Dinner Rolls 90
Fran's Bran Muffins 100
Gene's Dill Bread 83
Honey Whole Wheat Bread . .84
Raisin Bread 92
Shaun's Carrot Raisin
  Muffins 102
Sweet Potato Rolls 86
Yummy Morning Cereal 96
Zesty Corn Muffins 101
Zucchini Bread 104

Broccoli
Broccoli Dressing 42
Broccoli Marinara 218
Broccoli Strata 145
Pasta Broccoli and Tomatoes . .201
Sharon's Broccoli and
  Cheese Soup 79
Broccoli Dressing 42
Broccoli Marinara 218
Broccoli Strata 145
Butternut Bread 88
Butternut Squash Soup 78

C

Cabbage

Apple Coleslaw 44
Cabbage and Beer Soup 68
Cabbage Rolls 130
Cabbage Soup 80
Cabbage White Beans
   and Rice 168
Hermit Soup 73
Cabbage and Beer Soup 68
Cabbage Rolls 130
Cabbage Soup 80
Cabbage White Beans
   and Rice 168

Cakes

Applesauce Cake 228
Bob's Steamed Carrot Cake 250
Carol's Orange Cake 258
Carrot Cupcakes 242
Chocolate Cake 244
Estella's Chocolate Orange
   Cheesecake 240
Light Fruitcake 247
Moe's Pumpkin Cake 277
Nutty Apple Cake 252
Prune Cake 230
Rich Date Cake 232
Rose Mary's Apple Cake . . .236
Carol's Orange Cake 258

Carol's Santa Fe Casserole . . .156

Carrot

Al's Carrot Muffins 94
Bob's Steamed
   Carrot Cake 250
Carrot Cupcakes 242
Mashed Carrots 205
Shaun's Carrot Muffins . . .103
Carrot Cupcakes 242

Casseroles

Baked Bean Casserole 159
Baked Green Tomatoes
   and Zucchini 217
Barley Pilaf 212
Bev's Pasta Kraut Surprise .214
Broccoli Marinara 218
Broccoli Strata 145

Celery, Peppers and
   Pasta 200
Chickpea and Rice
   Casserole 192
Easy Pot Pie 186
Eggplant with
   Spiral Pasta 222
Elbow Macaroni Skillet
   Dinner 190
Enchilada Pie 164
Golden Harvest Casserole . .215
Helen's Barley Casserole . .121
Hominy Skillet Dinner 204
Imqarrun Fil-Forn 158
Jennifer's Spinach
   Lasagna 112
Lasagna Roll ups 134
Moussaka 208
Pizza Pasta Casserole 113
Potatoes, Peppers, and
   Asparagus 203
Reversal Moors and
   Christians 213
Sally's Potatoes 197
Sauerkraut Casserole 132
Sharon's Lasagna 112
Spaghetti Sauce
   Casserole 150
Vegetable Pie 202
Wild Mushroom and
   Red Pepper Bake 176
Vegetable Rice Casserole . .206
Zucchini Bake 221
Celery, Peppers and
   Pasta 200

Cereal

Edie's Granola 97
Yummy Morning Cereal 96

Cheese

Broccoli Strata 145
Dan's Grilled Cheese
   Sandwich 127
Enchilada Pie 164
Jennifer's Spinach
   Lasagna 112
Lasagna Roll ups 134
Lentil Loaf 133
Mexican Bean Dip 23

Sharon's Broccoli and
   Cheese Soup 79
Sharon's Lasagna 182
Stuffed Shells 143
Triple Deck Mexican
   Tortillas 30

Cheesecake

Estella's Chocolate Orange
   Cheesecake 240

Cherries

Lazy Cherry Cobbler 282

Chestnuts

Nutty Apple Cake 252
Chickpea and Rice
   Casserole 192

Chili

Black Bean Vegetable Chili .138
Donna's Vegetarian Chili . . .107
Jerry's Vegetarian Chili 122
John's Famous Chili 152

Chocolate

Chocolate Cake 244
Estella's Chocolate Orange
   Cheesecake 240
Chocolate Cake 244
Chop Suey 172

Cinnamon

Jerry's Cinnamon Biscotti .260
Pat's Cinnamon Rolls 278
Spice Cookies 275

Classic Molded Salad 45

Cobbler

Lazy Cherry Cobbler 282

Coleslaw

Apple Coleslaw 44

Cookies

Jerry's Cinnamon Biscotti .260
Marilyn's Oatmeal Cookies .284
Old Fashioned Oatmeal
   Cookies 276
Spice Cookies 275
Cooking with fat free
   ingredients 7

Corn

Hominy Skillet Dinner 204
Taco Chips 21
Zesty Corn Muffins 101

Cream Cheese

Cream Cheese Sauce 249
Estelle's Chocolate Orange
   Cheesecake 240
Mushroom Soup 65
Cream Cheese Sauce 249

Cupcakes

Carrot Cupcakes 242

Curry

Curried Yogurt Dip 24

D

Dan's Grilled Cheese
   Sandwich 127
Dave's Delectable Dessert 234

Desserts

Angel Food Fruit
   Pudding 254
Applesauce Cake 228
Bob's Steamed Carrot
   Cake 250
Bread Pudding 238
Carol's Orange Yogurt
   Cake 258
Carrot Cupcakes 242
Chocolate Cake 244
Cream Cheese Sauce 249
Dave's Delectable Dessert . .234
Easy Frozen Dessert 274
Easy Ice Box Pie 235
Estella's Chocolate Orange
   Cheesecake 240
Fake Shake 239
Fast Fruit Trifle 263
French Apple Dessert 264
Fruit Ravioli 262
Fruit Salad Dessert 227
Jerry's Cinnamon Biscotti .260
Lazy Cherry Cobbler 282
Light Fruitcake 246

Marilyn's Oatmeal
   Cookies 284
Moe's Pumpkin Cake 277
Nutty Apple Cake 252
Old-Fashioned Oatmeal
   Cookies 276
Pavlova 270
Pat's Cinnamon Rolls 278
Peaches 'n Cream 266
Pie Crust 283
Prune Cake 230
Pumpkin Pie 268
Raspberry Freeze 273
Rennet Pudding 280
Rice Pudding 272
Rich Date Cake 232
Rosemary's Apple Cake . . .236
Seven Minute Frosting 248
Spice Cookies 275
Strawberry-Rhubarb
   Squares 281
Whipped Topping 256
Deviled Eggs 29
Diane's Kidney Bean Loaf 124

Dill

Gene's Dill Bread 83
Lemon Dill Vinegar 54

Dinner Rolls

Estella's Fat Free
   Dinner Rolls 90
Sweet Potato Rolls 87

Dips

Curried Yogurt Dip 24
Garbanzo Ghanoush 32
Mexican Bean Dip 23
Salsa Grande 33
Spinach Dip 22
Tofu Cucumber Dip 28
Donna's Potato Soup 59
Donna's Vegetarian Chili 107

Dumplings

Jeanne's Chicken and
   Dumplings 184

E

Easy Recipes

Easy Frozen Desert 274
Easy Pot Pie 186
Easy Frozen Desert 274
Easy Icebox Pie 235
Easy Pot Pie 186
Edie's Granola 97

Eggplant

Black Bean Vegetable
   Chili 138
Eggplant with Spinach
   Spiral Pasta 222
Festival Couscous 140
Garbanzo Ghanoush 32
Golden Harvest Casserole . .215
Moussaka 208
Eggplant with Spinach
   Spiral Pasta 222
Egg Salad 43
Elbow Macaroni Skillet
   Dinner 190

Egg Whites

Deviled Eggs 29
Egg Salad 43
Enchilada Pie 164
Estella's Chocolate Orange
   Cheesecake 240
Estella's Dark Pumpernickel
   Bread 98
Estella's Fat Free
   Dinner Rolls 90
Ethel's Sweet Potatoes 198

F

Fifteen Minute Bean Soup 75
Fake Shake 239
Fast Fruit Trifle 263
Fran's Bran Muffins 100
French Apple Dessert 264
French Fries, Jerry's 195

Frosting

Cream Cheese Sauce 249
Seven Minute Frosting 248

Frozen Desserts

Easy Frozen Dessert 274
Raspberry Freeze 273

Fruit

Angel Food Fruit Pudding . .254
Applesauce Cake 228
Carol's Orange Cake 258
Easy Frozen Dessert 274
Fast Fruit Trifle 263
French Apple Dessert 264
Fruit Ravioli 262
Fruit Salad Dessert 227
Lazy Cherry Cobbler 282
Light Fruitcake 247
Moe's Pumpkin Cake 277
Nutty Apple Cake 252
Peaches and Cream 266
Prune Cake 230
Pumpkin Pie 268
Raspberry Freeze 273
Rice Pudding 272
Rich Date Cake 230
Rose Mary's Apple Cake . . .236
Strawberry Rhubarb
    Squares 281

G

Garbanzo Ghanoush 32
Garlic Pepper Sauce 142
Gene's Dill Bread 83
Golden Harvest Casserole 215

Granola

Edie's Granola 97

Gravy 210
Greek Lemon Rice Soup 70
Green Goddess Pasta Sauce . . .191

H

Hearty Stew 154
Helen's Barley Casserole 121
Helen's Stuffed Peppers 128
Hermit's Soup 73
Hominy Skillet Side Dish 204
Honey Whole Wheat Bread 84

Horseradish

Zesty Twice Baked Potatoes .216

I

Ice Cream

Dave's Delectable Dessert . . .234

Imqarrun Fil-forn 158

J

Jeanne's "Chicken" &
    Dumplings 184
Jennifer's Spinach lasagna 112
Jerry's Cinnamon Biscotti 260
Jerry's French Fries 195
Jerry's Sweet and Sour Beans . .114
Jerry's Vegetarian Chili 122
John's Famous Chili 152

K

Kathy's Grilled Cheese
    Sandwich 120
Key West Ten Can Soup 71

L

Lasagna

Jennifer's Spinach Lasagna .112
Lasagna Roll-ups 134
Sharon's Lasagna 182

Lazy Cherry Cobbler 282

Lemon

Greek Lemon Rice Soup 70
Lemon Garlic Dill Vinegar . .54

Lentils

Lentil Loaf 133

Light Fruitcake 246

M

Macaroni, see also pasta
Elbow Macaroni Skillet
    Dinner 190
Imqarrun Fil-Forn 158

Main Dishes

Basic Burgers 170
Baked Bean Casserole 159
Barbeque Sandwiches 175
Bean Burritos 162
Bean Stuffed Spuds 189
Best Ever Black-Eyes 118
Betty's Sausage Patties 148
Betty's Stuffed Peppers
    with Black Beans 116
Black Bean Vegetable Chili . .138
Broccoli Strata 145
Cabbage Rolls 130
Cabbage, White Beans
    and Rice 168
Carol's Santa Fe Casserole . .157
Chickpea and Rice Casserole 192
Chop Suey 172
Dan's Grilled Cheese
    Sandwich 127
Diane's Kidney Bean Loaf . . .124
Donna's Vegetarian Chili . . .107
Easy Pot Pie 186
Elbow Macaroni Skillet
    Dinner 190
Enchilada Pie 164
Festival Couscous 140
Garlic Pepper Sauce 142
Green Goddess Pasta Sauce .191
Hearty Stew 154
Helen's Barley Casserole . . .121
Helen's Stuffed Peppers 128
Imqarrun Fil-forn 158
Jeanne's "Chicken" &
    Dumplings 184
Jennifer's Spinach lasagna . .112
Jerry's Sweet and Sour
    Beans 114
Jerry's Vegetarian Chili 122
John's Famous Chili 152
Kathy's Grilled Cheese
    Sandwich 120
Lasagna Roll-ups 134

♥ ♥ ♥

Main Dishes, cont'd

Lentil Loaf 133
Meatless Sloppy Joe 146
Mickie's Gingered Asparagus
    Fettuccine 166
Pasta and Bean Stew 188
Pizza Pasta Casserole 113
Red Beans and Rice 144
Rice with Black Beans 136
Sandwich Spread 178
Sasaki 174
Sauerkraut Casserole 132
Sharon's Lasagna 182
Soft Soy Tacos 153
Southwest Spaghetti 179
Southwestern Baked Beans .123
Spaghetti Sauce 129
Spaghetti Sauce Calderone . .180
Spaghetti Squash Casserole . .150
Stuffed Shells 143
Tomato Relish 126
Vegetarian Meatloaf 108
Vic's Baked Beans 110
Vegetarian Stew 160
Wild Mushroom and Red Pepper
    Baked Pasta 176

Maple Glazed Winter
    Vegetables 199
Marilyn's Oatmeal Cookies . . .284
Mashed Carrots 205
Mashed Potatoes 211
Meatless Sloppy Joe 146
Mexican Bean Dip 23
Mickie's Gingered Asparagus
    Fettuccine 166
Mildred's Minestrone 66
Mixed Bean Salad 39
Mock Tuna Salad 41
Moe's Pumpkin Cake 277
Moussaka 208

Muffins

Al's Carrot Muffins 94
Apple Muffins 93
Bran Muffins 91
Fran's Bran Muffins 100
Shaun's Carrot Raisin
    Muffins 102
Zesty Corn Muffins 101

Mushrooms

Mushroom Soup 65
Vegetarian Portobella 189
Wild Mushroom and Red Pepper
    Baked Pasta 176

N

Noodles, see pasta
Nutrition Information 7

Nuts

Nutty Apple Cake 252

O

Oatmeal

Marilyn's Oatmeal Cookies .276
Old-Fashioned Oatmeal
    Cookies 276
Strawberry Rhubarb
    Squares 281

Orange

Carol's Orange Cake 258
Estelle's Chocolate Orange
    Cheesecake 240
Oriental Spinach Salad 46

P

Pasta

Bev's Pasta Kraut Surprise . .214
Broccoli Marinara 218
Celery Pepper and Pasta 200
Eggplant with Spinach
    Spiral Pasta 222
Elbow Macaroni
Skillet Dinner 190
Festival Couscous 140
Green Goddess
    Pasta Sauce 191
Imqarrun Fil-Forn 158
Jennifer's Spinach
    Lasagna 112
Lasagna Roll-ups 134
Mickie's Fettuccine 166
Pasta and Bean Stew 188

Pasta Broccoli and
    Tomatoes 201
Pizza Pasta Casserole 113
Ron's Pasta Salad 53
Sharon's Lasagna 182
Southwest Spaghetti 179
Spaghetti Sauce 129
Spaghetti Sauce
    Calderone 180
Stuffed Shells 143
Vegetable Pasta Salad 47
Wild Mushroom and
    Red Pepper Baked Pasta .176
Pasta and Bean Stew 188
Pasta and Broccoli
    with Tomatoes 201

Pat's Cinnamon Rolls 278
Pat's Potatoes 220
Pavlova 270

Peaches

Peaches 'n Cream 266

Pickled Plum Mayonnaise 25
Picnic Potato Salad 37
Pie Crust 283

Pies

Easy Pot Pie 186
Enchilada Pie 164
Peaches and Cream 266
Pie Crust 283
Pumpkin Pie 268
Vegetable Pie 202

Pineapple

Bread Pudding 238

Pizza Pasta Casserole 113

Potatoes

Babsi's Potato Soup 76
Donna's Potato Soup 59
Ethel's Sweet Potatoes 197
Jerry's French Fries 195
Mashed Parrots 205
Mashed Potatoes 211
Pat's Potatoes 220
Picnic Potato Salad 37
Potatoes, Peppers, and
    Asparagus 203

"Life Tastes Better Than Steak"

♥ ♥ ♥

Ruby's Potato Soup 64
Sally's Potatoes 198
Sweet Potato Rolls 87
Zesty Twice Baked
    Potatoes 216
Vegetable Pie 202
Vichyssoise Potato Salad . . .38
Potatoes, Peppers and
    Asparagus 203
Prune Cake 230

Pudding
Bread Pudding 238
Rennet Pudding 280

Pumpkin
Moe's Pumpkin Cake 277
Pumpkin Pie 268

R
Raisin Bread 92

Raspberries
Fruit Ravioli 262
Raspberry Freeze 273
Raspberry Fruit Salad 50
Raspberry Vinegar 55
Red Beans and Rice 144
Rennet Pudding 280
Reversal Moors and
    Christians 213

Rhubarb
Strawberry Rhubarb
    Squares 281

Rice
Babsi's Famous Rice Salad . .40
Cabbage Rolls 130
Chickpea and Rice
    Casserole 192
Chop Suey 172
Golden Harvest Casserole . .215
Greek Lemon Rice Soup 70
Hermit's Soup 73
Red Beans and Rice 144
Reversal Moors and
    Christians 213
Rice Pudding 272
Rice with Black Beans 136

Vegetable Rice Casserole . .206
Rice Pudding 272
Rice with Black Beans 136
Rich Date Cake 232
Rosemary's Apple Cake 236
Ruby's Potato Soup 64

S

Salads
Apple Coleslaw 44
Babsi's Famous Rice Salad . .40
Blueberry Spice Vinegar 52
Broccoli Dressing 42
Classic Molded Salad 45
Easy Trio Pasta Salad 53
Egg Salad 43
Lemon Dill Vinegar 54
Mixed Bean Salad 39
Mock Tuna Salad 41
Oriental Spinach Salad 46
Picnic Potato Salad 37
Raspberry Fruit Salad 50
Raspberry Vinegar 55
Taco Salad 48
Vegetable Pasta Salad 47
Vichyssoise Potato Salad . . .38
Sally's Potatoes 197
Salsa Grande 33
Sandwich Spread 178

Sandwiches
Dan's Grilled Cheese
    Sandwich 127
Egg Salad 43
Kathy's Grilled Cheese 120
Mock Tuna Salad 41
Sasaki 174

Sauces
Cream Cheese Sauce 249
Garlic Pepper Sauce 142
Green Goddess Pasta Sauce .191
Spaghetti Sauce 129
Spaghetti Sauce Calderone . .180
Tomato Relish 126
Sauerkraut Casserole 132

Sausage
Betty's Sausage Patties 148
Seven Minute Frosting 248
Sharon's Broccoli and
    Cheese Soup 79
Sharon's Lasagna 182
Shaun's Carrot Raisin Muffins 102

Side Dishes
Baked Green Tomatoes
    with Zucchini 217
Barley Pilaf 212
Bev's Pasta Kraut Surprise .214
Broccoli Marinara 218
Celery, Peppers and Pasta .200
Eggplant with Spinach
    Spiral Pasta 222
Ethel's Sweet Potatoes 198
Golden Harvest Casserole . .215
Gravy 210
Hominy Skillet Side Dish .204
Jerry's French Fries 195
Maple Glazed Winter
    Vegetables 199
Mashed Carrots 205
Mashed Potatoes 211
Moussaka 208
Pasta and Broccoli with
    Tomatoes 201
Pat's Potatoes 220
Potatoes, Peppers and
    Asparagus 203
Reversal Moors and
    Christians 213
Sally's Potatoes 197
Tangy Twice Baked
    Potatoes 216
Vegetable Pie 202
Vegetable Rice Casserole . .206
Vegetarian Portabella 196
Zucchini Bake 221
Soft Soy Tacos 153
Soup au Pistou 62

Soups
Babsi's Navy Bean Soup 74
Babsi's Potato Soup 76
Beet Soup 72
Beet Soup a la Doris 77
Butternut Squash Soup 78

Soups, cont'd

Cabbage Soup 80

Cabbage and Beer Soup 68

Donna's Potato Soup 59

Fifteen Minute Bean Soup. . .75

Greek Lemon Rice Soup 70

Hermit's Soup 73

Key West Ten Can Soup 71

Mildred's Minestrone 66

Mushroom Soup 65

Ruby's Potato Soup 64

Sharon's Broccoli and
Cheese Soup 79

Soup au Pistou 62

Vegetable Soup 60

Southwest Spaghetti 179

Southwestern Baked Beans . . .123

Soy

Barbequed Sandwiches 175

Basic Burgers 170

Betty's Sausage Patties 148

Betty's Stuffed Peppers 116

Cabbage Rolls 130

Chop Suey 172

Donna's Vegetarian Chili . . .107

Enchilada Pie 164

Hearty Stew 154

Imqarrun Fil-Forn 158

Meatless Sloppy Joe 146

Sasaki 174

Sauerkraut 132

Soft Soy Tacos 153

Southwest Spaghetti 179

Spaghetti Sauce Calderone . .180

Taco Salad 48

Vegetarian Meatloaf 108

Vegetarian Stew 160

Spaghetti

Green Goddess Pasta Sauce .191

Spaghetti Sauce 129

Spaghetti Sauce Calderone . .180

Spaghetti Sauce 129

Spaghetti Sauce Calderone . .180

Spaghetti Squash

Spaghetti Squash Casserole ..150

Spice Cookies 275

Spinach Dip 22

Squash

Baked Green Tomatoes
and Zucchini 217

Spaghetti Squash Casserole ..150

Zucchini Bake 221

Zucchini Bread 104

Stew

Hearty Stew 154

Pasta and Bean Stew 188

Vegetarian Stew 160

Strawberries

Strawberry Rhubarb
Squares 281

Stuffed

Betty's Stuffed Peppers 116

Helen's Stuffed Peppers 128

Stuffed Shells 143

Sweet Potatoes

Ethel's Sweet Potatoes 198

Sweet Potato Rolls 86

Sweet Rolls

Pat's Cinnamon Rolls 278

T

Taco Chips 21

Taco Salad 48

Tofu

Green Goddess
Pasta Sauce 191

Tofu Cucumber Dip 28

Tomato

Baked Green Tomatoes
and Zucchini 217

Bean Burritos 162

Betty's Stuffed Peppers 116

Black Bean Vegetable Chili . .138

Broccoli Marinara 218

Cabbage Rolls 130

Carol's Santa Fe Casserole . .156

Chickpea and Rice
Casserole 192

Donna's Vegetarian Chili . . .107

Eggplant with Spinach
Spiral Pasta 222

Elbow Macaroni
Skillet Dinner 190

Enchilada Pie 164

Golden Harvest Casserole . . .215

Hearty Stew 154

Imqarrun Fil Forn 157

Jennifer's Spinach Lasagna ...112

Jerry's Vegetarian Chili 122

John's Famous Chili 152

Lasagna Roll-ups 134

Meatless Sloppy Joe 146

Moussaka 208

Pasta and Bean Stew 188

Pasta Broccoli and
Tomatoes 201

Pat's Potatoes 220

Pizza Pasta Casserole 113

Salsa Grande 33

Sauerkraut Casserole 132

Sharon's Lasagna 182

Soft Soy Tacos 153

Southwest Spaghetti 179

Spaghetti Sauce 129

Spaghetti Sauce
Calderone 180

Spaghetti Squash Casserole ..150

Stuffed Shells 143

Taco Salad 48

Tomato Relish 126

Tomato Relish 126

Triple Deck Mexican
Tortillas 30

V

Vegetable Pasta Salad 47

Vegetable Pie 202

Vegetable Rice Casserole 206

Vegetable Soup 60

Vegetarian Meatloaf 108

Vegetarian Portabella 196

Vegetarian Stew 160

Vichyssoise Potato Salad 38

Vic's Baked Beans 110

Vinegar

Blueberry Spice Vinegar 52

Lemon Garlic Dill Vinegar . . .54

Raspberry Vinegar 55

W

Whipped Topping 256
Wild Mushroom and Red
   Pepper Baked Pasta 176

Y

Yogurt
   Curried Yogurt Dip 24
Yummy Morning Cereal 96

Z

Zesty Corn Muffins 101
Zesty Twice Baked Potatoes . .216
Zucchini
   Baked Green Tomatoes
     and Zucchini 217
   Vegetable Pie 202
   Zucchini Bake 221
   Zucchini Bread 104

Life Tastes Better Than Steak Cookbook: Heart Healthy Reversal Recipes

edited by Gerry Krag, MA, RD & Marie Zimolzak, DTR

Filled with delicious heart healthy reversal recipes, this new cookbook features dishes that come straight from the hearts of those who wrote it: the patients and their families of the successful Downriver Reversal Program. All of the recipes include complete nutritional information and preparation time. The contributors stories are sure to convince others that while steak may be great, *life* tastes better!

To order additional copies of *Life Tastes Better Than Steak Cookbook: Heart Healthy Reversal Recipes*

Telephone orders: 1-800-722-9925

Fax orders: 906-346-3015

Mail order: Avery Color Studios, Inc.
511 D Avenue
Gwinn MI 49841

Please send me:

_____ copies of *Life Tastes Better Than Steak Cookbook* at $17.95 each $ _____

Shipping and Handling $4.50 _____

MI residents only, 6% sales tax _____

Total _____

Payment: _____ Check _____ Visa _____ Mastercard

Card #_____ Expiration date _____ / _____

Name on card_____ Signature_____

Ship to:

Name _____

Address _____

City _____ State _____ Zip _____

Telephone _____

Avery Color Studios, Inc. • *511 D Avenue* • *Gwinn MI 49841* • *1-800-722-9925*